The OPEN Process Framework
An Introduction

The OPEN Series
Consulting Editor: Brian Henderson-Sellers

Related titles

The OPEN Process Specification, Ian Graham, Brian Henderson-Sellers and Houman Younessi

Documenting a complete Java application using OPEN, Donald G. Firesmith, Greg Hendley, Scott Krutsch and Marshall Stowe

The OPEN Toolbox of Techniques, Brian Henderson-Sellers, Anthony Simons, Houman Younessi

OPEN modeling with UML, Brian Henderson-Sellers and Bhuvan Unhelkar

The OPEN Process Framework

An Introduction

Donald G. Firesmith and Brian Henderson-Sellers

Addison-Wesley

London · New York · San Francisco · Toronto · Sydney
Tokyo · Singapore · Hong Kong · Cape Town · Madrid
Paris · Milan · Munich · Amsterdam

PEARSON EDUCATION LIMITED

Head Office:
Edinburgh Gate
Harlow CM20 2JE
Tel: +44 (0)1279 623623
Fax: +44 (0)1279 431059

London Office:
128 Long Acre
London WC2E 9AN
Tel: +44 (0)20 7447 2000
Fax: +44 (0)20 7240 5771

Websites: *www.it-minds.com*
www.aw.com/cseng

First published in Great Britain in 2002

ISBN 0-201-67510-2

British Library Cataloguing in Publication Data
A CIP catalogue record for this book can be obtained from the British Library

Library of Congress Cataloging in Publication Data
Applied for.

10 9 8 7 6 5 4 3 2 1

Designed by Claire Brodmann Book Designs, Lichfield, Staffs

Typeset by Pantek Arts Ltd, Maidstone, Kent
Printed and bound by Biddles Ltd of Guildford and King's Lynn

The Publishers' policy is to use paper manufactured from sustainable forests.

Contents

E Work Units 241

Preface

The OPEN Process Framework is a public domain framework for constructing processes for developing software-intensive applications and object-oriented business models. The OPEN Consortium is responsible for its development and maintenance. The OPEN Process Framework provides a template for generating flexible, yet disciplined, processes for developing high-quality software-intensive applications within a predictable schedule and budget. This book introduces to the reader the OPEN (Object-oriented Processes, Environment and Notation) Process Framework (or OPF) by documenting its underlying concepts, its predefined components, and the process construction and tailoring guidelines that can be used to create a well tuned process for specific projects.

Goals of this book

Using this book, you will:

- Learn what the OPEN Process Framework is and how its use differs from specific development methods, even those that permit some tailoring.
- Master the basic concepts of the OPEN Process Framework and understand their structure and interrelationships.
- Learn how to instantiate the OPEN Process Framework to construct a process that meets the needs of specific projects and organizations.

Intended audience

This book is not intended to be a manual containing *all* possible information on OPEN, particularly if utilized on a very large complex project. Rather it is intended to offer an *introduction* to OPEN, its contents and its underpinning philosophy (that of a framework). In parts, it synopsizes or just gives examples rather than giving a full inventory (e.g., of all possible Work Products). If you intend to use OPEN on commercial projects, you should also consult the other books in the OPEN series or access one of the Websites that many companies are increasingly making available either publicly as a product or on their own internal intranets.

This book was written in response to frequent requests that members of companies wished to get an overview of OPEN in order to assess whether it would suit their requirements *before* delving into the full process specifications as found in, for example, *The OPEN Process Specification* by Graham *et al.* (1997).

The book was primarily written for professionals who may be evaluating development processes with a view to their adoption for the creation of software-intensive applications, for business process reengineering or for process engineering:

- **Project managers** and **technical leaders**. This book provides a high-level description of a prototypical development process including development stages, work units, organizational structures, and the products to be produced.
- **Process engineers**. This book describes the basic process components and associated usage guidelines needed to begin constructing a project-specific development process.
- **Methodologists**. This book provides a generic metamodel for describing and comparing different system and software development methods.
- **Developers**. Requirements engineers, architects, designers, implementers, testers, strategists, and user-experienced personnel will learn the products they are to produce, the tasks they will perform, and how these tasks fit into the development life cycle.

This book is particularly relevant to those who are evaluating or adopting the OPEN Process Framework. It is not, however, intended to provide sufficient material with which to complete your own OPEN process instance in a commercial environment but, rather, to give those readers an overview to use in their own evaluation before investing in the full OPEN books, tools, Website information, consultancy etc.

This book is also aimed at a second group of readers – those wishing to study and learn about object-oriented processes:

- **University and college professors.** Those charged with constructing tertiary-level courses on object-oriented processes and component-based development.
- **Students** of object technology, software and systems engineering and process engineering.

Although this book assumes a basic understanding of system and software engineering, it does not require knowledge of any specific development method, modeling language or implementation language.

Organization

This book is organized into the following parts and associated chapters:

- Part I, *Introduction*, provides a foundation for understanding the OPEN Process Framework.
  - Chapter 1, *Processes and Process Frameworks*, documents the defining characteristics of a process, discusses why processes are so important and explains why a single standard process is inadequate. The need for a process framework is then justified, followed by a discussion of the defining characteristics of a process framework, listing requirements for an object-oriented process framework.

  - Chapter 2, *OPEN Process Framework Overview*, introduces the OPEN Process Framework, its components and how it is to be used.
- Part II, *Specifics*, provides details concerning the specific components of the OPEN Process Framework (OPF) and how to use them.
  - Chapter 3, *Work Products*, documents the OPF's class library of predefined Work Products.
  - Chapter 4, *Producers*, documents the OPF's class library of predefined Producers of the Work Products.
  - Chapter 5, *Work Units*, documents the OPF's class library of predefined Work Units performed by the Producers of the Work Products.
  - Chapter 6, *Stages*, documents the OPF's class library of predefined Stages including Cycles, Phases, Builds, and Milestones.
  - Chapter 7, *Languages*, documents the OPF's class library of predefined Languages for documenting and constructing Work Products.
  - Chapter 8, *Framework Usage Guidelines*, provides guidelines for the extension, construction, and tailoring of the OPF for use on specific development or business reengineering projects.
- The *Appendices* provide much more detailed and reference material.
  - Appendix A, *List of acronyms* – a list of all acronyms used.
  - Appendix B, *Glossary* – definitions of the most important technical terms used within OPEN.
  - Appendix C, *Work Products* – a full discussion on several groups of Work Products with special focus on Documents and Components.
  - Appendix D, *Producers* – detailed information on the full range of Producers, both Direct and Indirect.
  - Appendix E, *Work Units* – discussions on Activities and Tasks; list of OPEN Techniques.
  - Appendix F, *Example Work Flow* – one specific example related to the External Interface Specification Work Flow.
  - Appendix G, *Metamodel Diagrams* – the complete OPF metamodel.
- *Bibliography and References*, listing all cited references plus some relevant background reading.

How to use this book

Managers considering using the OPF should use this book to gain a high-level description of the framework and overview of its reusable component parts. They should read Part I and skim the chapters in Part II, starting with development stages, producers, and work products.

Process engineers need an in-depth understanding of all parts of this book if they are to successfully construct project-specific processes from the OPF. They should read the entire book including the appendices.

Methodologists, with their extensive knowledge of development processes, may profitably skim the entire book, focussing on those areas of primary interest.

After reading Part I, developers may wish to first read the description of their role in the Producer chapter and their tasks in the Work Units chapter and the corresponding appendix. If they have been assigned to produce a work product, they may wish to immediately read about it in the Work Products chapter and the corresponding appendix. As with the documentation for any class or component library or repository, one typically reads about the relevant classes (in this case process components) first and then studies the remaining classes on an as-needed and/or time-available basis.

One can either read Part II of this book in a top-down or bottom-up manner. If you want to start with a top-level overview and work down, read the following chapters in the following order: stages, producers, work units, work products, and languages. If you prefer to start with the most primitive concepts and build upon them, read these chapters in the reverse order.

History of OPEN Process Framework

OPEN was created by a merger of several methodologies in the mid-1990s by *active collaboration* between a number of methodologists. Primarily, OPEN brings together the SOMA (Semantic Object Modeling Approach), MOSES and Firesmith methodologies with later merging of ideas from the Synthesis methodology. As well as these methodologists, there are over 30 other OO "gurus" worldwide who are involved in establishing the strategic direction of OPEN and helping improve it through their membership of the OPEN Consortium.

The main initial reason for creating OPEN was to help industry move to OO by decreasing the choice of methodology from over 20 in the early 1990s to a single digit figure by the end of the millennium.

Second, the members of the Consortium are those international figures who prefer a responsibility-driven approach to OO software development rather than a data-driven or perhaps a use-case driven approach such as Objectory with UML.

OPEN began to take shape in early 1995 with the merger of MOSES and SOMA, and by mid-1996 the Firesmith method was fully integrated. In the same timeframe, the Object Management Group (OMG) was calling for proposals for ideas on which to base a standard for an object-oriented metamodel,[1] useful for OO analysis and design, which would permit CASE tool builders to create interoperable tools. This focus was very much smaller than a methodology and, although several members of

1 A metamodel is a model of a model. It delineates all the rules needed by which to construct models by creating instances of elements in the metamodel. These instances form the model.

the OPEN Consortium have spent time contributing to the OMG effort at standardizing an OO metamodel, it was clear to them that more than a standard metamodel was needed for efficient and effective OO software development. Thus OPEN was born, to encompass *all* the aspects of application development (including the modeling language being addressed by OMG and the UML Partners). The first book describing the elements of OPEN as a full life cycle methodology was published in September 1997.[2] In this book, we update the metamodel, expand the scope of OPEN (e.g., to better support Web development and business engineering) and summarize the easier elements of that more extensive and sophisticated book in order to provide information for those companies (and educators) about to embark on an OO path to the future. We will assume you understand basic OT concepts such as encapsulation, abstraction, classification, objects, interfaces, classes etc.[3] OPEN even has its very own modeling language[4] which is an alternative to UML – both are still supported and used, UML being by far the most commonly utilized by OPEN end-users.

Since that first book in 1997, the OPEN literature has grown, with a full book series being published with Addison-Wesley, a regular column in JOOP (*Journal of Object-Oriented Programming*) and an established and extensive Website (with mirrors) at http://www.open.org.au. A network of consultants, vendors, tools suppliers, and researchers offer worldwide support and the user base continues to grow. In 2001, a new initiative of the Object Management Group to create a standard metamodel for process has involved OPEN Consortium members as reviewers and the standards document cites OPEN in many places.

Finally, we note that OPEN supports true *OO ideas*. We believe that there are some very basic principles of object technology (OT) that should be your prime focus in developing software using OO principles. These are

- object modeling as a very general technique for knowledge representation
- encapsulation/information hiding
- polymorphism

together with

- clear, jargon-free and well founded definitions of all terms; and
- extensive use of abstraction techniques, a foundation for semantically cohesive and encapsulated process "objects".

2 Graham, I. *et al.* (1997) *The OPEN Process Specification*, Addison-Wesley.

3 If not, try reading Henderson-Sellers, B. (1997) *A BOOK of Object-Oriented Knowledge*, Prentice Hall.

4 Firesmith, D. *et al.* (1997) *The OML Reference Manual*, SIGS Books (republished more recently by Cambridge University Press). OML is now recognized as a formal variant of UML (Henderson-Sellers, B. *et al.* (1999) *Viewing the OML as a variant of the UML*, Springer, 49–66) and offers full UML support together with further capability not found in the basic OMG UML standard.

Acknowledgements

We wish to thank all our colleagues who have supported us over the years[5] and helped to promulgate OPEN as a viable OO/CBD process/methodology. We also wish to thank a number of our colleagues for reading an earlier draft of this book manuscript and providing invaluable comments. In alphabetical order, we wish to express our thanks to Richard Heycock, Klaas Koomen, David Lowe, Henrik Ortlepp (particularly for Figures 1.6, 2.4, 2.9 and for suggesting the style of Figures 8.3, 8.4 and 8.6), Thomas Passin, Vit Rudovich, Magdy Serour, Errol Thompson, Richard Veryard and Houman Younessi.

5 See the OPEN Website at http://www.open.org.au.

Part I

Introduction

Part I summarizes the essential concepts of the OPEN (Object-oriented Process, Environment and Notation) and the OPEN Process Framework (OPF). It consists of the following chapters:

- Chapter 1, Process and Process Frameworks, documents the defining characteristics of a process, discusses why processes are so important, and explains why a single standard process is inadequate for the majority of projects. The need for a process framework is then justified, followed by a discussion of the defining characteristics of a process framework, which lists requirements for an object-oriented process framework.
- Chapter 2, OPEN Process Framework Overview, introduces the OPEN Process Framework, its components, and how it is to be used.

1 Processes and Process Frameworks

1.1 Processes in Information Technology

The information technology industry cannot afford to rely on luck. Repeatability of success is vital, as is knowledge of reasons for failure. While building quality, small and simple, one-off software applications is possible without using a formalized, documented, and established process, we argue in this book that greater and continued success is achievable when a process is utilized in an effective manner.

Processes (sometimes called methodologies or methods) may have many scopes and thus they may be used for many purposes. Some processes only cover a few activities (such as requirements engineering and design), whereas other processes may cover the entire life cycle from initial visioning (the identification of a business opportunity) through construction, delivery, usage, and eventual retirement of a solution. A process may be restricted to the development of software applications, or may cover the development and maintenance of software-intensive system applications, which would also include significant hardware, data, personnel, and documentation components as well as software. A software development-focussed process may even be extended to support business modeling and business (re)engineering based on the development of such applications combined with appropriate changes to the business model including both organizational structures and business processes. Processes typically can also be used to develop individual reusable components, whether models, documents or executable software. Finally, processes may be restricted to a single project, or may support programmes of related projects and even entire enterprises. OPEN (Object-oriented Process, Environment and Notation) and the OPEN Process Framework (OPF) cover all of these areas, primarily in the context of object-oriented (OO) and component-based development (CBD).

A complete process is a collection of a number of things, including rules for application construction, sequencing rules within the process, a full description of deliverables and how they relate to other parts of the process producing them, guidelines on metrics, standards, test strategies, organizational roles and team structure the activities and tasks they perform, the tools they use, project management guidelines, construction and coding techniques, quality assurance tips, reuse strategies, underpinning metamodels (which describe the rules to be used in constructing models), and so on. Here, we focus on how we can use the OPEN Process Framework to create a process specifically attuned to the needs of either an organization or a single project. Such a process might be created at the organization level to cover the full life cycle of application development within the context of providing solutions to business problems (which may well include hardware, data, and documentation, as well as software components) or may be created incrementally as the project progresses, growing and maturing together with the increasing knowledge and skills of the development and management teams.

Processes are necessary to assist developers and managers in creating work products (i.e., artefacts), whether deliverable or only for informal internal use, over a wide range of scales and domains. In information technology, we can differentiate between products at different organizational-level scales such as project-level, programme[1] level and enterprise-level. We can also discriminate, inside the process itself, between the various phases and milestones within an application's life cycle.

The most common usage[2] of a process within information technology is for the construction or development of a software application. This may be for use within the development organization or for sale to another organization. For modern businesses, software, in some form, is essential. Furthermore, that software needs to adequately meet quality requirements (stated or perceived) as more and more businesses and even life-sustaining activities become dependent upon software for their successful functioning. Furthermore, clients seek software that is reliable, portable, maintainable, etc. These software characteristics can be enhanced by judicious adoption and use of a good quality process.

1.1.1 Software applications

In discussing processes in information technology (IT), *software development processes* usually spring first to mind. A development process for software describes the IT tasks and techniques necessary to build the product (the application or "app"). The process also includes advice on project management issues and quality engineering including evaluation techniques and metrics. It should even address the important people issues. The quality of a process may be reflected by the scope of its support for all these various elements. This characterization will be explored in more detail later in this chapter. Here, we simply note that by "process" we might well mean software development process – but there are other important interpretations in widespread use.

1.1.2 Software-intensive systems

While software is *the* most important enabling technology in practically every branch of business, whether in banking, commerce, insurance, manufacturing, telecommunications, or transportation, software by itself is insufficient. Today, soft-

1 A programme describes a suite of related projects.

2 While 'maintenance' costs are typically several times higher than development costs, in OO/CBD we prefer to think of maintenance as enhancing an existing product. Thus, the maintenance process becomes the repeated use of the process to produce new versions of the application.

ware is a major component of *software-intensive systems*. Software-intensive systems involve the integration of software, hardware, wetware (i.e., personnel), content (data) and paperware (i.e., documentation). In such systems, software may run on a single machine or across a distributed computer network containing simple clients, input and output devices, with Web access and various kinds of servers, and databases. Software is also embedded in everything from automatic teller machines to automobiles to microwave ovens. The list grows daily. Take away software – and our economy and society would rapidly collapse. This was never better demonstrated than through the societal reaction to the "Y2K crisis".

In discussing processes, therefore, we do not limit ourselves to *software* development processes, although this is one major application of processes. And in some areas, e.g. COTS (Commercial Off-The-Shelf) development, this may be the sole focus. Increasingly, however, we need to realize that software development is just one facet of overall *system* development. In this book, we thus discuss processes not only in the "software application development" sense but also in the software-intensive system (or just systems) sense. In fact, we cover not only development, but also delivery, usage and eventual retirement.

1.1.3 Business modeling

There is, in fact, a third domain of applicability for processes within information technology: Business Modeling and even Business Re-engineering. In modeling the business, we take a process approach that incorporates important system elements such as categories of stakeholders (e.g., users, buyers, sellers), available technologies and the current business context. If we utilize object technology (OT) in order to create the business model, which itself may or may not be subsequently implemented in one or more applications, then the use of a common (here object-oriented) model provides a degree of seamlessness that improves the likelihood that any applications developed will meet the true business need. With the advent of Web applications, it has become clear that processes should help organizations develop their overall digital strategy and associated digital branding strategy, each of which impacts application development.

1.1.4 Component-based development (CBD)

Using components to build software has been a major IT goal for many decades. Components are replaceable and reusable "parts" from which the application can be directly composed. To do this, components need to have well and clearly specified interfaces that delineate all the services offered by and needed by the component itself. Components need to be well tested and validated i.e., "trusted" components, since a component is essentially a "black box" and all that is typically known about it is what is specified in its interface. Knowing what is both needed and supplied by the component allows the components to be selected and "plugged" together.

While much of today's interest in components comes from the advent of binary executables such as Enterprise Java Beans (EJB) and COM components, the broader issues relate to application development focussed on the integration of third party packages (e.g., e-commerce engines, security engines, middleware layers, and personalization and internalization packages) and/or outsourcing rather than in-house development of software "from scratch".

1.1.5 Organizational scope

In developing either a software application or a software-intensive system application, the scope often initially envisaged is that of the single project that produces this particular application/system. For the developers, this might be appropriate but for project management and, at a higher level still, for strategic direction-setting of the business, system development on a larger scale must be considered. When several related applications are developed over a period of time, the goal is no longer a single application but a programme of related applications (sometimes called a product line or a "suite"). The process by which such a suite is developed must consider not just each project in turn but the synergies and cross-project similarities and dependencies that are inevitable in this programme of application development. A digital strategy based on customer, market, technology, and user analysis often leads to a programme that addresses several projects and needs additional programme management considerations (as compared to a single project). Reuse strategies play a much larger role, and domain modeling and amortization of capital across several projects become both feasible and advantageous.

Beyond programmes are enterprises, which may be at the organizational scale or even, these days, across several organizations, forming a virtual enterprise. Enterprise computing is to this decade what simple objects and components were to the last. Large-scale architectures need to be addressed, as does a tight integration between software support and the activities of the business itself. Enterprise computing is about a total integration of IT into the business domain, supporting larger scale architectural elements within and relating to the commercial and business activities of the organization. Enterprise-wide computing not only encompasses object-oriented (OO) process and component-based development (CBD) but also how these improve software that is designed to support not merely a single organizational unit, such as marketing, but a fully integrated enterprise. Typical examples are enterprise resource planning (ERP) packages which integrate the many previously disparate functions undertaken by an organization – marketing, finance, personnel and so on.

1.1.6 Stages in the life cycle

The word "process" is used in information technology (as elsewhere) with a plethora of meanings. Often it means simply "the way we do things" or "the way we accomplish this particular goal". In other words, the word may be used to describe something of short duration or of limited scope. We do not use the word in this sense here. Rather, we focus on the idea of a process as being aligned with the *full* life cycle of an application, from birth, through development and use, to retirement (or decommissioning). We also strongly advocate inclusion, within our definition of process, of ideas not just relating to software and systems but also to aspects of the business itself. We thus need to introduce terminology to describe the stages that comprise a life cycle or the stage which the life cycle has (currently) attained.

Processes in IT should, therefore, not focus solely on modeling or coding but on the totality. This starts with a vision, with strategic thinking and/or with business planning. Based on those business-focussed discussions, highlighting an opportunity or a problem within that business domain, it may be decided to create a system solution: hardware and/or software. If that is so, then the software-intensive part of the process is invoked. The activities in the life cycle relevant here are often called names like requirements engineering, architecting, design, code, implementation, and testing. Towards the end of "production", the application is delivered to the customer and deployed at their site. This often means working in collaboration with existing (a.k.a., "legacy" or "heritage") systems. The best way of getting synergy between existing investments and new systems is also a process issue.

Following implementation and testing, the application then typically goes into daily use. During its use by the client, some defects may surface. These are fixed and, perhaps more significantly, additional features are suggested. Together, defect fixing and enhancements have traditionally been labeled as maintenance. Today, we prefer to think of these as "enhancements" – further, more refined versions of an existing product. Often the budgetary responsibility for this maintenance has been distinct from that of development, frequently leading to tensions, particularly in respect of delivered quality, between the delivery team and the maintenance team. Also, the advent of Web applications have made it clear that ongoing content management (the creation, editing, approving, and publication of information) is also an important post delivery activity. Finally, the process life cycle ends when the system is retired i.e., its use is terminated. The process adopted needs to address each of these post-production activities.

1.2 The need for process

Whilst there is some discussion about exactly what a development process or method is or should be, as discussed above, it is generally agreed that it should encompass rules, suggestions, heuristics, guidelines etc. for building software and software-intensive systems. Indeed, its structure can be quite complicated. Many methods focus on the rules, tips, and techniques for modeling but do not address the larger-scale issues of people, activities and tasks, project management, quality assessment, metrics, standards and so on. Since successful projects are undertaken by *people* using *technology* in a *business* environment, then clearly a good method should encompass all of these facets.

Some software development seems to occur in a very *ad hoc* fashion, even today. When successes may occasionally occur, the underlying reason is not obvious, and there is no means to identify how to repeat the success. And conversely, when failures and severe cost overruns occur (as they inevitably will sooner or later in an *ad hoc* development organization), there is no way of identifying how to fix the process, learn from the failure and avoid a repeat failure in the future. A process of any sort lays down some guidelines to help developers set their own (personal and team) standards to follow. It is then possible for other personnel to temporarily or even permanently take over a role and for managers to control, monitor, and evaluate how well the development is progressing towards completion. A process thus identifies activities that need to be done, probably recommends means by which to achieve the associated goals and, most importantly, creates a sequence of tasks (or a set of sequences) which allows temporal planning.

The success rate for software and software-intensive systems development is appallingly low. There is still the feeling abroad that when things get tight, the process can be abandoned – and the development team reverts to hacking. Hacking, in this way, can of course occasionally lead to project success. But it often leads to corners being cut and patches being hastily added to the software. This means that maintenance/future enhancements can be excessively difficult, time consuming and costly. Eventually, the application is so brittle that its useful life is truncated. In contrast, with a process, whereas there are more up-front costs, the downstream benefits of better maintainability, enhanced lifetimes, etc. are significant. This claim should also be considered in the context that it is well known in IT that "maintenance costs" far outweigh development costs. So over the full life cycle of the application (a view we are advocating), using a process to get these improved quality attributes actually decreases total costs and is more likely to permit the organization to remain in business longer.

Costs of application production are notoriously difficult to predict. With no process, an up-front cost estimation, say during the requirements activity, must have large margins for error (although these are seldom stated). The use of a process permits cost estimation at the beginning of the project to be much more accurate. This means that costs can be predicted, budgeted for, monitored, and managed throughout the lifetime of each project. Schedules, whether denoted by milestones or timeboxed stages or work units, give a skeletal structure to the overall process and assist individual team members to manage their time in such a way as to help to optimize the overall process and application delivery. These work products may also assist the project manager in tracking and assessing the status of the project as it evolves.

So, using a process, and avoiding hacking, is a long-term investment to get better products. But it does more than that. It also increases the skills levels of the team members, and it creates an organizational culture in which mistakes of the past are heeded and avoided in subsequent projects and "things that worked" are clearly identified in order that they might be replicated in the future. Organizational learning can come from something as simple as a retrospective (sometimes called a post-implementation review). In other words, a process provides a personal and organizational "culture" in which good things can be leveraged and bad things noted, documented, and learned from. In addition, this learning at the organizational level will eventually lead to a feedback in which the organization's process will itself be improved – known as "software process improvement" or SPI.

Using an industry-standardized (rather than a proprietary) process enhances the transferability of personnel. If everyone knows the same process (not only the company's standard but also nationally and internationally recognized and regarded), not only can there be internal transfers but it is also highly likely that new hires (from industry or new university graduates) will have learned that same process at some stage in their career. Within the organization, this standard process then provides a common language and way of thinking and of doing. Most errors in application development (and actually in life!) come from miscommunication because the words sound familiar but the two participants in the conversation are putting their own semantics on the words. Expressed another way, they speak the same vocabulary without speaking the same language.

Since a good process should not restrict itself to discussing the technical aspects of application construction, the use of a process should also assist in the individual personnel and team levels of human interaction. Individual participants can clearly see their role, how they can best contribute and how the team itself may function more effectively.

The use of process supports not only maintainability and repeatability but also underpins scalability. In the dawn of the twenty-first century, businesses are rapidly moving to e-commerce, e-business and e-everything. Development by and for the Web in a commercial environment, where being first to market is often seen as *the* success factor, is often cited as a rationale for ignoring process. Rather, it is this very environment, critical as it is to the success of these businesses, that argues most strongly *for* process support. The existence of a process in an organization means that a newcomer can be told "this is how we do things here" and can be productive immediately. If the process of Web development is left to the individual developer (as it is, sadly too often, these days), then not only does the application need to be delivered on a short timescale but, in addition (and unbudgeted), the developer must create his own process before he starts the development itself.

An organization's process for software and software-intensive systems development therefore needs to offer support and guidelines for how to do things, as well as describing the style and content of work products; it must offer guidelines for monitoring and control through a strong project management flavor as well as emphasizing the all-important quality aspects. Small teams, working in "Web-time", do not of course need a "high ceremony" process with lots of seemingly bureaucratic reports and other document deliverables for project management and monitoring. However, process in the sense of a time-ordered sequence of events remains vital. Thus, despite claims that small processes such as XP (eXtreme Programming) are "hacking in disguise", in fact the process content is significant. The more important question is whether these so-called lightweight processes can scale up. Since they are not really focussed on scalability, it is perhaps not surprising that they typically do *not* scale to larger projects. On the other hand, some large projects might be better served by being split into a number of smaller projects. A wide spread of project size is, consequently, inevitable. Processes must therefore match this wide scope of project size. This can be done either by creating a suite of processes, each targetted at a specific project size, or by creating a single, yet highly flexible, process framework.

The scope of projects as well as their flexibility and scalability will be an ongoing theme in this book, particularly because the topic of Chapter 2 onwards is our selected flexible, scalable, and tailorable process framework, OPEN (Object-oriented Process, Environment and Notation) – but more of that later.

In summary, the adoption at an organizational level of a common "process" for developing software-intensive applications provides many benefits:

- a well-defined and well-managed process is a necessary, although unfortunately not sufficient, prerequisite for a successful development effort;
- a common process helps make the development of software-intensive applications more repeatable and forms the basis for process iteration to continually improve the process;
- cost and schedule can be more accurately estimated, tracked and controlled;
- managers can track the status of each project in terms of the status of work products and work units;
- producers (here people) can be transferred between teams without having to learn a new process;
- process training can be standardized within the organization.

A common process promotes understanding so that everyone involved in the endeavor knows what work products are to be produced and which languages are to be used to document those work products. They also know not only their own roles, responsibilities, and tasks but also how to collaborate with others to produce the work products. They are keenly aware of the roles, responsibilities, and tasks of others, whether on the same project, across multiple projects within a programme, across multiple programmes within an enterprise, or even across related enterprises. Finally, they have some understanding of how everyone should be organized into effective teams.

1.3 What is a process?

It is difficult to engineer a complex, business-critical, software-intensive system that must be cost-effective, timely and extensible as the marketplace and requirements rapidly evolve. Most systems are over-budget, delivered late, have poor quality and are expensive to maintain and enhance.

Given the critical nature of software in society, it is no wonder that mountains of books and articles have been written about software development. Because of this criticality and the increasing size and complexity of software-intensive systems, such systems must be engineered rather than informally hacked. Development processes typically codify a set of best practices as identified by individual methodologists or companies and, to this end, hundreds, possibly thousands, of software development methods have been produced and published over the last twenty years.

The identified problems with software intensive systems development stem from, first, poorly skilled participants in the development team and, second, from the lack of a good process for software construction. This led originally to the developments of process models or frameworks such as the waterfall model or, later, the spiral and fountain models. These are general descriptions of certain process elements and attempt to both identify the stages of development and to impose some sort of order, even if iterative and incremental, on to those life cycle stages. They are not really processes in that they do not provide guidelines on how to accomplish tasks, how to manage team members, and so on. They merely sketch the sequencing across the life cycle. Elaborated, as the waterfall model was in terms of SASD (structured analysis/structured design) in the 1970s and 1980s, they then become usable as a "method" or process. Indeed, there has been lengthy argument about whether processes must include methods or methods must include processes; or whether the terms are in fact synonyms. Since there are many types of processes, as we shall describe in this section, and many different definitions of the word methodology, we will not, in this book, be pedantic about the possible differences between the use of these two much-used words; methodology and process. Neither will we involve ourselves in the great methodology versus method terminology debate.

Traditionally, a development process is a cohesive set of steps to be performed in order to develop something. However, merely listing the steps of the process is inadequate. A complete process should specify not only what is done, but also who is doing it and to what, and what is the result of all this effort. It should clearly specify the inputs, outputs and ordering of each step. It should also document how the steps may best be performed (i.e., what tools and techniques should be used).

A process that describes, in detail, each of these elements (life cycle stages, producers, work units, work products, and so on) can indeed be called a process. The process thus "dictates" who does what to whom/what and when. Historically, a process such as this has tended to be derived for a specific purpose or by a specific individual and "frozen" by being fully documented. Devotees of this Process X thus either follow it slavishly or else say they do. This is easy since it is so well documented. Templates for reports and inspection check sheets are readily available and need only be filled in for the process to be deemed successful. In other words, it is all too easy for such a process to become a straitjacket rather than the flexible support that the contemporary software developer needs in a rapidly changing environment – as exemplified by changes in both technology (e.g., Java, XML) or in ways of doing business (the rapid rise of e-commerce and e-business in the late 1990s and early 2000s).

Processes may be in an individual's head or may be documented as an organizational (or international) standard to be followed on each project. Processes may be large or small, simple or complex, and "authoritarian" or flexible. Perhaps of greater importance is to ask whether the process is sufficiently mature to be repeatable. In other words, if the members of a project team say that they are applying a process, do they apply it the same way the second time and would a second project applying this same process have the same result as the first? This sort of repeatability leads to a more predictable application development environment. Data on time, effort, budget, and quality provide a coherent history upon which can be based reliable estimates for the future. In other words, the error bars in data from a repeatable process tend to become smaller. The process is "under control". This aligns well with one of the aims of the several software process capability assessment models such as ISO 15504 (SPICE[3]) and CMM. Here we use the latter as an example.

Table 1.1 The five-level capability maturity model (CMM)

	Level	Characteristics
5	Optimizing	Improvement formally fed back to process
4	Managed	Process quantitatively measured
3	Defined	Process standardized and institutionalized
2	Repeatable	Process documented yet dependent on individuals
1	Initial	Ad hoc

The five-level framework known as the Capability Maturity Model (CMM), illustrated in Table 1.1, is used to evaluate the maturity of an organization's processes. Each of the subsequent levels is cumulative, incorporating the characteristics and benefits of those preceding it:

- level 1 organizations use *ad hoc* development processes that are highly variable, individualistic, and rarely documented (the process is in the person's head; nothing is written down);
- level 2 organizations utilize processes that are documented and therefore, at least in theory, repeatable;
- level 3 organizations have institutionalized the use of a documented, repeatable process on each project. CMM Level 3 is generally regarded as the minimum level in which the use of process even approaches being satisfactory from a software engineering viewpoint. However, it is important to note that the "opposite" is also true. An organization with limited maturity (e.g., CMM Level 1) can readily adopt a process – and should do so. As a bonus, in so doing, their organizational maturity will slowly increase and they will find themselves "climbing the maturity ladder";
- level 4 organizations incorporate quantitative measurements so that the process can be managed (as opposed to "just happening" as in Level 3);
- level 5 organizations use the quantitative measurements, not only to manage the process, but also to implement a feedback loop to actually change and improve the process. This is an example of software process improvement (SPI).

Thus, the value of a process to the organization can potentially increase with an increase in the organization's maturity (e.g., CMM level, ISO 9000-accreditation). For instance, a process may be needed for managing development and for creating reusable assets, to underpin a measurement programme or for training new team-members in the ways of the organization. Process models underpin the capability of

3 SPICE stands for Software Process Improvement and Capability dEtermination.

a project manager to address their five main areas of responsibility: organizing, directing, staffing, planning, and control. This, in turn, leads to project management tasks such as scheduling, estimating, monitoring, contingency planning, and risk management. Each of these tasks needs to be an integral part of the process.

Flexibility is also sought in modern software engineering. Standardization at the international level of a single process is deemed unhelpful since it is generally regarded that no single *process* can satisfy everyone. But a single *process framework* can (see below).

For example, when circumstances are slow to change, as in the 1980s' COBOL environments in many large businesses around the world, a rigid process with clearly documented deliverables and a strict regimen can work well. When the world began to move to object-orientation and, later, component-based development, methodologies were developed with some of these "old-fashioned" characteristics. They were created largely by individuals or small teams working in specific domains. So, for instance, the ROOM methodology was created to address only real-time applications development. Such methodologies, being highly targeted, are highly applicable to those target domains. But they necessarily reflect the bias (perhaps we should say emphasis) of the methodologist responsible for the process's creation. For example, Responsibility-Driven Design (RDD), devised by Rebecca Wirfs-Brock and her colleagues, focusses on responsibilities and collaborations but is silent on issues such as requirements engineering, project management, and so on. Bertrand Meyer's persuasive arguments on Design By Contract (DBC) focus on quality issues through assertions – two ideas missing from almost all other contemporary OO methodology books. Objectory and now the Rational Unified Process (RUP) emphasize the use of use cases, which they see as a way of linking the main four views they identify within the process – but essentially ignore responsibilities, contracting, quality issues and real time issues. To each his own.

OO methods created and used in the timeframe of 1990–1995 were essentially incomplete (Figure 1.1). They perhaps omitted some technical aspects (such as responsibilities or assertions) or omitted any acknowledgement of business issues; perhaps they focussed on the software creation at the expense of the system development and the business issues (e.g., RDD); or neglected the team-building aspects of software viewed as a social construct (e.g., RUP). Their intended market might have been very specific, as in ROOM for the real-time market, or more general but still biased towards large, often defense applications, as in the earlier work of Booch, in HOOD (Hierarchical Object-Oriented Design) and so on. Some methods (such as Objectory and RUP) only give support for distinct individual "greenfield" projects; others highlight issues such as domain modeling.

Different problems, architectures, people, organizations, etc. need different process models. For example, the development cycle may be waterfall, spiral, or iterative, incremental and parallel (IIP). A project may be the first of its kind or just one in a programme of multiple projects. The focus may be a one-off development or the creation of reusable assets. This leads to the notion that there should be lots of processes, each applicable within often severe constraints. This, however, limits market share. Thus, many of the early object-oriented methods were touted as being

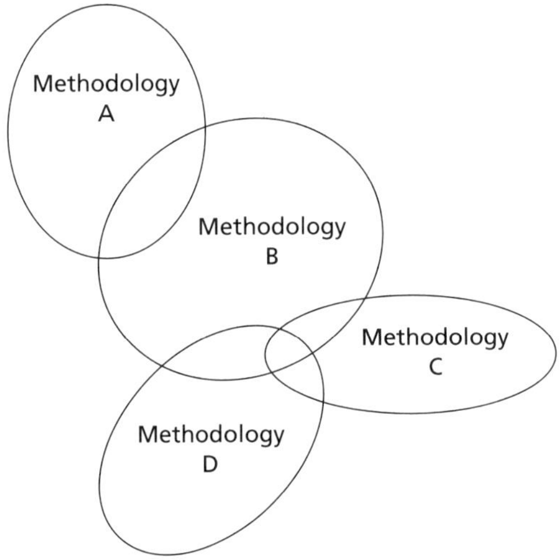

Figure 1.1 Methods from 1990–1995 were essentially incomplete with some overlaps

generally applicable – and certainly there has been a trend towards making that a reality. However, *any* process must, *de facto*, be pre-specified and pre-tailored, in the sense that every element has been laid down so that users of the method/process will be expected to adhere closely to the process as spelled out in the manual or (often) the internationally published best-selling book or embedded in some tool, e.g., Cool, Select Perspective.

But real projects do not, and should not, follow a book to the letter; they don't need *all* the elements as laid out so clearly in the manual. Software developers like to think of themselves as creative – as indeed the good ones certainly are. This led to individual organizations either "rolling their own" process or encouraging the group of OO/CBD methodologists to create a process that was, at the same time, a standard yet flexible. In other words, they seek some form of tailorability.

Tailorability, in the broadest sense of the word, permits the process/methodology to be modified to suit individual site circumstances in a supported and standardized way. Simply taking an OO method, say like Coad and Yourdon or Booch of the early 1990s, and picking out bits you like and using them as part of an in-house method which also uses parts of ROOM or HOOD, is unlikely to create a cordon bleu offering but rather a pot-pourri that might even be internally inconsistent – in detail or in philosophy. Even worse, taking one of these existing methods and tailoring it too much may even destroy it. For instance, selecting Design by Contract but then omitting any reference to or use of assertions is hardly Design by Contract; adopting XP (eXtreme Programming) but then omitting pair programming and testing means you are no longer using XP; RUP without use cases is not RUP; and so on.

So the extent to which you can change an existing *process* by tailoring is limited – without destroying the process, that is. Generic, "one-size-fits-all" processes are also less likely to cope with individual idiosyncrasies. The answer, as we shall see in the next section, is to tailor not a process but to use a *process framework* for process construction first and process tailoring second. In order to develop such a framework, we need to identify, at the most general (i.e., most abstract) level, what its components might be. And in order to do that (see below) we will first identify the components of a typical process.

A development process[4] is a cohesive aggregate of project-specific process components. It specifies three core (essential) process components and two other important components that play more of a support role.

Core

- the *work products* to be produced;
- the *producers* of these work products;
- the *work units* performed by the producers as they collaborate to produce the work products.

Support

- The *stages* that provide a macro organization to the work units;
- The *languages* in which the work products are documented.

Having identified these five high-level process components, we can now investigate how we can build a more flexible approach in terms of *process engineering*. In the next sections we demonstrate how to build a process framework from which individual, project-specific processes can be constructed.

1.4 From process to process framework

As we have seen, unfortunately no single development process can or should claim ubiquity and universal applicability because projects vary greatly along at least five dimensions: organizational constraints, domain influences, business constraints, technology issues, and application factors (Table 1.2).

4 In this book, a *development process* (a.k.a., development method or methodology) will mean a process, the objective of which is to develop an object-oriented or component-based (or, in the future, agent-based) model or a software-intensive application. We include in this definition processes focussed on so-called maintenance by regarding them as processes primarily aimed at developing new versions of existing products.

Table 1.2 Range of characteristics of projects

Organizational constraints:	Organizational structure Organizational culture (e.g. engineering, entrepreneurial) Organizational competencies (e.g., management, technology, strategy, user experience) Organizational maturity Availability of trained and experienced staff to play the roles needed
Domain influences:	MIS e-Commerce Real time Process control Embedded systems
Business constraints:	Time to market Cost (development and maintenance) Criticality Functionality Volatility of requirements Required interoperability with legacy and external applications and databases
Technology issues:	Commercial off-the-shelf components Development tools Infrastructure technologies (middleware) Web and wireless technologies Database technology Modeling and programming languages
Application factors:	Size Complexity Distribution, hardware, and network issues Required quality (e.g., operational availability, scalability, performance, etc.) Application domain

The first group of characteristics of modern software development environments likely to affect the sort of process that might be required are those organizational constraints that have so often been neglected in the past. In any organization there are people; and people are individuals despite the fact that in most software and system houses they work as teams. These teams operate within a specific organizational structure and organizational culture. There is a whole literature on teams and team building[5] which seldom sees the light of day in software books. OPEN, together with DSDM,[6] are process frameworks for application development that take the people and organizational issues seriously.[7] Organizational structures impose part of the culture, the rest being generated by the people employed there. For instance, an organization in which there is a distinct, and often lengthy, line of management – a highly hierarchical and bureaucratic organization – is unlikely to be at ease with a highly laid-back and informal process, like the one advocated in the XP approach. People in such an organization will feel happier with a very formal process with many reports and clearly specified deliverables. Contrariwise, an organization employing lots of "cowboy" (and presumably cowgirl) programmers – the so-called "heroes" of software development – are unlikely to accept a highly structured process. Indeed, they will likely rebel at the thought of using a process at all. They might even tell you they just don't believe in process (we've heard it often). What they don't realize or accept is that they *do* in fact use processes; they just happen to be their own personal ones "written down" in their heads rather than formalized and documented.

The other and final element found within the organization is again at the people level. The skills levels of individual computing professionals can be very different, even for two people with apparently the same background, training and experience. As they mature, they may develop a preference for particular techniques within the OO process – use cases or CRC card modeling, for instance. These choices are not necessarily right or wrong, better or worse, but simply personal preferences. A technique that is generally judged objectively as being in some way "better", yet used by a person with no skills in the application of that technique, is highly likely to have a detrimental effect on the success of the project. People are always more productive when using tools and techniques that they like; so, establishing what skills and preference sets are available within the team members is a wise management move. Such an analysis may well be attuned to one specific process and not another. So, once again, the specific process identified for use in the project team and/or the organization must be carefully determined.

The second set of project characteristics focusses on the impact of the domain itself. The kind of process that you may require for contrasting domains such as real-time process control, nuclear reactor monitoring, embedded systems, and business information systems is influenced by specific needs of these domains. These include the degree of safety criticality. Software used to fly aircraft, control nuclear devices and many embedded systems needs a process which has a much more formal approach to testing and support for the attainment of higher quality, perhaps in terms of reliability, security, operational availability and efficiency. Business systems can vary in these requirements. Clearly an information system supporting real-time settlement systems for a stock exchange or an online transaction system for a large bank needs many of these attributes because even a short downtime can result in the loss of millions of dollars. Other business software is more tolerant. Booking theater tickets, registering vehicles, and word-processing are areas where

5 Good examples are the books by Meredith Belbin republished in 1996.

6 DSDM stands for Dynamic Systems Development Method (Stapleton, 1997).

7 See also the People Management CMM of the SEI (http://www.sei.cmu.edu).

the user seems to be more tolerant of glitches in the system. Some Web applications may also require less testing and less formality in process although, of course, Web applications supporting core business elements need just as formal a process as would be used for a back-end transaction system (i.e., one *not* directly accessible to the Web-browsing public). On the other hand, if there is no human interface (e.g., in some embedded applications), then usability and personalization are not issues.

An example of an important business constraint (our third characteristic) might be where time to market is critical. In a highly competitive market or in one in which the software support products are needed rapidly and have a relatively short lifetime within the business, the time to market may be *the* dominating factor. In fact, many industries have adopted object technology primarily on its promise of delivering the product more rapidly to the user. At the same time, the project cost may be a major factor, coupled perhaps with quality requirements. Not all systems need to be built to the same quality. This, in part, depends upon the purpose to which the software will be put. Indeed, it is argued that quality is in the eye of the client and that there is no objective way to benchmark the quality of an application. Rather, from a list of quality factors, the client needs to choose those which are important to him/her. That then defines the quality that is to be sought and achieved by the development team. For example, the effort expended by the developers in order to achieve that agreed level of quality will depend upon whether the system is a rapid (and often dirty) prototype, perhaps as a proof of concept, or whether it is a production system designed to sustain the core business for the next decade; whether it aims to be reusable, or whether the client prefers to focus on characteristics such as efficiency, portability, security, maintainability, etc. The critical (or otherwise) nature of the software, perhaps in terms of reliability, is often a major influencing factor on the type of process to be used. For example, the extent of testing is higher for safety-critical software, for instance in the medical or aviation industry, than it would be for some of the office-based software, such as a word processor or an operating system for a home PC. In other words, the quality requirement depends significantly on the user's expectations across a wide range of characteristics.

An element often ignored in processes, but included in OPEN (see Chapter 2), is that of technology, our fourth category of project characteristics. Today, there are a plethora of commercial off-the-shelf (COTS) products and tools available to assist the developer. E-business applications may be composed largely of COTS packages such as e-business engines, security engines, personalization and internalization packages, Web servers, and application servers. Some tools have become so much a *de facto* part of our development environment that we cease to think of them as tools – although they are. Compilers are one such example, as are debuggers. While we might create a small design with paper and pencil or a crude documentation tool such as Powerpoint™, we would not dream of so doing for a huge safety-critical, core business application development. Here, we would expect tools to be provided to create large, interlinked and interchecked diagrams with full repository support and full life cycle seamlessness, possibly with reverse or roundtrip engineering between code and design.

At a slightly different level, in a distributed computing environment, we need to take into account in the process the availability of infrastructure technologies, so-called middleware, such as DCOM, CORBA or Enterprise Java Beans™. We might also take for granted that technologies to store persistent objects and components are readily available with relational and object-oriented database management systems. Finally, we expect to have tools to support our modeling and our programming ventures.

The fifth and final group of influencing characteristics relate to the specific type of application being developed. Size can be important. For a small system, a lightweight process may be adequate. Size brings its own complexity in addition to other complexity inherent in the problem. Complexity makes applications harder to understand, both by the developers themselves and, later in its life cycle, by the "maintenance team". A highly complex application is likely to need a larger degree of "ceremony" than a simple one. Finally, some application domains have idiosyncratic components that need special attention, resulting in the need for extra process elements or for specific tailoring of those process elements to the specific application domain.

There are thus many factors that influence the style and content of the most appropriate process. If such a process could be identified, it would need to be highly flexible to take into account factors such as

- *size* – small Web or e-commerce applications may require a "low ceremony" process in comparison to a large mission-critical banking application that is intended to support the core business and may therefore need a higher ceremony process;
- *complexity* – for highly complex developments, more attention will need to be paid to process elements such as quality assessment; more checks and balances will need to be installed to avoid relying on the intuition of an individual programmer;
- *business criticality* – reliability, scaleability, and operational availability mechanisms such as load balancing, failover, and redundancy are critical for applications that can never fail or be unavailable to their users.
- *safety* – quality and testing issues are more important for safety-critical software than for, say, a theater booking scheme;
- *schedule* – project management ideas, including timeboxing, may be more relevant for longer schedule projects, as might more formal and extensive levels of documentation;
- *domain* – the type of domain determines a number of high-level characteristics particularly in terms of safety criticality (see above) or technical expertise required;
- *skills set* – it is vital to match the process to the existing (or rapidly acquired) skills sets of developers. Mandating technique A to a team with no skills or training in that area will lead to failure;
- *corporate culture* – identification of the culture in terms of closed/hierarchical versus visionary/synchronous versus random versus open/consensus-driven has a significant influence on the process style. Designing a highly bureaucratic process will suit the first group (closed/hierarchical) well but will be anathema to the third (and therefore if imposed would be soon ignored);
- *maturity level* – as assessed by ISO 15504 (SPICE) or CMM (or in the future OOSPICE),[8] the extent to which an organization and its members can appreciate the need for process. A low maturity organization will find the idea of process almost untenable; a highly mature organization will find the idea of *not* using a process infeasible.

8 http://www.oospice.com.

A single process can never satisfy all these criteria under all circumstances. A structure is needed that is more flexible than a process. This leads to the identification that what is really needed is a *process framework*, probably described in terms of a metamodel.[9] A framework is a skeleton which describes the overall architecture and makes recommendations for its instantiation. Being defined in terms of a metamodel, a framework thus consists of a set of concepts (such as "activity", "work product", "role") and a set of rules governing the relationships between these concepts. In order to use this framework on a real project, we must therefore transform these *concepts* into something more concrete.[10] To do this, we create or reuse *instances* of each of the concepts of the framework or metamodel together with instances of the rules and relationships that govern how the instantiated process elements can interrelate. These instances are in fact descriptions of process components (such as the Activity of Requirements Engineering, or the Technique of CRC cards). These are best stored in a repository (Figure 1.2). Putting together these individual elements (or process components) from the repository creates a specific process instance targeted at the needs of the particular project or organization.

The process framework approach embodies both standardization and flexibility. The former results from the fact that the framework prescribes a standard and fixed (in the minimalist sense) set of terminology together with predefined semantics of metalevel concepts such as Activity, Task and Technique. It does not impose order; nor does it impose constraints such as "this process metamodel must be use-case driven". This means that biases of particular authors or developers are not frozen into the process framework, although they may be added as part of the instantiation process. Creating a specific process requires selection of actual activities, tasks, etc. together with sequencing rules, choices to be made regarding emphasis (e.g., use-case driven versus responsibility-driven), choices regarding maturity levels, skills demands, and so on. Yet despite there being no sequencing rules, we can in fact say that the metamodel conforms to and can therefore be labeled as depicting a "contract-driven" life cycle. This was originally proposed by Ian Graham based on his work with the SOMA methodology[11] which in turn was based on the second-generation MOSES methodology.[12] The idea is that by using a framework and depicting elements of the process/method as a set of interacting objects, we can actually use object technology to model the object-oriented process itself. Objects interact. They

9 We note the likely use of metamodels since we are aware that there are current deliberations within the Object Management Group that also focus on the potential use of metamodels for process descriptions and eventual standardization. The direct depiction and use of metamodels will, however, be avoided as much as possible in the main text of this book. If you find that metamodels offer greater clarity than text, see Appendix G.

10 A process framework has some similarities to the ideas of a whitebox framework in object-oriented programming i.e. a set of classes or types which are generally abstract and which are then made concrete. The concrete classes then form the software application. However, in this programming context, the concretization results from the use of inheritance, whereas in the process construction approach discussed here the mechanism is instantiation.

11 Graham, I. (1995) *Migrating to Object Technology*, Addison-Wesley.

12 Henderson-Sellers, B. and Edwards, J.M. (1994) *BOOK TWO of Object-Oriented Knowledge. The Working Object*, Prentice Hall.

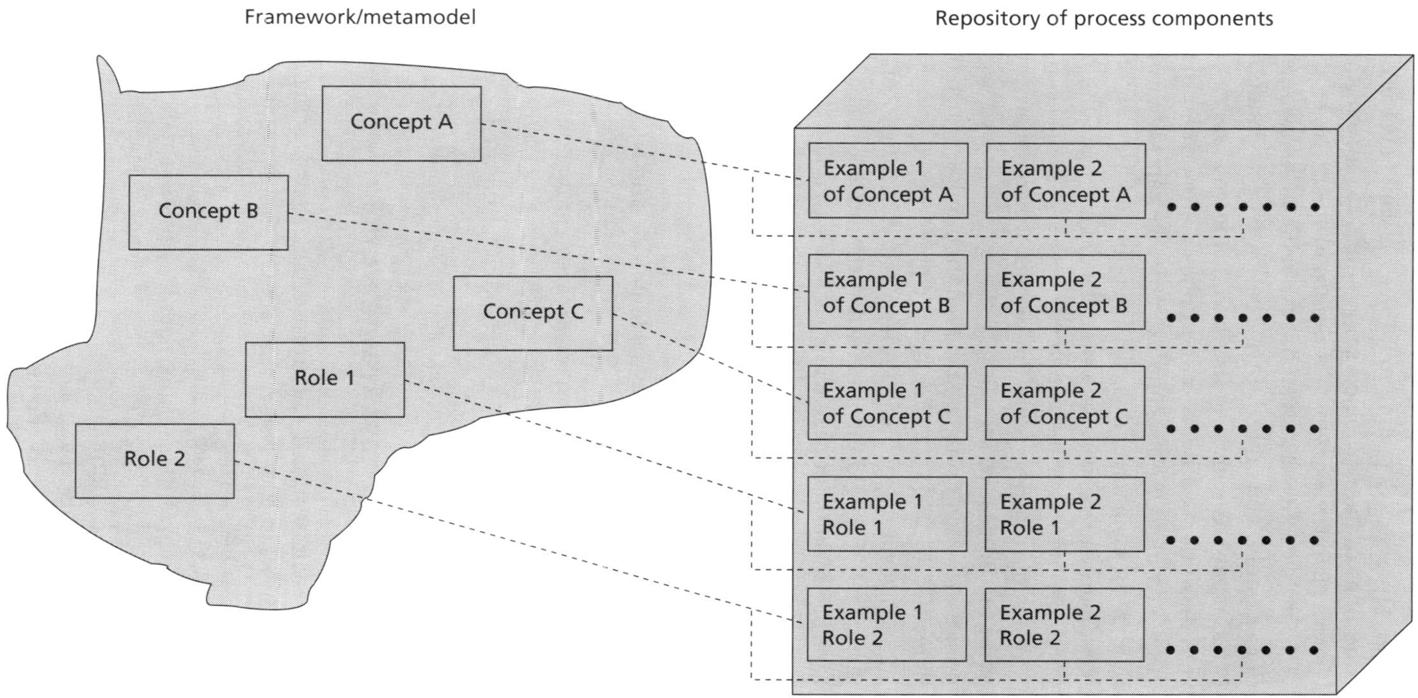

Figure 1.2 Creating an instance of a process from its metamodel

do so by sending requests with information (messages, in the OO jargon) to each other. Control therefore passes between objects. Now apply this to the process life cycle. The contract-driven life cycle model says that we can move between life cycle objects (perhaps depicting Activities) in whichever way we like *so long as* the pre-conditions of the new object's operation are met and the post-conditions of the old object's operations are met. This aims to ensure high quality of the process itself.

That this contract-driven life cycle (CDLC) subsumes others is also easily seen. For example, consider the waterfall life cycle model. This is an instance of the CDLC model in which no iteration is allowed and the pre- and post-conditions of activities (mapped one-to-one to phase) are written in terms of deliverables being 100% complete. As a second example, we can see a use-case driven approach (like RUP) is an instance of this CDLC model in which one particular technique is mandated, i.e., the use case *must* be selected as one of the primary technique instances when the process is instantiated.

We should further note that within this standardization there exists flexibility since the process of selection of the activity instances that make up the life cycle process depends strongly on the required process characteristics (as discussed above in relation to Table 1.2). Each of the process components in the repository of Figure 1.2 has a clearly specified interface so that putting together these components as you incrementally build the process is very much "plug and play". Overall, it is therefore clear that, for the wide variety of reasons as outlined above, a process framework is more flexible than a prespecified process, which tends to have many "hard-wired" cross-component connections.

Finally, we note that the framework approach offers three modes of extensibility (and thus flexibility):

- additional concepts may be identified and added to the metamodel;
- more commonly, additional examples (or instances) of existing concepts can be added to the repository of process components (Figure 1.2), thus swelling its capability; and
- existing examples can be extended (or tailored).

1.5 What is a process framework?

As we saw in section 1.4, a process framework is actually defined by a special model called a metamodel (see Appendix G). The concepts of the metamodel need to be instantiated in order to create process components, and these are used to construct an actual process. In fact, the framework/metamodel defines the rules of any and all instantiated processes – rules both for selecting and creating process model elements from the framework as well as their semantics and interconnectability. This approach is essentially a componentized one which provides the basis for the creation of an actual software development (or other) process from the individual process components in the repository (Figure 1.2). That creation process describes, *inter alia*, how the selection of process components is made from the library or repository. These existing components are each instances of one of the concepts[13] described in the metamodel. They may be newly created specifically for the current project process or they may have been accumulated there from past projects and, most importantly, from the published literature or existing websites.[14] Dozens of instances will have already been created by other companies and process specialists and made widely available. Reusing these historically proven process component instances is clearly beneficial. Selection from this existing library or repository of (predefined) process components permits creation of *your*, organization-specific or project-specific process (Figure 1.3).

Thus a process framework is *not* a process. It is more of a process to create a process. It *must* be instantiated before it can be used for developing real applications – in OPEN, for instance, this is called process construction. Preferences are added at this process creation stage by the process engineer users and *not* by the methodologist responsible for the process framework. Thus the framework approach to process has a potentially wider market since there are no inbuilt constraints or (personal) biases. Since it is based on a metamodel and componentized approach, it can *and should* be as complete as possible – although because of its component nature, additional clearly specified components can readily be added at a later date. The framework should also include support for the various "factions" outlined earlier, e.g., use case or responsibility driven, hard real time through to financial transaction management, and so on. It needs to address equally and fully the range of domains identified at the beginning of this chapter: software applications, software-intensive applications and business modeling.

This inbuilt flexibility comes at some cost, of course. There is the cost of doing the instantiation and/or process construction – but with the benefit that the result is a 100% fit to *your* needs (Figure 1.4) as compared to the null cost[15] of using a more highly constrained (and thus potentially inappropriate) productized process. In this latter case, the process vendor has done the instantiation and the selection of components and rules for component interaction, particularly at the life cycle scale of granularity. They have made one specific choice for all these. This saves you, the developer, spending time and energy doing this job. If the result (the productized process) is exactly what you require, then you are very lucky and should use the product. If, on the other hand, the match is not perfect, then you may end up spending even more dollars (more than needed in the alternative framework approach) tailoring the product, typically by subtracting pieces from the highly integrated full process (instance) and/or making small changes at the task, technique level, work product, role, and team of granularity

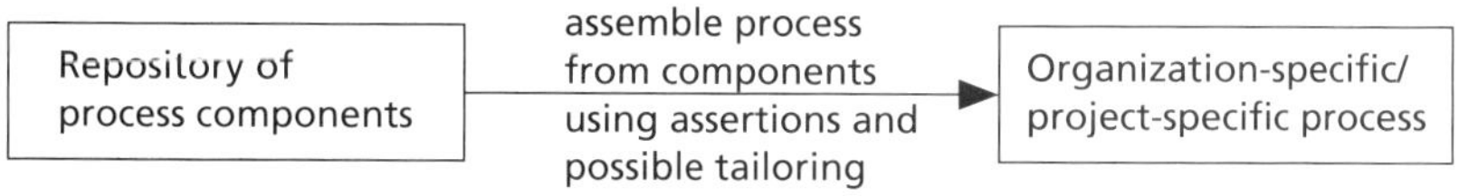

Figure 1.3 Process assembly and possible tailoring

13 Represented by metaclasses in the metamodel.

14 Such as those described in Henderson-Sellers, B. *et al.* (1998) *The OPEN Toolbox of Techniques*, Addison-Wesley.

15 Other than the capital acquisition cost, that is – which may, itself, be non-trivial.

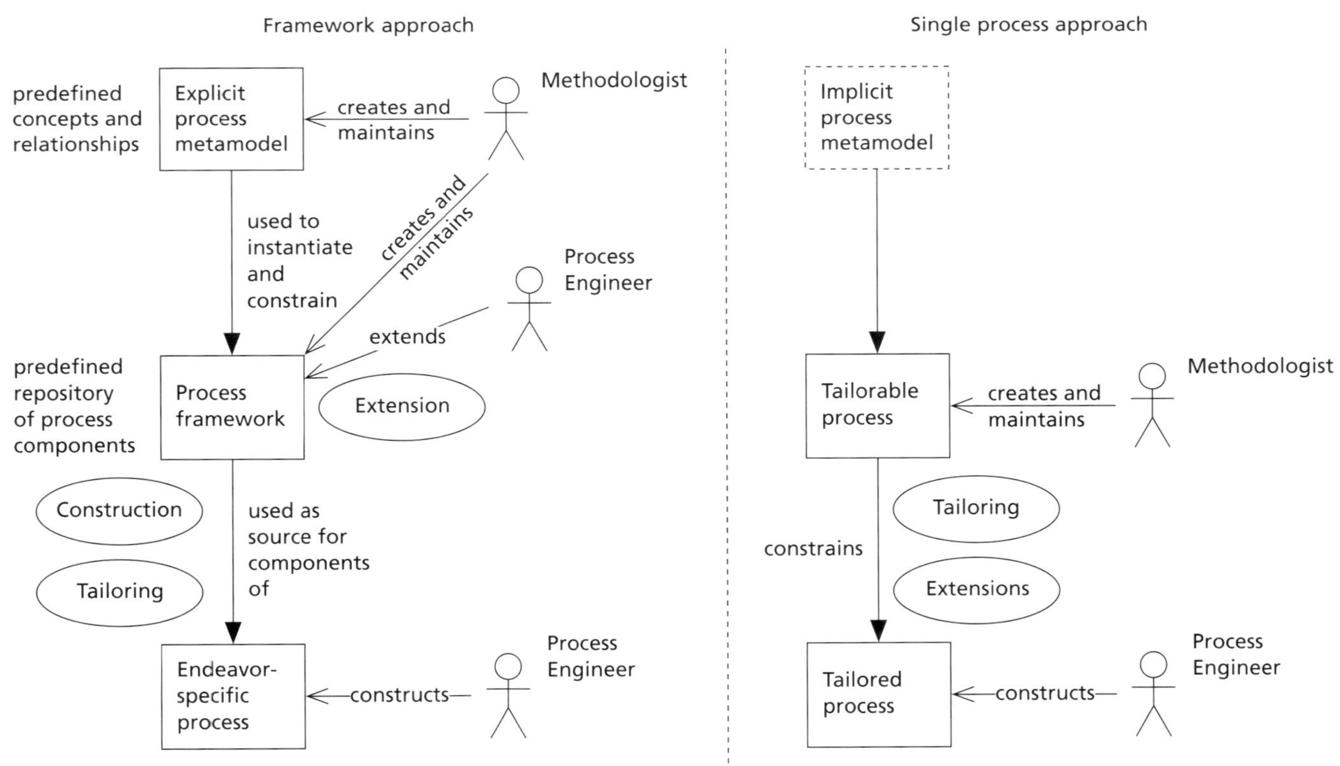

Figure 1.4 Comparison of framework and single process approaches

(Figure 1.4). This is because the productized process wasn't really designed to be flexible so patches are often necessary beyond those envisaged and supported by the productized process. As well as being potentially brittle, these patches are also non-standard so that the benefits of using a standardized process begin to fade, and upgrades to the product are not easily accommodated in your tailored version of it. Upgrades of a productized process could result in additional costs when tailoring has to be repeated.

In using the framework approach, there is also a need for a slightly deeper understanding of process. No longer is it adequate to pick up a manual, follow the process slavishly and "tick the boxes".[16] In other words, a framework is not something you learn by rote and follow mechanically. On the other hand, it isn't necessary to understand 100% of the framework (e.g., its architecture and elements) since no one project will use 100% of the framework. For instance, if you are working on banking software, the elements concerning hard real time are unlikely to be of value to you; digital branding is unnecessary for an embedded controller.

So how do you use a process framework?

As illustrated in Figure 1.5, a development process framework consists of a metamodel defining the concepts plus a class library of process components and an associated set of usage guidelines. The extensible class library provides predefined instances of all standard process components including descriptions of work products, producers of these work products, the work units performed by the collaborating producers (Figure 1.6) and, probably, descriptions of both languages used to document the work products and of various life cycle stages. The usage guidelines contain advice for extension of the class library and construction and tailoring of the associated processes. The process engineer would use the usage guidelines to extend, instantiate and tailor the predefined process components to produce a process (method) that is appropriate for a specific endeavor (a collective name for project, programme or enterprise). Thus, as we noted earlier, a development

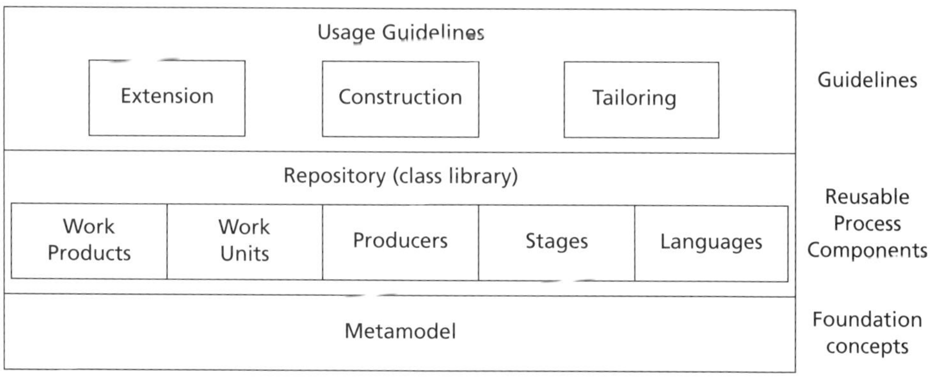

Figure 1.5 A framework consists of a set of process components in a repository, underpinned by a metamodel and complemented by a set of usage guidelines

16 Actually, it never was adequate to do this, although many companies deluded themselves.

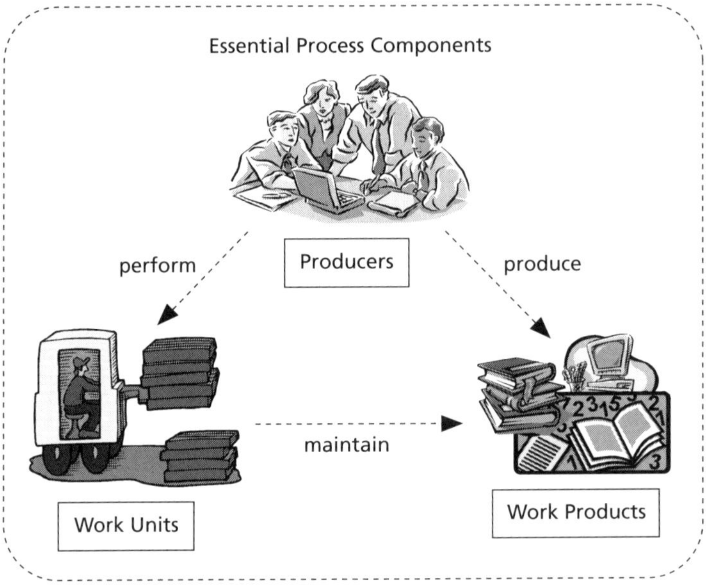

Figure 1.6 Three major process components are Producers, Work Units and Work Products

process framework provides a process for producing development processes. This process, once constructed and tailored, is the process that is used by that organization or project. It is their local standard and "way of doing things". However, for a specific project with identified people, calendar dates and dollar amounts, the process must be *enacted,* i.e., put into operation with specific data values (people's names, actual costings, etc.). Successive enactments will be similar but not identical.

Since a process framework must be instantiated before it can be used, a requisite component is a set of usage guidelines for the framework. Usage guidelines are required for instantiating the framework to construct a process instance, tailoring the resultant process instance and, possibly, creating extensions to the existing set of predefined process components. These are discussed in Chapter 8.

1.6 Specification for a process framework

Any standard process framework, for object-oriented development or otherwise, should meet a number of requirements. As a framework, it does not define a specific, cast-in-concrete process but rather defines the framework components (actually defined as metalevel concepts) that need to be selected in order to create the process. With that in mind, we realize that the process framework needs to provide an all-inclusive approach and be, as far as possible, complete. In other words, it needs to contain a large class library of process components together with a manual of usage guidelines. Each of these framework components and the way they are to be put together needs to be *rigorously defined* whilst at the same time providing flexibility in the way the components interlink to each other. This can be accomplished, much as with component-based specification and development in general, by specifying the components (here *process* components) and their interfaces as formally as possible. One excellent approach to that, and one adopted fully in OPEN, is that of contracting, derived from the "design by contract" discussions by Bertrand Meyer in the late 1980s and since elaborated upon by many authors.

The framework itself should ideally be object-oriented rather than, say, control-flow-oriented as might be the case for a process designed within the mindset of a top-down functional decomposition waterfall model (a traditional approach). The process framework model should thus emphasize classes of objects, collaboration, inheritance and polymorphism and be documented in terms of a simple, understandable object model based on standard object-oriented techniques and patterns. Although the process framework represents process elements, it should also emphasize the modeling of things (e.g., deliverable products and the people who produce them) over the decomposition of functions (e.g., activities into tasks) and, more importantly, the way these things interact, or *collaborate* in order to get things done, i.e., the work products produced and delivered to the client.

The process framework should support a range of popular development cycles such as an iterative, incremental and parallel (IIP) OO development cycle, a component-based development cycle and prototyping, as well as the traditional waterfall approach.

Let us examine each of these facets in turn.

1.6.1 Completeness

Any standard object-oriented process framework and its repository should be relativoly complete so that process engineers do not have to develop a lot of (process) components from scratch. It should come with a large class library of standard predefined process components, as we noted above. These include (i) Work Products; (ii) Producers of Work Products; (iii) Work Units to be performed by the producers; (iv) descriptions of the various developmental Stages that provide an overall organization of the process and full support for project management; together with (v) Languages with which to implement the Work Products.

Work Products include a wide range of artefacts that might be needed by the development team themselves, by the development team as documentation of internal milestones to be presented to management for review, or artefacts to be delivered to the customer, either for review or as documentation of the final application. Thus Work Products need to include the software, hardware and data components, analysis and design diagrams (visual representations), documentation which is textual, rather than visual, in nature and a wide range of other models, including use case models, prototypes and so on.

The second kind of library components listed above are the producers needed in the process. Naturally people are involved as Producers, but so sometimes are software tools and other systems. People may be producers because they are people or, more commonly, because they are playing a specific role. Or they may be producing not individually but as a team or at an even larger scale such as that of an organization. Inside the organization, we can also consider production at the scale of a single project or across a program of related projects. We can divide all the producers into (a) Direct Producers and (b) Indirect Producers.

Producers produce products[17] by means of effort applied in the context of one or more Work Units. There are a range of Work Units needed in a process framework. Work Units such as large-scale Activities and smaller-scale Tasks describe the aims of the process users: the "what is to be done". The achievement of such goals is undertaken using specific and selected Techniques. Work Flows may be considered as groupings of Tasks plus Performers (Task Performances) where a single Activity may contain several Work Flows. Work Flows focus on the products of the Activities as performed by Producers over a specified time period. The work of developers has traditionally been divided into major Activities (historically mapped to phases) that can be functionally decomposed into minor Tasks. For example, the Requirements Engineering Activity includes the requirements elicitation, requirements analysis and requirements specification tasks. To provide this overview level of abstraction, a process framework should recognize these activities and tasks, although possibly modified for consistency with the object-oriented development cycle and development methods. However, instead of being functionally decomposed in a top-down manner, activities and tasks should be identified by methodologists or process engineers in a bottom-up manner based on the products to be developed and the roles that develop them.

A process framework needs some way of organizing the overall flow of the process elements. A framework may use the notion of stages i.e., cycles divided into phases, builds and milestones. Other terms that may be useful include releases and drops. Sequencing is done using some sort of constraint such as pre- and post-conditions or triggering events.

Although when we think of languages in a computing context, we usually think only of the programming language used for the final implementation; in fact, developers use a far wider range of languages than just the coding language. As well as *implementation languages* there are *modeling languages*. Modeling languages have gained much more credibility and importance over recent years as the value of modeling has been realized. Modeling is the creation of a simpler substitute for the real world in order to understand, analyze, and finally to create a solution. A model is an abstraction. It highlights certain aspects of the thing being modeled at the expense of diversionary detail. In the context of OO, a modeling language is usually thought of as the (graphical) language used to depict the development teams' deliberations over the problem and the resulting solution or business model. Generally some form of notation is used – frequently graphical. However, a notation is inadequate unless it has meaning (semantics) as well as a syntax (i.e., rules for its usage). Often metamodels are used to provide the syntax and some of the semantics – although a criticism of modern modeling languages is that they focus on the syntax

17 In OPEN, these are called Work Products.

at the expense of the semantics. The metamodel is a model of the model. It encapsulates the rules (grammar) of the notation and depicts them graphically using object-oriented concepts such as classes and relationships but expressed at the metamodel level rather than the more normal modeling layer. Much of the rigor of OPEN comes from its underpinning metamodels. Despite this rigor and available formality, some practice in reading metamodels is needed so we collect together some of the more important metamodels for the OPEN process framework into an appendix as an additional resource for those who are metamodel-literate.

The third kind of language is *natural language*, perhaps surprisingly – since it is often forgotten as being a formal part of the process. Clearly, natural language is important, perhaps *the* most important language of all. It is needed for lots of annotations and labels in the modeling language. It is the prime means of communication[18] in any requirements specification documents, and it is the main tool used in software manuals and other supporting documentation.

All these elements of the process framework require supplementing and complementing by a set of usage guidelines which describe to the project manager or process engineer just how to tailor the process framework, how to select appropriate Activities, Tasks, and Techniques, and just what set of deliverables or Work Products seems reasonable according to the scope of the particular project or programme of projects.

1.6.2 Flexibility

Any standard object-oriented process framework should be flexible in terms of:

- **extensibility**. Because no class library can ever be totally complete, any standard object-oriented process framework should be extensible, allowing the process engineer to add new items to the library of predefined process components;
- **construction**. Any standard object-oriented process framework should allow the process engineer to instantiate (construct) a process that is appropriate for a specific project. He or she should be able to (i) choose the Work Products to develop; (ii) choose the Languages with which to document and implement the Work Products; (iii) choose the Producers (e.g., roles, teams, organization, and tools) to develop the Work Products; (iv) allocate Tasks and associated Techniques to the Producers; (v) group the Tasks into Activities and Work Flows; and (vi) choose the development Stages (cycles, phases and milestones).
- **tailoring**. Any standard object-oriented process framework should permit the process engineer to tailor the process initially and, iteratively, to modify the process to meet the changing needs of the project and incorporate lessons learned during the process. In particular, the process engineer should easily be able to tailor the Work Products by adding, deleting, and modifying their contents. Tailoring is thus typically not a one-off event.

18 Developer to developer or development team member to end-user/client.

1.6.3 Rigor

While providing the necessary flexibility, a process framework must provide an appropriate amount of rigor. Specifically, it should provide:

- **contractual basis**. The resulting process must make development manageable e.g., by allowing the process engineer to specify the relationships between work units (and stages) via assertions. One of the primary managerial concerns regarding object-oriented development is that the iterative, incremental and parallel life cycle may be misused as justification for the methodological equivalent of hacking. Whereas all requirements need not (and probably should not) be completely specified before the start of architecting and design, neither should requirements be analyzed after the associated software design is implemented in tested code. Contractual agreements between the different roles played on the project must be specified, and developers and managers must be able to agree on incremental milestones and completion criteria for the various Work Products. Otherwise, the entire project becomes unmanageable.
- **formality**. Most processes in use on industrial development projects are relatively *ad hoc* and documented using narrative text with all of the associated possibilities for human error in interpretation and execution. The use of a standard and formally specified framework for object-oriented processes ensures a standard terminology and standard definition of terms. The resulting object model clearly specifies the essential process components (roles, teams, organizations, products, tasks, techniques, activities, and phases) and the relationships between them. The use of assertions on tasks clearly specifies the contractual relationships between roles and teams. Ultimately, the use of a standard framework can signify the development of a documented, manageable, repeatable, extensible development process that would score well on the CMM scale.

1.6.4 Object orientation

Use of object models to model the process framework

An *object-oriented* process framework is one that has been analyzed, designed and modeled using the techniques of object-oriented analysis and design. Thus, an object model of the development process would consist of collaborating polymorphic classes organized into inheritance hierarchies. It is therefore clearly well aligned to create OO process instances but can equally be used to create processes for non-OO software development.

Object-oriented methods

Methods (sometimes known as methodologies) have been around a long time; but it is only since around 1990 or so that they have been available to support the majority of object-oriented development. An object-oriented approach relies on notions such as abstraction, strict modularization and information hiding, and polymorphism. Requirements, design, and code all use the same model of the "object" which encapsulates together state and behavior with a tightly controlled interface. The initial emphasis is always on the "what", not the "how" within the development life cycle. With this more holistic view of modeling and software design, it is beneficial to ask about the high-level responsibilities that an object has: responsibilities for doing, for knowing, and for enforcing business rules. In later design and coding, these responsibilities are translated into operations and then methods of the classes. Whilst using a responsibility-focussed approach is found to be highly useful, object orientation can also give good results using a data-driven approach or a use-case driven method, depending on the particular problem and problem domain.

Object-oriented development cycles

In an OO development environment, many of the traditional process and associated project management techniques are applicable. However, in order to provide the necessary flexibility, an object-oriented development cycle should typically be described using the following three attributes:

- **Incremental**. The development cycle of most object-oriented projects is *incremental* because non-trivial products are so large and complex that they would take too long to deliver if developed and tested in a big bang manner. By the time the application was delivered, their original requirements typically would be obsolete. Today's competitive marketplace will often no longer support the inherent delays of the traditional waterfall cycle. An OO development should deliver products to the users incrementally, possibly as frequently as at the end of each build, say every few weeks. Incremental delivery keeps the customer in the loop, ensuring that they always have in their possession a delivered and running version that is at worst a few weeks old. They can thus give immediate feedback rather than waiting for a one-time delivery of the full system perhaps as much as three years after they first made the request for its development. They will also end up with a valuable partial system if the project must be terminated prior to completion.
- **Iterative**. The development cycle of most object-oriented projects is also *iterative*. As time goes on, some or all of the development process will be repeated on the evolving partial products to improve them as requirements change and defects are identified and fixed. At the beginning of a project, the requirements are rarely completely known and they will often change during the course of development. Humans develop software, which means that developers make mistakes and are not omniscient; they should learn during development. The traditional waterfall life cycle dictates a number of phases that are sequentially completed and, once any given step is finished, it is theoretically never returned to. In contrast, an iterative life cycle is one in which development activities are repeated on the same Work Product to change (i.e., iterate) it. Iterations need to be planned and often go across all life cycle activities (user requirements elicitation, analysis, design, code, and test). However, iteration is no excuse for hacking, and eventually the current version of the application must be completed and deployed.

- **Parallel**. Finally, the development cycle of most object-oriented projects is *parallel.* There is typically a great deal of overlap in development activities in which requirements analysts develop requirements, architects architect, designers design, programmers code and testers test, all of these activities occurring simultaneously during most of the project. Even within a single activity such as OO modeling, multiple teams will typically be working in parallel on different packages.

Work Products and their producers

Remember that a major difference between a functionally decomposed design and an object-oriented design is in what they emphasize. Whereas a procedural design emphasizes the functions to be performed and the relationships between them, an object-oriented design emphasizes the classes of objects and how they collaborate to perform useful work. Thus, a traditional process model would emphasize software development activities (mapped one-to-one with phases) and their decomposition into lower-level activities and tasks. On the other hand, an object-oriented model of the software development process would emphasize the major classes of objects such as the Work Products to be produced and the teams of people that produce them. Individual tasks would be merely the operations performed by the "developer" objects and overall development activities could be seen as analogous to the realizations of use cases, being implemented by the collaboration of many "developer" objects performing their individual development tasks.

The primary reason development projects exist is to produce applications and their associated documentation. Any standard object-oriented process framework should therefore be based on the products to be developed because it ultimately depends on the size, complexity, criticality, and number of Work Products to be produced. All other decisions are secondary and a function of the Work Poducts. Therefore, the most important objects in the model are the Work Products that must be produced by the object-oriented development method that is instantiated from the process framework.

Some methodologists (especially those burned by the over-production of documentation on traditional military or governmental projects) might object that this emphasis on products would encourage a document-driven process that wastes valuable development time and effort on the development of large, complex, but relatively useless documents. However, one would better argue that by emphasizing the development of *appropriate* products, one avoids both wasting time on irrelevant documentation as well as wasting time on unproductive activities and tasks that are performed merely because they have been mandated as part of the process. Better to decide first what you need to produce before you worry about how to produce it.

Second, the development of software-intensive systems will be a labor-intensive activity for the foreseeable future. Such systems are developed by people who play various, sometimes multiple, roles on the project. Management needs to know how to staff the project, what roles the staff will play, the level of their necessary expertise and training, and how these roles should be aggregated into teams and organizations. An object-oriented process metamodel would also concentrate on these active producer objects that collaborate to produce the more passive Work Product objects.

1.6.5 Component-based development (CBD)

Although we have discussed *object-oriented* approaches to software intensive system development, another technology which is currently of much interest is that of component-based development (CBD). There is much debate whether CBD is (a) another name for OT, (b) an extension (i.e., a more sophisticated version of) OT, or (c) something completely different. Potential confusion comes in part from the emphasis in CBD on the idea of a component as a source-code level module. Components emphasize pluggability of binary-level modules of code – for example, the use of JavaBeans, ActiveX and so on. Components must be able not only to be plugged into your next application but should be able to be traded on the open market. This emphasis on the use of encapsulated and pluggable modules as units of deployable code characterizes component technology as different from, perhaps even orthogonal to, object technology. More important than the development of fine-grained components is the production of applications by integrating a relatively small number of large commercial-off-the-shelf (COTS) components (packages). At a minimum, the two technologies co-exist but with a major difference in granularity. At the same time, although components exist in other than object-oriented contexts, it is our forecast that over the next decade the use of CBD will, in almost all cases, involve some aspect(s) of object orientation – for example, the realization of a component by one or more classes.

Component technology[19] naturally emphasizes interfaces and the level of trust that one can place in such specifications as being truly indicative of the behavior of the component. Thus projects such as "Trusted Components" began in the late 1990s. Furthermore, the emphasis on deployable code units has tended to mean that discussions of "analysis and design" have been largely ignored in the literature, although some CBD advocates comment that this means that OOAD is an unchanged component of CBD.

In Chapter 2 we will show how CBD and OT co-exist in OPEN, and in Chapters 3 to 8 we show how a relevant process can readily be created from the OPEN Process Framework elements.

Summary

In summary, we can characterize a process by the following statements:

- A development process is a process that develops either a model (e.g., of a business during business modeling/business engineering) or an application (during a development project).

19 See, for example, Cheesman, J. and Daniels, J. (2001) *UML Components: A Simple Process for Specifying Component-based Software*, Addison-Wesley and http://www.cbdinforum.com.

- Having a well-defined standard development process has numerous advantages:
  - It is a necessary prerequisite for a successful development effort.
  - It provides repeatability and forms the basis for process improvement.
  - Cost and schedule are more accurately estimated and tracked.
  - Managers can track status.
  - It promotes understanding among stakeholders.
  - Producers can be transferred without having to learn a new process.
  - Process training can be standardized.
- No single development process is appropriate for all endeavors because of differences in:
  - Organizational constraints.
  - Domain influences.
  - Business constraints.
  - Technology issues.
  - Application factors.
- A development process specifies:
  - Work Products to be developed.
  - Producers who produce the Work Products.
  - Units of Work to be performed by the Producers as they collaborate to produce the Work Products.
  - Stages that provide a macro organization to the Work Units.
  - Languages used to document the Work Products.

The alternative to a single, highly specified process is the process framework. It is this approach that is recommended in this book. A process framework provides a large, relatively complete repository (or class library) of predefined process components including Work Products to be produced; Producers of Work Products; Work Units performed by Producers as they collaborate to produce the Work Products; Stages that provide a macro organization to the Work Units; and Languages in which these Work Products are to be implemented. It is this set of components that now offers ultimate flexibility. Components are selected from this library and a specific process constructed in a bottom-up or top-down fashion. A set of usage guidelines is required to describe three major aspects of this approach: constructing the process instance; extending the process metamodel; and tailoring the process instance to specific circumstances and organizational or project requirements.

Thus the 'process' is in fact 'standardized' at a higher level of abstraction – at the framework or metalevel rather than at the process level. The standard process framework remains unaltered as a result of specific instantiations of it being created, thus permitting a cohesiveness between groups of developers all using the same process framework yet using (slightly) different instances of that framework.

Finally, an (object-oriented) process framework should fulfill certain requirements:

- It should provide concrete and useful support for everyday activities and tasks of people working on a project.
- It should be relatively complete in terms of predefined process components and usage guidelines.
- It should be flexible in terms of extensibility, instantiation and development, or life cycle.
- While providing flexibility, it should nonetheless provide the necessary rigor to make development manageable (e.g., by allowing the process engineer to specify the relationships between Work Units via assertions).
- It should (preferably) be object-oriented, emphasizing classes of objects, collaboration, inheritance, and polymorphism.
- It should provide a formal framework for the specification of system or software development methods and the specification of individual project-specific processes.

2 OPEN Process Framework Overview

Abstract

After reading this chapter, you should have a good general idea of what the OPEN Process Framework is about. However, a detailed understanding of its components and usage guidelines will require reading Part II of this book.

2.1 OPEN

Object-oriented Process, Environment, and Notation (OPEN) is the premier third-generation, full Life cycle, process-focussed, object-oriented development methodological approach that was designed for the development of software intensive applications, particularly object-oriented and component-based endeavors. OPEN was developed and is maintained by the not-for-profit OPEN Consortium, an international group of over 35 methodologists, academics, CASE Tool vendors, and developers.

OPEN is defined as a process framework, known as the OPF (OPEN Process Framework) and defined by a metamodel.[1] From it can be constructed many OPEN-compliant processes (or, more strictly, process instances) by the instantiation of elements in the metamodel, these instantiated elements being the predefined process components stored in a repository. Each individual process is then created by selecting appropriate process components from this OPF repository of predefined elements – or, indeed, creating your own process component instances directly from the metamodel. These process components (in the OPF respository: Figure 2.1) are specific examples of Work Units, Producers, Work Products, etc. Process components known as Stages are then used to configure the other process elements together (using the Construction Guidelines in the OPF: Figure 2.1), thus adding sequencing, timing and life cycle information. This is process construction[2] (Figure

1 The M2 level in OMG parlance.

2 In contrast to a tailorable process in which there is only one *prescribed* process which is then tweaked. Tailoring is thus described in terms of (relatively small) modifications – see e.g. Ginsburg, M.P. and Quinn, L.H. (1995) *Process Tailoring and the Software Capability Maturity Model.*

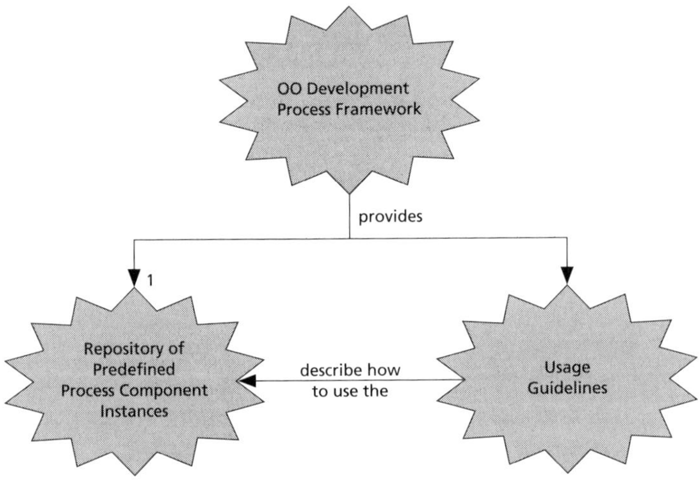

Figure 2.1 Using a framework approach requires selection of Instances of Process Components from the repository by use of the Construction Guidelines

2.2). Since this configuration activity can result in one of very many possible arrangements of the process component pieces, we can think of OPEN not just as a process framework (its primary role) but also, more loosely, as a (family of) processes, each meeting the needs of a specific company, domain etc. (Figure 2.3). On both counts, it is a *highly flexible* componentized methodological approach to building software and software-intensive systems as well as offering support for business engineering and modeling, including digital strategies and digital branding.

OPEN is broad in scope. It addresses not only software modeling but also business, quality and reuse issues within its end-to-end life cycle support for application development. OPEN provides flexibility. Its metamodel-based framework can be tailored to individual domains or projects taking into account personal skills, organizational culture and requirements peculiar to each industry domain. It is thus useful for not only application development projects but also for business process re-engineering and for process creation.

Specifically:

- *OPEN is third generation.* The first OO methods, created about 1990, were primarily sets of tips and techniques rather than true methods. However, they are often referred to as first-generation OO methods. They were constructed by individuals or small groups and used in pilot projects in industry and in teaching. By about 1994, two things were happening. Methodological writing increased so that the original methods developers of 1990, along with an increasing number of others, started to read widely and incorporate good ideas from a wide variety of sources into their own methodologies. The methods began to look more and more like each other, supporting common ideas and common principles. Once published, these became known as second-generation methods. Typical examples are Booch's 1994 approach, OMT, the SOMA approach, Firesmith's 1993 approach and MOSES (the last three being direct precursors of OPEN).

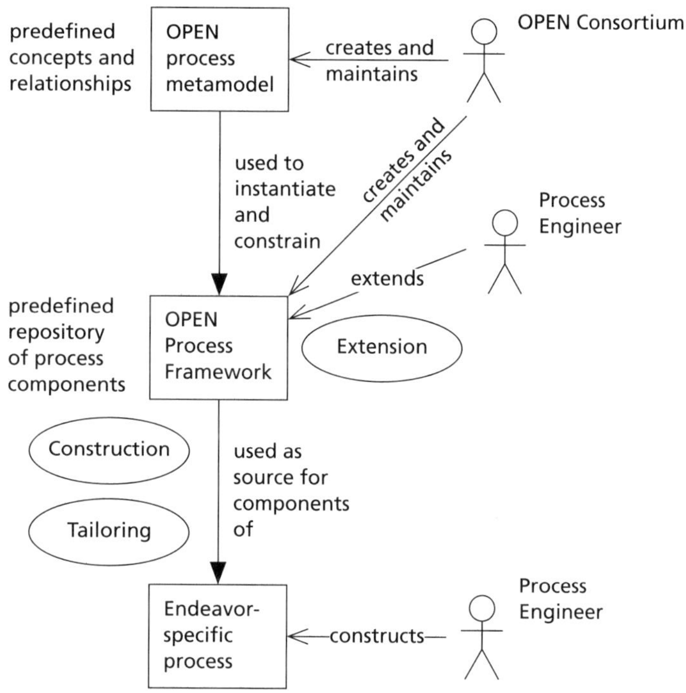

Figure 2.2 The OPEN Process Framework approach (cf. Figure 1.4)

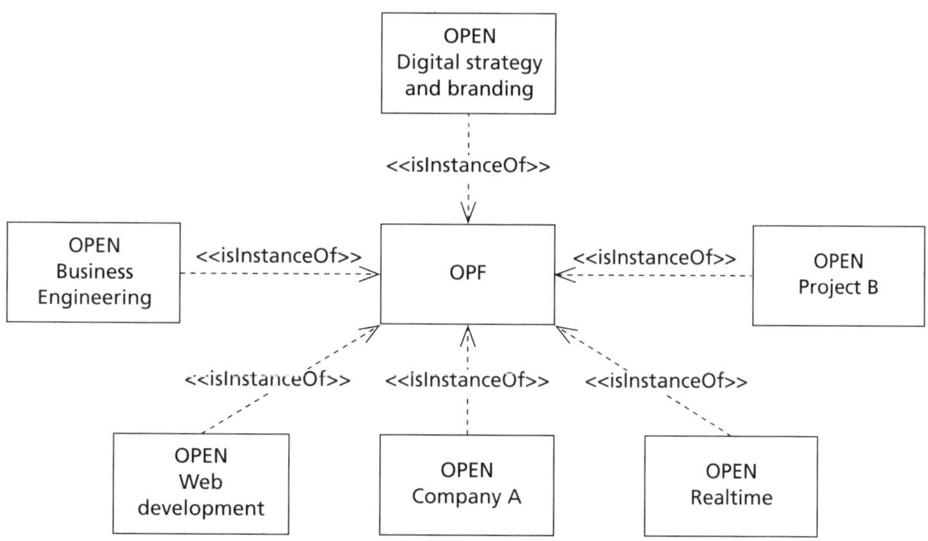

Figure 2.3 OPEN provides a family of processes (six examples are depicted), each process configured to meet exactly the requirements of a specific domain, company, project or application type

Despite the publication and teaching of these second-generation methods, it soon became clear to these methodologist authors that the software industry in general still seemed reticent to adopt their ideas. One reason was perceived to be the lack of standardization and support in the sense that second-generation methods were still under the control of only one person or, at best, a small group of people. Furthermore, CASE tool vendors found it difficult to support a large number of methods. In addition to good tool support, for large-scale industrial usage an industrial user needs to be sure that, if one provider of support vanishes, alternative sources will remain. This led to the active collaboration of methodologists in order to create more broadly supported third-generation methodologies. Begun in late 1994, OPEN is the premier example of a third-generation methodological approach. As well as being a methodological approach, thus supporting your organization's process, OPEN goes one better by specifying a *process framework* which is able to generate a wide number of processes from its metamodel.

- *OPEN is full Life cycle.* OPEN covers the complete development cycle including the strategy, initiation, construction, delivery, and usage phases through to the retirement of the application. OPEN also covers all engineering activities including requirements engineering, architecting, design, coding, integration, and testing. OPEN even covers such activities as project management (planning, staffing, and scheduling), metrics, configuration management, risk management, training, digital branding, quality engineering, and content management.

  OPEN provides strong support for process modeling and requirements engineering, and has an embedded project management and reuse framework. It also supports business process modeling, offers guidelines on migration strategies and supports links to human relations issues. A prime concern of OPEN is software quality and the use of metrics. To that end, there are close links with quality frameworks including the Software Engineering Institute's Capability Maturity Model, ISO 9000 and ISO 15504 (SPICE) as well as to the newer OOSPICE software process improvement project.

  Applications can be considered to have a life cycle from birth to death. The need for software can arise when business problems need a solution. Therefore, the first step (the birth) occurs when a business problem is identified. This problem must be clearly enunciated and may involve customer analysis, market analysis, technology analysis, user analysis, cost/benefit analysis, and business strategy. And although application need not be mandated at this Stage, for those problems that *do* require them, the Requirements Engineering Activity, which focusses on elucidating the business problem, is clearly a vital part of the Application Life Cycle. Business decision-making, requirements engineering and systems analysis are all "early life cycle" activities. OPEN includes Tasks and Techniques that are useful in these early stages, thus providing support for business modeling and reengineering. Few other OO/CBD methods pay more than lip service to these more business-focussed issues. Yet in the real world, if technology (here object technology or component-based development) is to be relevant to commercial environments, an OO method *must* consider these early life cycle issues and not just assume that the life cycle begins with the handing over of a clearly and uniquely defined requirements definition to the software development team.

Similarly, a methodology should cover the late life cycle activities. Whilst most are good at program design and coding, they tend to tail off in their coverage of issues such as deployment, user training and future enhancements/maintenance. It is just as important that a method addresses these issues, perhaps using testing metrics to do fault detection and usability studies to evaluate customer acceptance of the delivered product, for instance.

- *OPEN is process-focussed.* Process is a key to successful application development. It imposes order and rigor that permits and encourages repeatability of outcomes and continuous improvement. Sophisticated processes are highly compatible with measurement and with use of the resulting metrics to manage, control and improve the process.

- *OPEN is object-oriented.* OPEN is object-oriented in two ways. First, its heredity is that of the many OO methodologies that have been developed over the last decade of the twentieth century. It was originally designed to answer the question "How should we build object-oriented systems and software?" and then extended to support other software development paradigms such as CBD, traditional non-OO development and Web development (see below). It is object-oriented in a second way: ideas from object technology have been used to construct the metamodel underpinning the OPEN Process Framework (OPF). This is done by objectifying (or reifying) all the elements of the process and permitting them to interact in any reasonable way wherein their interaction is governed and constrained by whether the objects do or do not meet the *assertions* (pre-conditions, post-conditions and invariants) declared in the (process) objects. This use of contracting, originally introduced in object technology by Bertrand Meyer through the Eiffel Language, gives this approach its name: the contract-driven life cycle (CDLC) approach. While this is the preferred model of the life cycle, others, such as a risk-driven spiral or even a waterfall, can be supported since they can all be viewed as subsets of the contract-driven approach.

- *OPEN provides a flexible development process framework.* OPEN is essentially a framework for creating third-generation, object-oriented methods/processes for developing software, for software-intensive systems and for business modeling and engineering. These processes are constructed from the framework by creating a specific instance of that framework. The specificity is reflected in the choice of which instances of Work Unit, Work Product, Producer etc. are selected. Each process constructed in this way is highly configured to a particular domain or Project. It can thus be used to create a process instance to support component-based development and can be used for traditional software development (see discussion below).

  It provides a suite of Tasks and Techniques from which a set can be chosen to use to create a process *specifically* for each individual Organization or each Application development i.e., to each individual Project as described in Chapter 1.

The framework approach adds the capability of being able to support several "styles" of OO development. Although the recommended style is that of a responsibility-driven approach, other styles such as document-driven, data-driven and use-case driven are equally easily accommodated.

- *OPEN is useful for component-based development (CBD).* As well as object-oriented systems developments, OPEN is also highly useful for component-based development (CBD) approaches which are just beginning to be developed. In particular, the process strongly supports ideas of reuse; both in terms of how to create reusable components and how to locate, integrate, and use reusable components.

  In CBD, the focus is on the use of encapsulated and pluggable components as units of deployable code. Thus, while additional support is needed in a process to discuss these implementation issues, the "analysis and design" issues for CBD using OT are exactly the same as for traditional OO developments, although the emphasis in build versus buy is, of course, somewhat different.

  In CBD, there is also a greater emphasis on interfaces. Interfaces must be trusted, clearly specified and useful. Ways of "glueing" the components together are needed both diagrammatically, leading to the need for minor enhancements or variations in use with current OO modeling languages, and at the code level. Outgoing and incoming ports are equally relevant since the client object is as likely to be componentized, and hence immutable, as is the server object/component. OO methods such as Catalysis were specifically designed for this type of approach and ideas from this approach have been borrowed for use in OPEN. While the idea of a Component as a pluggable part is orthogonal to the technology which may be used to achieve it, in reality the most used technology for components is object technology.

- *OPEN is useful for traditional software development* since its metamodel-based framework generates high-level process elements independent of the implementation technology and because any OO-specific process components stored in the OPF repository can be neglected in building a software process for traditional, non-OO software development. Specific legacy technologies can equally easily be supported directly by creating a new process component specifically tailored to the situation from one of the existing OPF metalevel elements. In other words, the metamodel is independent of development approach; only the process components in the repository are directly influenced. And since these are fully componentized, building processes of any kind is easy.

- *OPEN is useful for development of Web-enabled systems.* With the advent of business-critical Web-based applications in recent years, it is now evident that a Web-focussed process (an OPEN instance) is needed. This is created in exactly the same way as all other examples of the OPEN family of processes. For Web development, new process components have been added to the OPF repository to support those aspects of Web development unique to that environment – for example, digital branding, website design, usability testing, data components, content management, and Web development roles and teams.

- *OPEN is highly appropriate for distributed systems.* Development in the new millennium with new technologies such as .NET HTML, XML, and WAP will incorporate distributed architectures almost by default. With the advent of the Internet and industrial strength middleware to support distributed architectures, a good methodology has the responsibility of providing the detailed process of architecting and designing fully encapsulated components that can be deployed over a company's network or on the web. OPEN provides detailed support for such applications via hardware architecting, hardware and network roles etc.

- *OPEN is useful for business modeling* and business reengineering as well as for software intensive applications, component-based exercises and the integration of hardware systems and software systems. OPEN goes further than many other OO processes by including significant support for business modeling and business decision-making, well prior to any software solution being sought. It can be used therefore not only in business modeling but also for business process reengineering. It includes support for programme management, digital strategies and branding, which are all applicable both outside the software domain as well as inside. At the same time, it is fully comprehensive in terms of supporting the *software* development environment with a full set of requirements engineering, modeling and implementation Techniques and Activities.

- *OPEN is notation-independent.* OPEN supports both the UML notation, the OML notation, and any other good OO notation of your choice in order to document the work products that the OPEN process produces.

2.2 The OPEN Process Framework

Unlike an individual development process, the OPEN Process Framework (OPF) consists, not of a single integrated product, but of a metamodel together with a large extensible class library of reusable process components that can be used to meet the needs of multiple, often quite different, projects. Process construction may be per project or per organizational unit depending upon the variability of project characteristics within the organizational unit. To provide flexibility, a process framework library/repository will typically include far more components than will be used on any one project rather than a minimal or "optimal" set of components.

Figure 2.4 illustrates the high-level structure of the OPF. It defines three kinds of essential or core process components: Work Products, Producers that produce Work Products, and Work Units that are performed by Producers when they create, evaluate, or document Work Products. These are supported by Stages, which provide a macro-organization to the process, and by Languages, which are used to document the Work Products.

We will now give an overview of each of these five component types in turn – details are deferred to Part II and the Appendices.

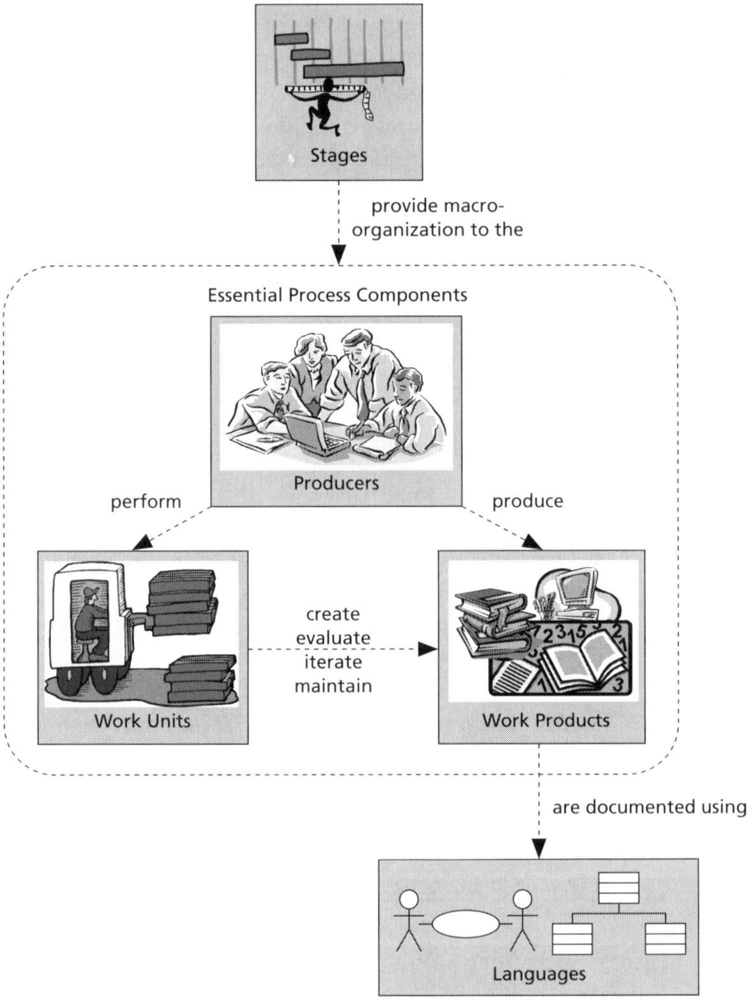

Figure 2.4 The components of the OPEN Process Framework

2.2.1 Work Products

A *Work Product* is anything of value (e.g., Application, Document, Model, Diagram, or Class) that is produced during the development process. Direct Producers produce Work Products as they perform their Tasks. During the evolution of a Work Product, Work Product Versions are created. Therefore, each Work Product has an associated time-ordered set of Work Product Versions.

Process engineers must instantiate the development process framework to meet the needs of the specific Project. Primarily, they select those Work Products that are useful and cost-effective to produce. They may also extend the process framework by adding any additional Work Products that are needed but were not predefined in the class library. This is possible with the process framework approach as a direct result of its componentized nature.

Sets of Work Products

Work Products can often be usefully organized into sets, based on the activities that produce them; for example:

– Management Set
– Configuration Management Set
– Quality Set
– Training Set
– Process Set
– Metrics Set
– Environments Set
– Security Set
– Digital Branding Set
– Requirements Set
– Architecture Set
– Design Set
– Implementation Set
– Integration Set
– Test Set
– Deployment Set

where the first four refer to management-oriented Work Products and the last eight refer to the engineering perspective. We briefly examine some of these in the following subsections.

Management Set

The management set of Work Products includes planning, staffing descriptions, and schedules (Table 2.1) – mostly textual documentation. Plans and Work Schedules are normal components of any management strategy. Unlike many other OO methods which ignore the project management aspects of developing applications, OPEN specifically includes extensive discussions and Work Products relating to Project and Programme Management.

Configuration Management Set

The Configuration Management Work Products include a Configuration Management Plan that describes how configuration management is to be undertaken and using what Tools as well as other Configuration Management Documents.

Quality Set

Much of the Quality Set of Work Products involves Quality Metrics. It is clear that appropriate metrics need to be identified and a plan put in place to ensure that they are collected and analyzed and that the resulting analysis is used for timely decisionmaking. Other quality Work Products include the quality plan, inspection checklists, and audit reports.

Table 2.1 Management Set of Work Products

Planning work products:
– Management plan – Build plan – Conversion plan – Risk management plan – Disaster recovery plan
Staffing work products:
– Job description – Organization chart
Scheduling work products:
– Project schedule – Component schedule – Team schedule
Other documents:
– Contract – Statement of work – Work breakdown structure (WBS) – Budget – Status report – Project debrief report

Training Set

Training Work Products include training plans by which all personnel will receive adequate training and education in the technical or management areas relevant to them. Other Work Products include reports of employees after attending training, handouts and manuals acquired as part of training, as well as assessment documents for future tendering and outsourcing, when appropriate.

Process Set

The *Process Set of Work Products* is the set of engineering Work Products primarily developed by the Process Team. It includes Procedures, Guidelines, Standards, Templates and Inspection Checklists.

Since OPEN is a tailorable framework, one of the important Work Products is a Process Description Document that defines and describes the results of that tailoring; in other words, an agreed manual for *your* version of the OPF (Figure 2.3).

Requirements Set

The *Requirements Set of Work Products* includes all Work Products directly produced during Requirements Engineering, both for the application development and any business modeling or business engineering work. The OPF contains definitions for a number of kinds of Requirements Activity Work Products, including Vision Statement, Glossary, System Requirements Specification, External Interface Specification, and Software Requirements Specification. For business engineering projects, the Requirements Set can include customer, market, technology, and user analyses, application cost/benefit analyses, and business strategies.

It is important that any project have a number of documents clearly specifying aspects of the project identifiable and assessable by the client. The developer needs to have an agreed vision of the project – one that is shared with the customer! At a lower level, the requirements also need to be well specified, although of course these work products will be built up iteratively.

Architecture Set

The OPF contains a number of predefined classes of Architecture Work Products: documents that describe the Enterprise Architecture, the Programme Architecture, the Business Architecture, the System Architecture, the Software Architecture, and the Information Architecture. Architecture can also refer to databases, websites, hardware, and networks and information.

It is increasingly being recognized that one (but not the only) driving factor for a good application development is a sense of the overall architecture. Akin to a building architecture, system architecture relates to large-scale logical and physical architectures as well as architectural mechanisms and technology choices.

Design Set

The OPF contains advice on a number of manuals and documents that can collectively be called the "Design Set". These include the Database Design Document, the Framework User's Manual, the Package Design Document, a GUI Prototype, the UI Design Document, and (when using the Java Language) JavaDoc.

The smaller-scale configuration of the objects and components is documented, including how the system being created will interact with databases, relational or object-oriented according to taste. Here also are Work Products for the user interface and, in a Java development environment, documentation created using the very useful JavaDoc tool.

Implementation Set

For application development projects, the Implementation Set of Work Products defined in the OPF fall into three categories: Software Components, Hardware Components and Data (Content) Components. Software Components covers the areas of Frameworks, Packages, Classes, and Stored Procedures. Hardware Components include Devices, Computers, Networks, and Storage Devices. Devices include Actuators, Input Devices and Output Devices such as Displays, Printers, and Sensors. Computers themselves may be classified as Clients, Firewalls, Routers, or Servers (Application, Database, and Web Servers). Networks may be the Internet or a corporation's Intranet. Storage devices include Disk and Tape Libraries. Data Components describe the data that are part of the system.

For business engineering Projects, the implementation set includes Organizations, Facilities, Applications, and Business Enterprise Data.

Implementing the designed system requires the use of Coding Languages, Interface Definition Languages for distributed applications, web-based considerations and so on. These must all be documented, although of course the code itself will serve as its own definition – but not, of course, for the whole of the design Work Products!

Integration Set

As an application is developed within an iterative and incremental environment, new components must be integrated with existing systems, possibly with appropriate integration test results. Integration of individual components, integration of new components into the system itself, and integration with legacy systems are key issues. These are covered by several OPEN Tasks and Techniques as well as these specific Work Products.

Test Set

The OPF contains the following predefined classes of test Work Products, including Test Harness, Test Cases, Test Suites, Test Data, Test Procedure, Test Report, and Defect Report. Testing a software application is important, yet often skimped both in theory and practice. Testing (together with maintenance) is not seen as "sexy". OO testing is in fact somewhat different in detail from traditional testing. Components need to be evaluated from both a blackbox (external/interface) and a whitebox (internal) viewpoint. Test harnesses, created in parallel with the application itself, are very important Work Products, as are the results of testing in terms of defect reports.

Deployment Set

The application, installation guide, release notes and the user manual form the Deployment Set of predefined OPF Work Product Components. Transitioning an application from the development environments to the user's site (called deployment) is little different using object technology than a traditional approach. As well as the fully documented application itself, other user manuals and guides, created preferably by a Technical Writing Team, not the developers, may make or break the successful deployment and extended use of any application. Poor documentation at this stage can easily turn users off. This set also includes more management-focussed Work Products such as a deployment plan and a disaster recovery plan.

Classes of Work Products

In the discussion above, we have grouped Work Products roughly in line with Activities of the software development. As an alternative, we could group these Work Products by regarding them by type rather than by the Work Unit that produces them. With this alternative classification structure, we can identify seven groupings in the OPF (see Table 2.2).

Table 2.2 Classes of Work Product according to type

Applications:
– Software application – System application
Diagrams
Documents:
– Technical documents – Management documents
Metrics:
– Process metrics – Quality metrics
Models:
– Object models – Use case models
Increments
Requirements:
– Operational requirements – Quality requirements – Design constraints – Prototype
Component
Architecture

2.2.2 Producers

A *Producer* is responsible for creating, evaluating, iterating, and maintaining Work Products. The OPF distinguishes between Direct Producers (Persons as well as Roles played by the people and tools that they use) and Indirect Producers. This second category consists of teams of people (the membership of Teams strictly being Roles) and Organizations (the membership of which are Teams). Producers are modeled as concurrent objects that proactively collaborate to produce the more passive Work Products.

As with Work Products, process engineers would expect to instantiate the appropriate Producers by selecting Producer classes from the class library. If the class library is incomplete, they may also extend it by defining new classes of Producers.

Let us now explore each of these categories of Producer in a little more detail.

Direct Producers

As the name implies, a *Direct Producer* is any Producer that directly produces Work Products. These are often people but, more importantly, people playing Roles. They may also be other non-living entities, such as software Tools, other systems or, sometimes, hardware e.g., sensors collecting data.

Persons

Because most of the interesting behavior (Tasks) is performed by the Role objects *Person* objects can be thought of as relatively passive information holders with attributes such as name and contact information and operations such as allocating time to its competing Roles based on their Task completion due dates. However, Role objects are active objects with many responsibilities for performing Tasks, knowing how to do Tasks, and following relevant business rules.

Roles

A *Role* is a functionally cohesive part that may be played by a Person on a Project (or even by an Organization). On small projects, the same developer often wears many hats, performing requirements engineering, architecting, design, coding, and testing. On larger projects, there is typically considerable specialization but, even then, the same Person may play different Roles at different times. The OPF repository provides a large number of different Roles that may be played on an Endeavor, keeping the Roles separate from (but related to) the People who play them (see Appendix D for full details). Two examples of Roles in the OPF repository are:

- **architect.** the role of one who creates and specifies an architecture. The responsibilities of an architect are to develop the architecture and to inspect relevant products;
- **class owner.** the role of one who develops and maintains an individual class. The responsibilities of a class owner are to develop the class and to inspect relevant products.

Based on their assigned responsibilities, operations and properties are also assigned to Roles. As we shall later see, operations are the Tasks performed by the Roles. The common properties of all Roles would include:

- the Person who plays the Role;
- the Team to which the Role belongs;
- the required and actual expertise (and training);
- the schedule of the associated Tasks.

Tools

A *Tool* is a software application that is used to generate, document, or manage a Work Product. The OPF contains definitions of several kinds of Tools: (i) a Documentation Tool, such as a word processor, which is used to generate Documents, (ii) a Process Engineering Tool that is helpful in constructing processes from the process components in the repository, (iii) Database Management Tools (for relational, OO and object-relational databases) and (iv) a *Computer-Aided Software Engineering (CASE) Tool* which is a Tool specifically designed to support software engineering. Two kinds of CASE Tool are generally recognized: upper and lower CASE Tools. An *upper CASE Tool* is a CASE Tool that works above the code level. Examples include Configuration Management Tool, Documentation Management Tool, Modeling Tool and Requirements Management Tool. In contrast, a *lower CASE Tool* is a CASE Tool that works at the code level, e.g. Compiler, Browser, Debugger, Interpreter, and JavaDoc.

A *development environment* is a collection of Tools used to develop an application. An *Integrated Development Environment* (IDE) is a development environment in which the Tools are integrated to work together (e.g., the output of one Tool is the input of another).

Indirect Producers

As implied by the name, an *indirect Producer* is any Producer that indirectly produces Work Products via its associated Direct Producers. Indirect Producers may be Teams or Organizations. These are briefly described in the next two sections.

Teams

The OPF comes with a full suite of predefined Teams in its repository. These are outlined in Chapter 4 and described in detail in Appendix D. This prescribed suite can be regarded as a maximal set – usually only a smaller subset will be necessary.

Teams are critical in application development. Much is known about team formation and team successes[3] but little of this non-software knowledge was available to OO practitioners until recently. A dysfunctional team may be one of the main reasons for the large percentage of failures within the software industry where, unfortunately, there seems to be more emphasis on individualistic achievement than on team playing.

3 See Belbin, R.M. *Management Teams: Why They Succeed or Fail* and *Team Roles at Work*, both reprinted many times recently.

Organizations

The OPF also comes with a number of predefined Organization instances in the repository, although these could easily be extended. They are listed in Chapter 3 along with a brief comment, and fully described in Appendix D. These Organization types span not only development organizations but also client businesses and others with whom the development organization are likely to have to interact during the normal course of business. An Organization is to business what a Role is to a Person. The same business may play the "Role" of multiple Organizations or different parts of a business may be modeled as different Organizations, e.g., development, customers and user.

2.2.3 Endeavors

An *Endeavor* is associated with Producers, representing as it does a high-level venture undertaken to develop and maintain one or more related Applications. Endeavors may be categorized as *Projects*, which either produce an Application or reengineer a business; *Programmes*, which are aggregations of two or more related Projects; or *Enterprises*, which are aggregations of one or more related Programmes.

The mission of a Project is typically the creation of a software or software-intensive Application. A Project exists for as long as it is resourced (e.g., time, people, money) and no longer. Projects are often the sole focus of other methods in which the ideas of cross-project relationships (called Programmes in OPEN) are studiously ignored. The existence of Programmes makes possible effective reuse and is facilitated, at least in part, by the effectiveness of domain analysis or business engineering.

A Programme describes a suite of related Projects, thus permitting sharing of resources, utilization of a reuse strategy, and domain modeling.

An Enterprise is the name used for a collection of Programmes which may cross organizational boundaries, e.g., a venture between three companies.

2.2.4 Work Units

The OPF defines a *Work Unit* as a functionally cohesive operation that is performed by a Producer during an Endeavor and that is reified as an object to provide flexibility during the construction and tailoring of a process. There are three kinds of Work Unit: Activity, Task, and Technique, which are interconnected.

Activities

An *Activity* is a major Work Unit consisting of a cohesive collection of Tasks that produce a related set of Work Products. Activities in OPEN are coarse granular descriptions of what needs to be done. If this were a waterfall process (which it isn't) these Activities might be called Phases. The Activities identified at this high level for OPEN are, in many senses, fairly traditional. A few examples are (see also Appendix E)

- Project management
- Configuration management
- Process engineering
- Quality engineering
- Training
- Digital branding
- Requirements engineering
- Architecting
- Design
- Implementation
- Testing
- Deployment
- Content management

Which activities you choose depends on a number of things such as the size of the Project, the maturity level of the Organization, and the safety-criticality aspect of the system. For small non critical projects undertaken by a small number (one or two) of people, you will probably not have a Project Management Activity and even the Requirements Engineering Activity may be absent, particularly if you, the developer, are also the user, so that the requirements are in your head. Even for a small project destined for outside use, however, you would wish to retain the Requirements Engineering Activity. In other situations, you may choose to retain the Activity, but the intensity with which it is performed is low.

Tasks and Techniques

Since Activities are, generally, large-scale descriptions of what is to be done, i.e., they describe long-term objectives that are difficult to manage because of their potential duration. To *manage* the "what", a finer discrimination is needed. In Project Management thinking, a Task is the smallest unit of work that is worth assigning or requested and that can be evaluated as either complete or not complete. Tasks are thus smaller-scale "jobs to be done" associated with each of the activities in the life cycle.

A *Task* in the OPF is described as a functionally cohesive operation (reified as a Work Unit) that is performed by a Producer. A single responsibility of the Producer will be fulfilled by the execution of one or more Tasks. A Task results in the creation, modification or evaluation of a Version of one or more related Work Products.

But Tasks don't say "how" the jobs are to be done. This is the role of the Technique (Figure 2.5). The Technique describes in full how we might use object technology, object-oriented concepts and years of experience of users to accomplish the Tasks we have set ourselves. Since Techniques are just ways of doing things, they can be thought of as the "tools of the trade". Just as the tools of the trade of a plumber include hammers, screwdrivers and wrenches, the tools of an object technologist include knowledge about the use of, for instance, CRC card modeling, aggregation modeling, and OO team

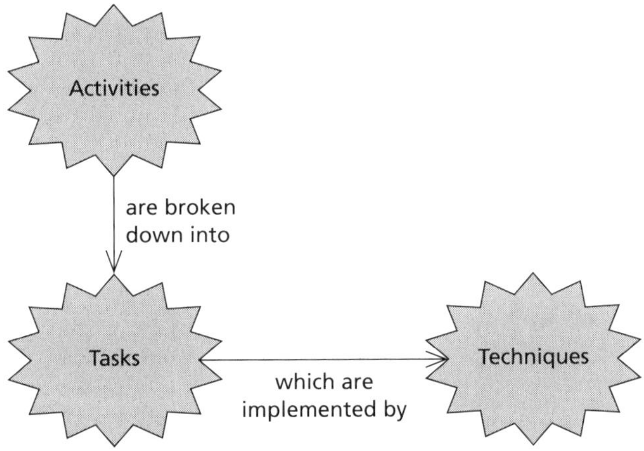

Figure 2.5 Activities are broken down into Tasks, which are implemented by Techniques

building.[4] Different Roles typically perform different Tasks and an experienced developer often knows multiple ways (Techniques) to perform these Tasks. Just as the value of a plumber is the knowledge and experience in choosing which of the screwdrivers and wrenches are needed to solve any particular problem, a skilled technologist is one who is able to choose the best Technique to accomplish the specific OPEN Task being worked on. Choosing the correct Technique is largely a matter of experience, real or surrogate. The latter is encapsulated in the OPEN tailoring matrices described in Chapter 8.

An example of a Task and associated Techniques include:

- Role: OO Modeler:
  - Task: Identify Classes – can be performed using the following Techniques:
    - Reification of domain concepts
    - Reification of nouns as classes (i.e., perform lexical analysis)
    - Reification of externals as interfacer classes
    - Reification of states using the State Pattern
    - Reification of operations using the Command Pattern
    - Reification of transactions

Full details are to be found in other books in the OPEN series (see Bibliography).

Work Performance

The OPF defines a *Task Performance* as the combination of a Producer and the Task that they are responsible for. It is a kind of Work Performance. It emphasizes that it is not just the Task that is important to model but the *interaction* of the Task

4 There are over 150 techniques documented in *The OPEN Toolbox of Techniques* (Henderson-Sellers *et al.*, 1998) so we won't describe them all here. However, for the curious, we do include the full list in Appendix E.

and its performer (the Producer). Task Performances provide the basis for the Work Flow concept (q.v.). They bring together synergistically the human side (in Producer) and the technical side (the Task).

The OPF defines a *Work Flow* (the second kind of Work Performance) as a sequence of Task Performances (see above) whereby Producers collaborate to produce a Work Product. Typically, a Work Flow involves multiple Producers (Teams, Roles), thus providing a collection of time-ordered[5] Task Performances combining Producers and Tasks.

Examples of Work Flows include the following Requirements and Architecture Work Flows:

- Vision Statement Work Flow
- System Requirements Specification Work Flow
- External Interface Specification Work Flow
- Software Requirements Specification Work Flow
- System Architecture Document Work Flow
- Software Architecture Document Work Flow

2.2.5 Stages

A *Stage* is a formally identified and managed duration within the process or a point in time at which some achievement is recognized. Stages provide a *macro* organization to the Work Units. They prescribe calendar dates. A *Cycle* is the largest kind of Stage. It is decomposed into *Phases*, each of which consists of one or more *Builds*, some of which may be released to the customer or user organizations.

The OPF repository contains instances created from one kind of instantaneous Stage (Milestone), while there are several examples of Stages with Duration. These include Cycles (e.g. a Life Cycle or a Development Cycle), Phases, and Builds.

We now briefly consider each of these kinds of Stage in turn (further details are given in Chapter 6).

Cycles

The term "Life Cycle" is used to describe a sequence of Phases that cover the extent of the temporal existence of whatever is being described. Thus a *Project Development Cycle* describes the duration over which the Project is conceived and constructed (called, together, "development"). The *Project Life Cycle*, on the other hand, includes not only the Project Development Life Cycle but extends far beyond it, including its on-site usage and ending when the Application becomes redundant and is no longer used.

At a larger scale than Project Life Cycles, there are Cycles relative to Programmes (of Projects) i.e. multiple project considerations such as domain analysis and reuse

5 By constraint, not by sequence – multiple task performances occurring simultaneously on the same work product.

strategies. Thus we can describe the *Programme Life Cycle* as consisting of the sum of all the Project Life Cycles.

We noted much earlier that OPEN was useful not only for software and software-intensive (i.e. software plus hardware) systems but also for business modeling at the enterprise scale. OPEN thus describes a further type of life cycle, the *Enterprise Life cycle*, in which business modeling and business re-engineering occur.

Each of these Life Cycles can be broken down into a number of Phases, as described below.

Phases

A *Phase* is a Stage (with duration) of development consisting of a sequence of one or more related Builds and Releases. The OPF provides, within its repository, five Phases appropriate to the Application Life Cycle:

- *Initiation* is the Phase during which the Endeavor is started and sufficient Requirements Engineering and Architecting are completed to estimate the following two phrases.
- *Construction* is the Phase during which the Work Products are developed and prepared for release.
- *Delivery* is the Phase during which the Work Products are deployed to the end-user.
- *Usage* is the Phase during which the Work Products are placed into service with the user Organization(s).
- *Retirement* is the Phase when the software is withdrawn from service. This is likely to result in strategies for a switch-over to a new system, checks for other software dependent upon this obsolete software, and so on.

Prior to Application Development, there are also two Phases which might make a useful contribution to the Enterprise Life Cycle:

- *Business Strategy* is the Phase in which the processes involved with the customer, market, technology, and users are analyzed and the business and digital branding strategies are developed, usually resulting in significant restructuring. Object technology is seen as an enabler here, with significant business object and process modeling ocurring.
- *Business Optimization* is the Phase in which the business and digital branding strategies are put into effect by implementing the new business Models and creating new Applications.

For some Enterprise Life Cycles, an alternative viewpoint might be equally useful and that is to view the Enterprise Life Cycle as if it were an example of the Development Life Cycle and therefore use the same five Phases as described above.

Each of the Phases outlined above contributes to one or more of the Life Cycles as described in the previous section. For example, the Project Development Cycle consists of three Phases, Initiation, Construction, and Delivery whilst the Programme Life Cycle consists of the Project Development Cycle's three Phases together with the Usage and Retirement Phases (Figure 2.6).

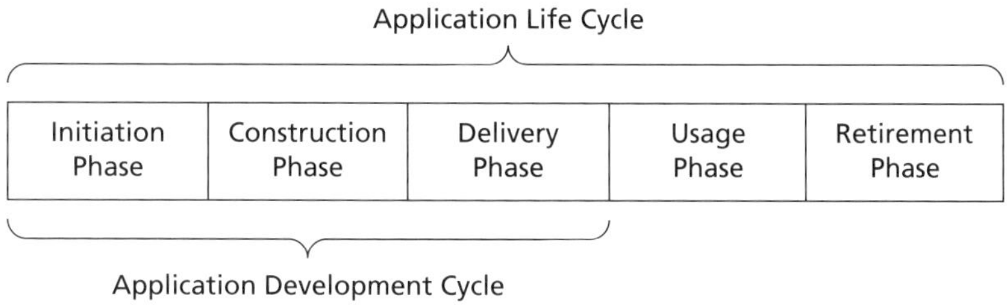

Figure 2.6 Phases in the Programme Life Cycle and Project Development Cycle

An important point needs to be made here in our description of Life Cycles being made up of or containing several Phases. That is, the bland statement with no further constraints might easily be misconstrued as support for a waterfall sequence of events. Far from it. The number of times that a given Phase is entered (and exited) is not restricted – although when using the normal OO-style contract-driven approach, these entrances and exits *are* constrained – by the contracts between the Activity and Task objects. Thus, for example, Initiation may be performed only once at the beginning of an Endeavor, whereas Development and Delivery may be performed for each release of the related Work Product (Model or Application).

Builds

A *Build* is a Stage describing a period of time during which Tasks are undertaken. It typically has a duration of a month or a quarter (i.e. three months), but may only last a few days on a rapidly reiterating Project. A *release* is a special kind of Build. It occurs less frequently than Builds. In it, the Work Products of the Build are released by the development Organization to another entity (e.g., an internal client, the customer, or user Organization) for evaluation or use (Figure 2.8).

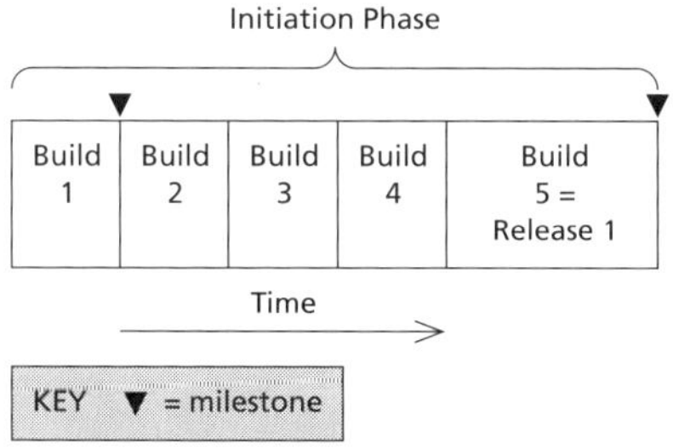

Figure 2.7 Builds occurring within the Initiation Phase

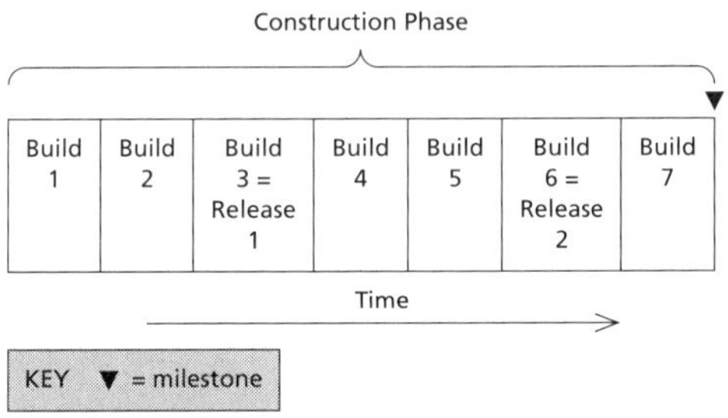

Figure 2.8 In the Construction Phase, Builds are supplemented by Releases and Milestones

Milestones

A Milestone is a kind of Stage with no duration. It marks an event occurring. Milestones are usually recognized as 'achievements' i.e., a time for celebration that some part of the Endeavor has been successful. There are two types of Milestones: Management Milestones and Technical Milestones.

Example Milestones recognized in the management domain are:

- Vision statement baselined
- Application released to customer

Some example technical Milestones are

- Requirements relatively stable and complete
- Architecture relatively stable and complete
- Document Drop
- Code Drop.

During development, there are likely to be frequent drops, recognized internally by Team members as an achievement. These are the Work Products typically put under configuration control. The management Milestones, on the other hand, are usually identifiable once per Project (depending upon the iterative, incremental and parallel strategy of course) – or at least once per major Life Cycle Increment.

2.2.6 Languages

A *Language* is the medium used to document a Work Product. For example, Documents are mostly written in a natural language such as English. Use Case Models and Object Models are written using a Modeling Language such as the Unified Modeling Language (UML)[6] or the extensions to it found in the OPEN

6 OMG (1999) OMG Unified Modeling Language Specification, Version 1.3, June 1999, OMG document ad/99-06-09, 808 pp.

Modeling Language (OML).[7] Finally, code is written in an Implementation Language such as Java, SQL or CORBA's Interface Definition Language (IDL).

The most important Languages (in the metamodel) are:

- **Natural Languages** (such as English) that are used to capture narrative information in Documents.
- **Modeling Languages** that are used to document Use Case and Object Models. A Modeling Language consists of two parts:
  - A notation – a (usually graphical) communication and documentation approach, underpinned by
  - A metamodel – a higher level model, often described using its own notation, which defines the modeling rules concretized by the notation.
- **Constraint Languages** such as OCL (Object Constraint Language). OCL is useful not only in helping clarify the UML metamodel but directly in the design Diagrams to add further information and resolve potential ambiguities.
- **Implementation Languages** that are used to implement software, such as:
  - Coding Languages, such as Java, C++, Eiffel, Smalltalk, HTML, XML, WML, CSS
  - Database Languages, such as SQL
  - Interface Languages, such as IDL

OPEN supports a wide range of Languages, viewed as framework components. Granted at the detailed level, programming tips in specific Languages (using idioms) need individual support per Language. However, if the overall design to be coded is of high quality and high integrity, then the choice of Language is less important. OPEN can be (and has been) used in OO/CBD developments using various Languages and is appropriate irrespective of whether you are using Java, C++ or OO COBOL. Similarly, the choice of Modeling and Constraint Languages is also flexible within the OPF.

2.3 Framework usage

As we noted at the beginning of this chapter, the OPEN Process Framework, defined in terms of its metamodel, cannot be used as is. Rather, its meta-elements must first be instantiated and then a resultant process constructed to meet the needs of the specific Endeavor (see Figure 2.2). There is no unique way to do process construction. A top-down or a bottom-up approach may both succeed depending on both the prevailing organizational culture and the demands of the project. For example, using the OPF to produce a project-specific process may include the following steps:

- Identify the Work Products that are to be produced by the Project and select the Languages to be used when creating them.
- Select the appropriate Tasks that will therefore need to be performed to produce them.

7 Firesmith, D.G. *et al.* (1997) *The OML Reference Manual*, SIGS.

- Assign these Work Products and Tasks to the appropriate Producers, whereby a single Task may be performed by one or more Roles or Teams.
- Select recommended Techniques for the Producers to use when performing their Tasks (they may choose).
- Using Assertions to constrain the dependency relationships between (e.g., sequencing of) the Tasks.
- Organize these Tasks into cohesive Activities.
- Select the relevant Cycle, Builds, and Milestones.
- Tailor these Work Units to meet the specific needs of the Project.
- Document the process so that the Producers will understand what is expected of them.
- Iterate the process components as lessons are learned and situations change.

In contrast, creating a process for a process management-focussed team in a "novice" OO context may look more like this

- Identify current skills set.
- Identify aim of creating new process.
- Start small by identifying small number of relevant Activities.
- Within constraints of initial Project, select a minimal number of Tasks for the selected Activities.
- Using assertions to constrain the dependency relationships between (e.g., sequencing of) the Tasks.
- Taking cognizance of skills available, recommend appropriate Techniques.
- Tailor these Work Units to meet the specific needs of the Project.
- Identify appropriate Work Products.
- Identify Roles and Teams (Producers).
- Allocate Tasks and Work Products to Producers.
- Project-manage at the Stage (Milestone) level and Team-manage at the Task level.
- As the Team's maturity grows, iterate by adding more Activities and Techniques and more detail to previously selected ones – be more adventurous!

The process engineer thus requires *usage guidelines* covering three areas:

- *Process construction*: Choosing the best process components from those already in the OPF repository.
- *Tailoring*: Changing the fine detail inside the chosen process components.
- *Extension*: Enhancing the existing class library of predefined process components or even extending the metamodel itself.

Details of these three sets of usage guidelines are to be found in Chapter 8.

2.4 OPEN compliance

Since there are an indefinitely large number of processes (process instances) that can be generated from the OPF, the question arises: "What does it mean to be OPEN-compliant?"

1. The process users must adopt and use OPF's metamodel, possibly with consistent extensions (see Extension Guidelines).
2. All process components must be instances of a class in the OPF metamodel.
3. Instances thus generated comprise a large set, kept in a repository or class library, from which the set of elements for the specific process are selected. In other words, an actual organizational process must utilize examples/component instances available either in the predefined OPF repository or must have been added to it in accordance with the compliance test (Guideline 2 above).
4. Since an organizational process should be useful for a large range of projects *within your organization*, each specific enactment of the standardized project process must be an instance of that standard process. In OMG parlance, the M0 process enactment must be an instance of the M1 process (your organizational process or a predefined default) which in turn is an instance of the OPF metamodel (see Figure G.1 in Appendix G). Some default process configurations are given in the various OPEN books and some examples are also shown in this book in Chapter 8. "Default" processes may be lightweight, heavyweight or intermediate, for instance.

Summary

The goal of this book is to distill the accumulated wisdom of the IT community by documenting a process framework called OPEN (standing for Object-oriented Process, Environment and Notation) from which can be constructed appropriate, production-quality development processes that are useful for engineering high-quality object-oriented software-intensive systems or business. In other words, this book provides a way of producing object-oriented, Component-based and traditional (non-OO) development processes, which can be tailored to your own individual requirements.

In summary:

- The OPEN process framework consists of three main elements:
  - A metamodel;
  - A repository (or class library) of predefined components designed to work together; and
  - A set of construction, tailoring, and usage guidelines.

- The essential components in the framework can be categorized as either Work Products, Producers of Work Products or the Work Units performed by Producers to produce the Work Products.
- Additional, support classes in the metamodel are Languages and Stages.
- The OPEN process framework must be instantiated and components selected to produce a project-specific process. Figure 2.9 illustrates some example components and their relationship to the essential and support types.
- An OPEN process must be created and possibly tailored initially and then can be refined over time, thus opening up opportunities for Software Process Improvement (SPI) – and better yet Process Framework Improvement (PFI)!

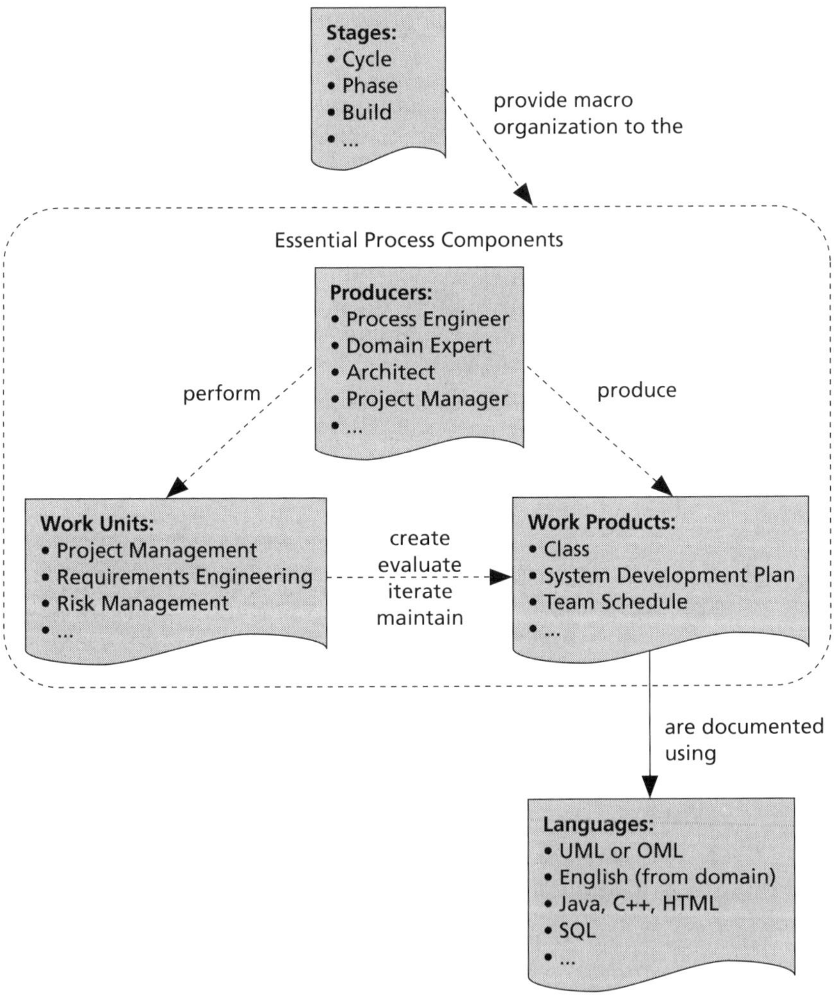

Figure 2.9 Example component instances set in the context of the overall metamodel architecture of the OPEN Process Framework

Part II

Process Components and Usage Guidelines

Part II contains the following chapters:

- Chapter 3, *Work Products*, Documents the OPF's predefined class library of Work Products.
- Chapter 4, *Producers*, Documents the OPF's class library of predefined Producers of the Work Products.
- Chapter 5, *Work Units*, Documents the OPF's class library of predefined Work Units performed by the Producers of the Work Products.
- Chapter 6, *Stages*, Documents the OPF's class library of predefined Stages.
- Chapter 7, *Languages*, Documents the OPF's class library of predefined Languages for documenting Work Products.
- Chapter 8, *Framework Usage Guidelines*, provides guidelines for the extension, construction, and tailoring of the OPF for use on specific Endeavors.

3 Work Products

The primary objective of any development process is to develop one or more related Work Products. Thus, customer organizations primarily pay development organizations to develop the products they require, not merely to perform a development process. The process is a means to an end (the developed products), not an end in and of itself. However, no customer organization wants to pay for the development of unnecessary Work Products or ones that are not cost-effective to develop and maintain. Thus, an essential early Task in any Project is to identify exactly which of the many possible Work Products are to be produced.

Different kinds of Projects develop different kinds of Work Products. For example, a business [re]engineering Project develops a business object model, a business process and data model and several other Work Products. A systems development Project develops a system Application (hardware, software, and data) and its related documentation, and a software development Project develops a software Application and its related documentation. Projects can develop many different kinds of products. Whereas the most important products are eventually released to the customer or user organizations, other intermediate products are only temporarily useful as inputs to create other products.

A *Work Product* is any significant thing of value (e.g., Document, Diagram, Model, Class, Application) that is developed during an Endeavor. One or more *Producers* develop a Work Product during the performance of one or more *Work Units*. During the evolution of a Work Product, *Work Product Versions* are created. Therefore, each Work Product has an associated time-ordered set of Work Product Versions, produced incrementally and iteratively.

3.1 Classes of Work Products

The OPF contains the following predefined classes of Work Products:

- Applications (both Software and System)
- Architectures (e.g. Software, System and Information Architectures, Business, User Interface)
- Components (e.g. Data, Hardware, Paperware,[1] Software and Wetware[2])

1 Documentation.
2 Personnel.

- Metrics (e.g. for Process and Quality)
- Models (e.g. Object Models and Use Case Models)
- Increments
- Requirements (Operational and Quality Requirements and Design Constraints)
- Diagrams (for both Static Architecture and Dynamic Behavior)
- Documents, such as Plans and Schedules, Conventions (for Procedures, Guidelines, Standards, Templates and Inspection Checklists), Requirements Specifications and Architecture Documents.

Each of these predefined classes of Work Product will now be discussed in turn.

3.1.1 Applications

An *Application* is a Work Product consisting of one or more integrated Components that implement a complete set of a customer's operational and quality requirements. An Application is developed by a development Organization, supported by a support Organization and funded by one or more customer Organizations for use by one or more user Organizations.

The OPF comes with the following predefined kinds of Applications in the repository:

- Software Application – an Application consisting of only software and associated data Components.
- System Application – an Application consisting of hardware, software, wetware (i.e., personnel) and paperware (i.e., documentation) Components.

3.1.2 Architectures

An *Architecture* is the strategic "design" of a major Work Product such as an Application, Business Model or a set of related reusable Components. Thus, an Architecture is an abstraction, capturing only the most important aspects of the design: those aspects that significantly influence and constrain the detailed (tactical) design and implementation. Getting the Architecture right is one of the biggest and most valuable challenges, in that a well-designed Architecture will make the final product more extensible and flexible, thus giving it a longer lifespan. The essential features of an Architecture include its overall style embodied in its overall architectural pattern together with the essential Application abstractions (not only Objects but also Components), their responsibilities, how they are related, their interfaces, and how they collaborate. Other important elements of an Architecture are the architectural mechanisms, technology selections, strategic design decisions, and their rationales.

An Architecture is verified in the following two ways:

- Evaluate the Architecture Document to determine if the architectural abstractions, components and patterns are properly documented and collaborate properly to fulfill the architecturally significant operational and quality requirements. It should also be asked whether the Architecture can be implemented within the existing business and technological constraints. Examples of business constraints are those of cost, schedule (time to market) and available development staff; whereas typical technological constraints are the capabilities of Implementation Languages, browsers, operating systems, databases, and other infrastructure products.

- Test the executable architectural prototype for conformance with its associated requirements.

Having a well-designed, well-documented Architecture is a critical Project success factor. Such an Architecture provides a wide range of benefits. For instance, good Architectures are resilient to change and are easily extensible as Requirements evolve. They allow the development Organization to deal with the size and complexity of Applications by allowing them to:

- Modularize the Applications into major blackbox Components with well-defined interfaces.
- Separate concerns so that the different Teams with different areas of expertise (e.g., GUI design, distribution, and persistence) can be allocated to appropriate Components.
- Perform incremental, iterative, parallel development of the Components.
- Estimate the development effort based on the Components.
- Reuse existing Components.
- More easily perform integration testing and fix defects.

Good Architectures also allow their stakeholders to understand the overall structure and behavior of large complex Applications and how the Applications fulfill their Requirements. They are also highly successful in minimizing both development and maintenance costs.

The choice and creation of an Architecture is driven by multiple, often conflicting, factors. These factors include (i) the architecturally significant operational and quality Requirements, (ii) the Components that are to be reused, (iii) the commercial off-the-shelf products (e.g., middleware) to be used, (iv) the experience and training of the associated Architects and Developers, (v) the standards and company policies to which the Architecture must conform, (vi) the maturity of the development, component, and infrastructure technology and (vii) the organizational structure of the development Organization (i.e., Conway's Law[3]).

The OPF comes with a number of predefined instances of Architecture, including the following:

- Software Architecture is the Architecture of a software Application or the software Components of a system Application.
- System Architecture is the Architecture of a system Application (including hardware, software, and data components).

3 The structure (Architecture) of an Application tends to mirror the structure of the Organization(s) that produce it.

- User interface (e.g. Website) Architecture is the Architecture of the user interface (Website) together with any remote services it may require. For both traditional and Web Applications, this outlines the large-scale architectural aspects of the way that people will interact with the software system.
- Business Architecture is the Architecture of a business, captured in terms of an Object Model.
- Hardware Architecture describes the Architecture of all hardware elements including those devoted to networking.
- Information Architecture refers to all data aspects of the Application development.
- Database Architecture describes the kind of database structures that are to be used.

3.1.3 Components

A *Component* is a major, architecturally significant part of an Application or Framework. Components are therefore the configuration items of an Application. Components should be cohesive in the sense of implementing a well-defined set of related responsibilities. Components should also be usable as blackboxes that hide their implementations behind a well-defined set of interfaces and associated protocols. These interfaces thus allow a Component to be replaceable within the context of a well-defined Architecture.

The OPF comes with the following predefined Components:

- hardware Components (e.g. devices, computers, networks and storage);
- software Components (e.g. class, package, database, Web script);
- data Components (e.g. content);
- wetware Components (e.g. Administrator, Operator);
- paperware Components (various Documents).

Hardware and software Components are identified explicitly in the OPF metamodel. Wetware Components offer another viewpoint on Roles occupied by people and Paperware Components are really Documents (Work Products).

3.1.4 Metrics

Metrics are means by which aspects of software may be quantitatively assessed.

The OPF comes with two predefined classes of Metrics in the metamodel:

- Process Metrics;
- Quality Metrics.

Process Metrics

Process Metrics relate to elements such as time, resources and resource allocation, cost and effort estimation, tracking and control. In object-oriented and component-based developments, these Metrics are generally poorly developed and inadequately validated.

Quality Metrics

Quality Metrics involve measuring size and complexity of both code and design and are complemented by Models that link these "internal factors" to the "external factors" which are characteristic of aspects of quality. These external factors, often called the "ilities", include maintainability, flexibility and so on. External factors are of most interest to developers but can rarely be measured and, even if they can, their measurement only becomes possible at a significantly later Stage in development than when the information is required. For instance, we can only measure code size once the software has been coded, whereas we probably wish to "know" the size of the system during the initiation Phase in order to understand how long it will take to build it. Since direct measurement is impossible, estimates have to be made from artefacts that *are* measurable at that point in time. These are known as Internal Metrics.

Internal Product Metrics are those which can be determined *directly* from the artefact, be it code or design. The better understood and accepted OO Metrics all pertain to the code level although Design Metrics are also slowly beginning to emerge. Product measures, aimed at quality, involve various forms of complexity (where complexity loosely means the difficulty of understanding) through to evaluations of the quality of designs and business analyses, the latter expressed in, say, atomic Task Scripts.

3.1.5 Models

A *Model* is a cohesive, organized set of Requirements, Architecture, or design information that captures the significant abstractions of all or part of a problem domain. Models are only approximations and thus purposefully ignore certain diversionary details. They often represent specific views of the system under construction. The most common Models used in OO are Object Models and Use Case Models. Other kinds of Model are used in traditional, non-OO design (see below).

Models in the software domain are documented using Modeling Languages such as the Unified Modeling Language (UML) or its extension,[4] the OPEN Modeling Language (OML) – see Chapter 7 for further details. Models, therefore, are typically documented using a graphical notation (the vocabulary), grammar, and semantics, which are defined in the associated metamodel.

4 Henderson-Sellers, B. *et al.* (1999) Viewing the OML as a variant of the UML, in *<<UML>>'99. The Unified Modeling Language – Beyond the Standard*, Springer LNCS 1723, 49–66.

Object Models

When constructing a Model, Object Model or otherwise, to assist in designing and implementing an Application, it must be remembered that the best approach is to build a *single* Model of the Work Product in question. Obviously, displaying every facet of a large commercial model is overly complex. Thus, each of the OO Diagrams (see below) highlights and focuses on just one aspect of the model, seeing it from different angles, as it were. In this context, the aspect of an Object Model that is most relevant might well be different at different Stages in the Life Cycle.

Object Models use Techniques generally regarded as object-oriented, focussing on modularity and semantic cohesion in which the Object/Component is a close fit to the business concept being modelled rather than just a fraction of it. This means that an Object Model emphasizes Objects and Components and their interactions. Object modeling focuses on the specification of services offered in the interfaces as well as pluggability. An Object Model attempts a holistic synthesis between the data aspects and functional or behavioral aspects that must exist in any system.

Use Case Models

A *Use Case Model* is a Model of the functional Requirements of an Application or business in terms of the Application's externals, their associated use cases, and the relationships and interactions between them. A Use Case Model can have the following compositional structure:

- *Context Specification* – this includes the Context Diagram and the External Specifications (External Description and External Responsibilities) together with the Use Case Diagrams themselves.
- *Use Case Specifications* – in this case, the Use Case Requirement, the Business Justification and the Use Case Path Specifications, including Use Case Path Requirement, Preconditions, Sequence Diagram, Post-conditions and Categorization.

Although Use Case Models represent the functionality of a system, when using an OO approach, care should be taken not to decompose these functions into smaller functions. Doing this leads to traditional, non-OO data flow diagrams (see below) rather than object diagrams.

Structured Models

When developing in a traditional, non-OO environment, a standard Object Model is unlikely to be useful. Instead, a data model such as an ER (Entity-Relationship) diagram can be most useful. There is a distinct similarity between an ER diagram and an object diagram from which the operations (representing the behavioral aspect of an object) have all been removed. In that sense, traditional and OO modeling approaches have much in common. A second traditional model is the data flow diagram (DFD), which parallels the use case. In fact, a use case could be regarded as a parent to the DFD in that if the functionality modeled in a use case is decomposed (as it should *not* be in an OO environment), then the traditional DFD will result. A third kind of traditional model is the flow diagram, paralleled by the Activity Diagram of UML. This represents the flow of control through the whole program and has been used for many years in a traditional development environment along with structure charts and other visualizations.

3.1.6 Increments

An Increment is a Work Product or, more likely, a combination of Work Products, that is delivered as a "partial" product i.e., there is no need to wait until the Work Product(s) is complete before being made available to the "client" (who might be external, internal or even yourself). An Increment is thus strictly a kind of Work Product Version rather than a kind of Work Product and is made up of one or more other Work Products, i.e., it is a compound Work Product.

3.1.7 Requirements

A *Requirement* is a capability or condition to which an Application must conform. A Requirement is thus a formalization of a need of a customer, user, or other stakeholder. The OPEN Process Framework repository contains the following predefined classes of Requirements:

- Operational (a.k.a. functional) Requirements: a Requirement that specifies a required blackbox stimulus/response behavior of an Application. An operational Requirement therefore specifies a function or action that the Application must be able to perform.
- Quality Requirements (a.k.a. factors): a Requirement that specifies a necessary property of an Application (e.g., correctness, operational availability, portability, reliability, robustness, safety, security).
- Design Constraints: a design decision that is treated as a Requirement (e.g., must operate on a Unix platform, must interface with Simply Objects™, must use a specific relational database product).
- Interface Requirements: a Requirement that specifies some particular characteristics of the user interface, most commonly graphical user interface.
- Data Requirement: a Requirement that determines constraints on any data held or manipulated by the proposed Application.

Importance of Requirements

Requirements are statements of what the Application is intended to accomplish in a user-centred or business-focussed sense. It is therefore critical to determine *exactly* what is required by the future users. In previous decades, Application development timelines were often lengthy (perhaps several years) so that by the time the Application was delivered to the user in line with their Requirements (stated some years ago) they were of course outdated. In an iterative, incremental and parallel framework, this is less likely to happen since user Requirements can be reevaluated on a shorter timescale.

Sources of Requirements

Requirements often come from users; but users may be management or end-users, as well as possibly marketing in the case of shrink-wrapped software. Requirements may be documented in existing business processes or they may be "gleams in someone's eye" for future new business opportunities. They may be written or verbal. They may even be determined by an interaction with another piece of software or hardware. For instance, a Requirement may be that the input information needs to be compatible with particular word-processing or graphical layout software.

3.1.8 Diagrams

Object orientation typically uses modeling Techniques that rely heavily on graphical Models. A *Diagram* is a graphical representation of a part of a Model drawn using the notation of a specific Modeling Language. The OPF describes two major subtypes of Diagrams that can be used, for instance, to capture Use Case and Object Models: Static Architecture Diagrams and Dynamic Behavior Diagrams.

Static Architecture Diagrams

A *Static Architecture Diagram* is a Diagram that Documents a cohesive set of elements and the static relationships between them. OPEN recommends using a number of variations of the semantic net – a general name for a Static Architecture Diagram that uses a graph structure to represent the semantics of a set of nodes in terms of the referential and definitional relationships between them. This includes not only UML Class and Object Diagrams but other Static Diagrams currently not part of the OMG standard, e.g., context Diagrams, Inheritance Diagrams. Different styles of Semantic Net may be useful at different stages in the life cycle. Here are some of the more useful types of diagram included in the OPF repository:

- **Context Diagram**: a semantic net that documents the context of an Application in terms of its externals and the relationships between it and its externals.
- **Configuration Diagram**: a semantic net that documents the configuration of an Application in terms of its Components and the relationships between them; whereas the special kind of Configuration Diagram known as a *Layer Diagram* is a Configuration Diagram that documents the relationships between layers in an Application.

- **Class Diagram (a.k.a. Package Diagram)**: a semantic net that documents the elements of a package and the relationships between them.
- **Inheritance Diagram**: a semantic net that documents all or part of an inheritance structure.
- **Aggregation Diagram**: a semantic net that documents all or part of an aggregation structure.
- **GUI Navigation Diagram**: a semantic net that documents the screens at a site and the navigation paths between them.
- **Component Diagram**: a semantic net in the UML that shows dependencies between software Components. It describes source code Components, binary code Components, and executable Components. These may exist at compile time and/or run time. The Component Diagram in UML has only a type form and not an instance form. (To show Component instances in UML, a deployment Diagram should be used.)
- **Deployment Diagram**: a semantic net that Documents the static allocation of distribution units to hardware Components in a distributed Application.

Dynamic Behavior Diagrams

A *Dynamic Behavior Diagram*, on the other hand, is a Diagram that documents the dynamic behavior of a Component in terms of the interactions or state transitions. The OPF comes with the following predefined classes of Diagrams, the first three of which correspond directly with those in the UML, for instance.

- **Use Case Diagram**: a Dynamic Behavior Diagram that summarizes the operational Requirements of an Application or business in terms of its externals, its use cases and the relationships between them.
- **Interaction Diagram**: a Dynamic Behavior Diagram that documents the interactions between a set of collaborating objects, classes, types and/or packages. There are two styles of Interaction Diagram: the *Collaboration Diagram,* which emphasizes the architectural context of the object interactions (actually potential interactions) and the *Sequence Diagram,* that documents a sequence of actual interactions in the form of arcs between the time lines of collaborating objects, classes, types, and/or packages.
- **Statechart Diagram or State Transition Diagram**: a Dynamic Behavior Diagram that documents the states of an object or class, the associated transitions between those states and the triggers that fire the transitions.
- **Migration Diagram**: a Dynamic Behavior Diagram that documents the movement of distribution units between Hardware Components in a distributed Application.

3.1.9 Documents

Whilst a typical Object Model has many aspects which can readily be documented using a graphical Modeling Language such as UML, there are a range of other Documents, text-based, that are also Work Products. The main categories of predefined Document types of Work Product in the OPF include:

- Plans
- Conventions
  - Procedures
  - Guidelines
  - Standards
  - Templates
  - Inspection Checklists
- Requirements Specifications
- Architecture and Design Documents
- Schedules
- Reports
- Staffing Descriptions
- User Documentation

These are discussed in more detail in the following sections 3.2 and 3.3 (for a fuller discussion of Work Products, see Appendix C). These sections describe an alternative classification of Work Products in the repository, where they are grouped into two sets (Management and Engineering), based on the activities during which they are produced.

3.2 Management Set of Work Products

The *Management Set of Work Products* (Table 3.1) is the set of Work Products primarily used by management rather than the engineering staff. It includes a number of predefined classes of Work Products which cover the areas of planning, staffing and scheduling. The planning Work Products include plans for system development, (system) build, for configuration management, metrics, risk management, testing and finally for training. The staffing Work Products are those for job descriptions and the Organization chart. Scheduling Work Products are those focussing on Component schedules and Team schedules as well as on the overall Project schedule.

Table 3.1 Management Set of Work Products

Management Set of Work Products	Producer
Plans:	
• Management Plan	Management Team
• Build Plan	Development Team
• Conversion Plan	Development Team
• Configuration Management Plan	Configuration Management Team
• Quality Plan	Quality Team
• Metrics Plan	Metrics Team
• Risk Management Plan	Management Team
• Security Plan	Security Team
• Test Plan	Test Team
• Training Plan	Training Team
• Disaster Recovery Plan	Development Environment Team
• Change Request Forms	Management Team, Test Team, Quality Team
Staffing Work Products:	
• Job Description	Management Team
• Organization Chart	Management Team
Schedules:	
• Project Schedule	Management Team
• Component Schedule	Management Team
• Team Schedule	Management Team
Other Documents:	
• Contract	Management Team
• Statement of work	Management Team
• Work breakdown structure	Management Team, Project Team
• Budget	Management Team
• Status report	Project Team
• Metrics report	Metrics Team
• Project debrief report	Management Team, Project Team

Table 3.1 Management Set of Work Products *continued*

Management Set of Work Products	Producer
Business Modeling Work Products:	
• Application business case	Business Strategy Team
• Brand strategy Document	Branding Team
• Brand communication plan	Branding Team
• Brand style guide	Branding Team
• Client analysis report	Business Strategy Team
• Market analysis report	Business Strategy Team
• Programme and Project recommendations	Business Strategy Team
• Proposed Applications list	Business Strategy Team
• User analysis report	Business Strategy Team
• Technology strategy Document	Technology Strategy Team

3.3 Engineering Work Products

Engineering Work Products are focussed upon the software development side both in terms of process (Process Set, including guidelines, standards, templates etc. – see Table 3.2), user-interaction in terms of the Requirements Set (Table 3.3) and several sets relating to the modeling and implementation Components of the Life Cycle. These are the Architecture Set (Table 3.4), Design Set (Table 3.5), Implementation Set (Table 3.6), Integration Set (Table 3.7) and Test Set (Table 3.8). While the Architecture Set is focussed on both business and software issues, the Design and Implementation Sets are clearly attuned solely to those demands of software development, including database design, UI design and coding issues. Test and integration must not be neglected. Finally, the Deployment Set (including deployment plans, installation guides and so on – Table 3.9) again focusses on interactions with clients and end-users.

These tables give a range of typical examples in each set of Work Products. They are not intended to be complete. More details of the Work Products summarized in these tables can be found in Appendix C.

Table 3.2 Process Set of Work Products

Process Set of Work Products	Producer
Procedures:	
• Configuration Management Procedure	Process Team or Configuration Management Team
• Metrics Procedure	Process Team or Metrics Team
• Requirements Procedure	Process Team or Requirements Team
• Architecture Procedure	Process Team or Architecture Team
• Design Procedure	Process Team or Development Team
• Implementation Procedure	Process Team
• Integration Procedure	Process Team
• Testing Procedure	Process Team or Test Team
• Deployment Procedure	Process Team
Guidelines:	
• Use Case Modeling Guidelines	Process Team or Requirements Team
• OO Modeling Guidelines	Process Team
• GUI Design Guidelines	Project Team

Table 3.2 Process Set of Work Products *continued*

Process Set of Work Products	Producer
Standards:	
• Vision Statement Standard	Process Team
• Glossary Standard	Process Team
• System Requirements Specification Standard	Process Team
• External Interface Specification Standard	Process Team
• Software Requirements Specification Standard	Process Team
• Use Case Specification Standard	Process Team
• Enterprise Architecture Document Standard	Process Team
• Programme Architecture Document Standard	Process Team
• System Architecture Document Standard	Process Team
• Software Architecture Document Standard	Process Team
• CRC Card Standard	Process Team
• Database Design Document Standard	Process Team
• Framework User's Manual Standard	Process Team
• UI Design Document Standard	Process Team
• Package Design Document Standard	Process Team
• Modeling Language Standard	Process Team
• JavaDoc Standard	Process Team
• Coding Standard	Process Team
Templates:	
• Vision Statement Template	Process Team
• Glossary Template	Process Team
• System Requirements Specification Template	Process Team
• External Interface Specification Template	Process Team
• Software Requirements Specification Template	Process Team
• Enterprise Architecture Document Template	Process Team
• Programme Architecture Document Template	Process Team
• System Architecture Document Template	Process Team
• Software Architecture Document Template	Process Team

Table 3.2 Process Set of Work Products *continued*

Process Set of Work Products	Producer
Inspection Checklists:	
• Vision Statement Checklist	Process Team
• Glossary Checklist	Process Team
• System Requirements Specification Checklist	Process Team
• External Interface Specification Checklist	Process Team
• Software Requirements Specification Checklist	Process Team
• Enterprise Architecture Document Checklist	Process Team
• Programme Architecture Document Checklist	Process Team
• System Architecture Document Checklist	Process Team
• Software Architecture Document Checklist	Process Team

Table 3.3 Requirements Set of Work Products

Requirements Set of Work Products	Producer
Enterprise Documents:	
• Enterprise Vision Statement	Enterprise Requirements Team
• Enterprise Glossary	Enterprise Requirements Team
• Enterprise Requirements Specification	Enterprise Requirements Team
Programme Documents:	
• Programme Vision Statement	Programme Requirements Team
• Programme Glossary	Programme Requirements Team
• Programme Requirements Specification	Programme Requirements Team
Project Documents:	
• Application Vision Statement	System Requirements Team
• Project Glossary	System Requirements Team
• System Requirements Specification	System Requirements Team
• External Interface Specification	System Requirements Team
• Software Requirements Specification	Software Requirements Team

Table 3.3 Requirements Set of Work Products *continued*

Requirements Set of Work Products	Producer
Use Case Model Elements:	
● Context Specification	
– Context Diagram	System Requirements Team
– External Description	System Requirements Team
– Use Case Diagram	System Requirements Team
● Use Case Specification	Requirements Team
● Use Case Path Specification	Requirements Team
● Sequence Diagram	Requirements Team

Table 3.4 Architecture Set of Work Products

Architecture Set of Work Products	Producer
Enterprise Architecture Document	Enterprise Architecture Team
Programme Architecture Document	Programme Architecture Team
Business Architecture Document	Business Architecture Team
System Architecture Document	System Architecture Team
Software Architecture Document	Software Architecture Team
Website Architecture Document	Website Development Team
Database Architecture Document	Database Team
Information Architecture Document	Several Teams

Table 3.5 Design Set of Work Products

Design Set of Work Products	Producer
Class Responsibility Collaborator Card	Class Owner
Database Design Document	Database Team
Package Design Document	Package Team
Reusable Components Manual	Reuse Team
Framework User's Manual	Package Team
UI Design Document	User Interface Team
JavaDoc	Class Owner
GUI Prototype	User Interface Team
Metrics	Metrics Team
White site/Wireframe Prototype	Web Development Team

Table 3.6 Implementation Set of Work Products

Implementation Set of Work Products	Producer
Hardware Components:	
● Devices	Hardware Team
– Convertor	Hardware Team
– Input Device	Hardware Team
– Input/Output Device	Hardware Team
– Output Device	Hardware Team
– Sensor	Hardware Team
● Computers:	Hardware Team
– Client	Hardware Team
– Firewall	Hardware Team
– Router	Hardware Team
– Servers	Hardware Team
● Networks:	Hardware Team
– Internet	Hardware Team
– Intranet	Hardware Team
● Storage:	Hardware Team
– Disk Library	Hardware Team
– Tape Library	Hardware Team

Table 3.6 Implementation Set of Work Products *continued*

Implementation Set of Work Products	Producer
Software Components:	
● Deliverable Software	Software Team
● Framework	Software Team
● Test software	Test Team
● Package	Software Team
● Class	Software Team
● Stored Procedure	Database Team
● Web page	Web Development Team
Data Components	Various Teams

Table 3.7 Integration Set of Work Products

Integration Set of Work Products	Producer
Increment	Software Team
Integration Test Results	Test Team

Table 3.8 Test Set of Work Products

Test Set of Work Products	Producer
Test Harness	Class Owner, Test Team
Application Testing Procedure	Test Team
Website Testing Procedure	Test Team
Test Report	Test Team
Defect Report	Test Team
Test Script	Test Team
Test Suite	Test Team
Test Case	Test Team
Test Data	Test Team
Usability Testing Pre-test Questionnaire	Test Team
Usability Testing Post-test Questionnaire	Test Team
Master Test List Questionnaire	Test Team

Table 3.9 Deployment Set of Work Products

Deployment Set of Work Products	Producer
Application	Software Team
Website	Web Development Team
Deployment Plan	Management Team
Disaster Recovery Plan	Management Team
Installation Guide	Documentation Team
Release Notes	Documentation Team
User's Manual	Documentation Team
Support Plan	Documentation Team
Support Reference Materials	Documentation Team
Job Aids	Documentation Team

Summary

Work Products are at the core of any software development process since the aim of this endeavor is to produce a software (or software-intensive) Application for delivery to the client, *not* to merely enact a process. Thus, Work Products form one of the cornerstones of the OPEN class library of Process Components.

Work Products need to be specified according to the needs of the specific Project and Organization. Here we have discussed a wide range of possible Work Products for use in the OPEN approach. They range from planning Documents to detailed Model descriptions, from Metrics to Change Management.

Work Products can also be grouped according to their style. For instance, we may group together Management Work Products versus Engineering Work Products. Some examples of this grouping have been discussed here.

We may also group Work Products in terms of whether they relate to hardware, software, or data documentation.

Any grouping we use is simply a matter of convenience. What is important is that the *appropriate* Work Products are chosen and enacted. It would indeed be an extremely rare Project that used *all* of the Work Products described in this chapter and in Appendix C.

4 Producers

A *Producer* is anything that produces (i.e., creates, evaluates, iterates, or maintains) Versions of one or more Work Products. The OPF comes with two metalevel classes of Producers: Direct and Indirect Producers. Direct Producers are those that are themselves responsible for the creation of one or more Work Products. These include people, the Roles played by people and non-people Producers such as other software Tools. Indirect Producers exist at a higher level of abstraction and include Teams and Organizations.

4.1 Direct Producers

Direct Producers are those Producers that directly create, update, and evaluate Work Products. The OPF comes with the following predefined classes of direct Producers in the metaModel:

- Person
- Role
- Tool.

4.1.1 Person

A *Person* is an individual human being involved with an Endeavor. Persons must have the experience and training to perform the Roles assigned to them. Also, because a single Person can only do so many things at once, a Person playing multiple Roles must time-slice and prioritize their efforts.

4.1.2 Roles

A Role is a well-defined, cohesive part played by an individual Person on an Endeavor. Remember that a single Person will often play multiple Roles (i.e., wear multiple hats), either simultaneously or at different times, and multiple Persons may play the same Role. While a Role may be a position in an Organization Chart, a Role is usually not a job title.

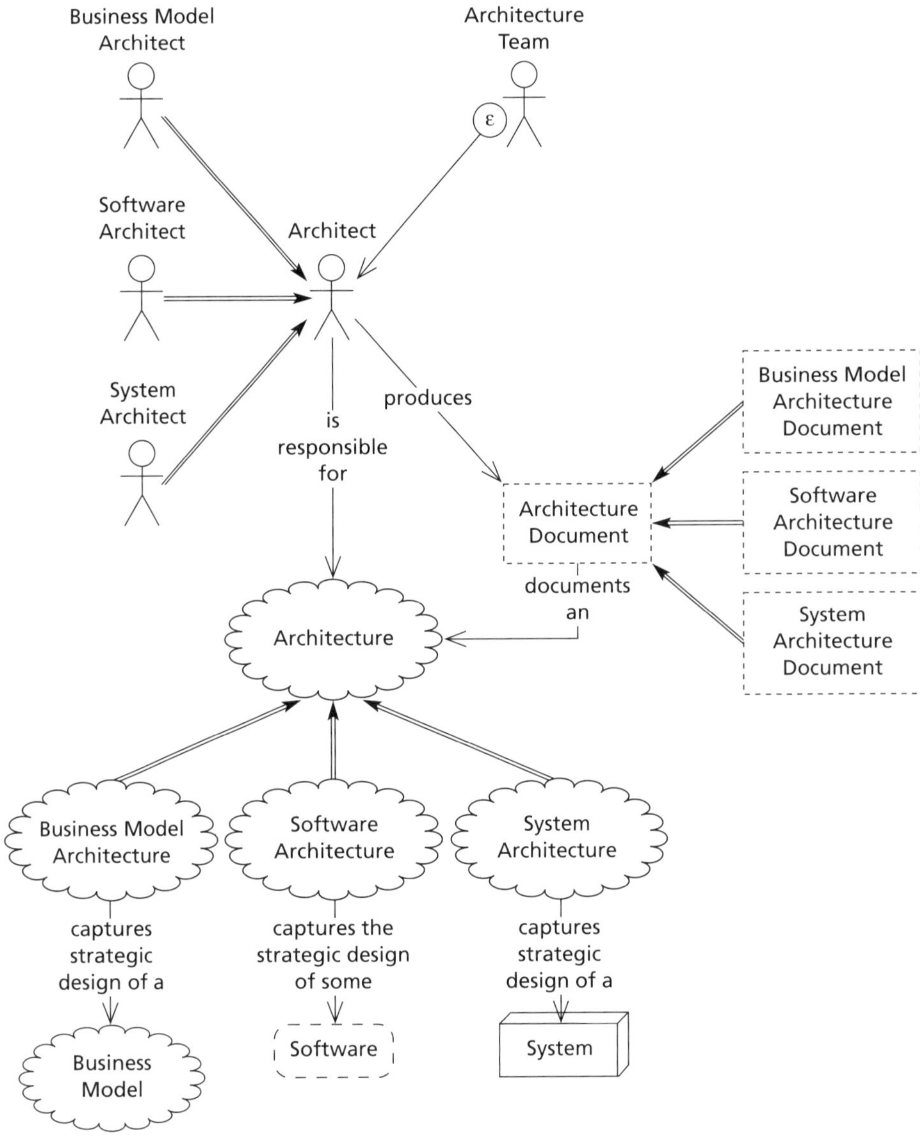

Figure 4.1 Architects and their Work Products [Note that here we demonstrate OPEN's independence of modeling language by using OML]

The OPF describes and defines a significant number of major Roles, although in many Organizations the names may be different and sometimes several Roles will be combined. For each Role, we can identify responsibilities and required abilities. These are summarized below, and described in detail in Appendix D.

In addition, we can sketch how the Roles interact with their respective work products. One specific example (for the Role of Architect) is shown in Figure 4.1.

The OPF comes with the following predefined classes of Roles in the repository:

- **Architect** – the Role played by a Person who is responsible for an Architecture (strategic design):
  - *Business architect* – an Architect who is responsible for the Architecture of the business Model.
  - *Database architect* – an Architect who is responsible for the Architecture of the database.
  - *Hardware architect* – an Architect who is responsible for all hardware aspects.
  - *Information architect* – an Architect who is responsible for the data and informational Components of the Application.
  - *Security architect* – an Architect who is responsible for the software and hardware security of the system.
  - *Software architect* – an Architect who is responsible for the Architecture of the Application software.
  - *System architect* – an Architect who is responsible for the Architecture of the overall Application including hardware, software, personnel, and Documentation.
- **Application Conscript** – the Role played by a developer when temporarily assigned to the reuse Team.
- **Class Owner** – the Role played by a Person responsible for the production of an individual class including designing, coding, unit testing, and debugging as well as developing the related unit test software.
- **Configuration Manager** – the Role played by a Person responsible for the configuration management program including configuration identification, configuration control, configuration auditing, and configuration status accounting.
- **Content Worker**:
  - *Content approver* – the Role played by a Person who approves content for incorporation into an Application and release to the users.
  - *Content creator* – the Role played when a Person creates or obtains new content for one or more Applications.
  - *Content editor* – the Role played when a Person copy edits textual content prior to approval.
  - *Content publisher* – the Role played when a Person publishes approved content to an Application, such as to a Website.
  - *Content writer* – the Role played when a Person enters content for one or more Applications into a content management system.
  - *Content translator* – the Role played when a Person translates the content of one or more Applications between different natural Languages.

- **Database Administrator** – the Role played when a Person administers one or more databases in the production environment.
- **Database Engineer** – the Role a Person plays when designing, implementing, and installing an Application's databases.
- **Designer** (sometimes called modeler) – the Role played by a Person who creates, Documents, and maintains the tactical design of an individual Component, package, or class:
  - *Class designer* – a Designer who designs an individual class including how the class design implements its abstraction, responsibilities, and contractual obligations.
  - *Component designer* – a Designer who designs components for third-party reuse.
  - *Database designer* – a Designer who designs the various parts of the database used to store, retrieve and delete persistent objects or data.
  - *Package designer* – a Designer who designs a package of collaborating classes and interfaces.
  - *User-interface designer* – a Designer who designs, prototypes, and leads the evaluation of user interfaces.
  - *Website designer* – a Designer who designs the technical aspects of the Website e.g. in terms of HTML, XML, and page construction as well as remotely called executable software.
- **Domain Expert** – the Person with knowledge of the business domain.
- **Graphic Designer** – the Person responsible for the visual content and layout of the Website interface.
- **Hardware Engineer** – a Person who produces the Hardware Components of an Application.
- **Integrator** – a Person who integrates baselined Components into builds.
  - *Component integrator* – an Integrator who takes third-party supplied Components and integrates them into the current Application.
  - *Software integrator* – an Integrator of software classes, components, packages etc.
  - *Systems integrator* – an Integrator of system Components.
- **Methodologist:**
  - *OO methodologist* – a Person with extensive knowledge of a wide range of OO methodologies.
  - *CBD methodologist* – a Person with extensive knowledge of a wide range of Component-based development methodologies.
- **Metrics Analyst** – a Person with extensive knowledge of software and system engineering Metrics.

- **Modeler**:
  - *OO modeler* – a Modeler who specializes in object-oriented requirements engineering, architecting, and design Techniques.
  - *Use case modeler* – a Modeler who specializes in use case analysis techniques.
- **Network Administrator** – the Role that is played when a Person administers one or more networks in the production environment.
- **Process Engineer** – a Person who is responsible for creating and maintaining the development process.
- **Programmer** – a Person who writes, unit tests and debugs source code:
  - *Peer programmer* – a Programmer who is part of a programming team of two.
- **Project Manager** – the Person responsible for all management aspects of a single Project.
- **Prototype Developer** – the Person responsible for evaluating prototypical ideas, often used in the context of Website development but also relevant to Rapid and Joint Application Development (RAD and JAD) approaches.
- **Quality Engineer** – the Person responsible for all the quality aspects of the software development.
- **Requirements Engineer** – the Role played by a Person who performs Requirements elicitation, Requirements analysis, Requirements specification, and Requirements management:
  - *Business Requirements engineer* – a Requirements engineer who deals with the overall Requirements of a business.
  - *Software Requirements engineer* – a Requirements engineer who deals with the software Requirements of an Endeavor.
  - *Systems Requirements engineer* – a Requirements engineer who deals with the system-level Requirements of an Endeavor.
- **Reuse Librarian** – the Person responsible for adding classes/Components to the reuse library, for maintaining the quality of the library contents, and for making developers aware of what is already available.
- **Scheduler** – the Role played by the Person who identifies work schedules and delivery dates, taking into account available personnel.
- **Security Analyst** – the Role played when a Person engineers an Application's security requirements.
- **Security Engineer** – the Role played when a Person engineers Components, Applications and Data Centers to meet their security requirements.
- **Stakeholder** – the Role played by any Person who is significantly affected by an Application:
  - *Administrator* – a Stakeholder who is responsible for one or more aspects of system construction.
  - *Customer* – a Stakeholder who purchases an Application from a development organization.

- *Developer* – a Stakeholder who invests effort in system construction.
- *Manager* – a Stakeholder who invests effort in managing the construction of the system.
- *Operator* – a Stakeholder who invests effort in running the hardware and network.
- *Subcontractor representative* – the Role played when a Person represents a Subcontractor Organization in interactions with members of the development Organization.
- *User* – a Stakeholder who uses the Application.
- *Vendor representative* – a Role played when a Person represents a vendor Organization in interactions with members of the development Organization.

- **Strategist**
  - *Brand strategist* – the Role played when a Person develops the digital brand strategy for a customer's business.
  - *Business strategist* – the Role played when a Person develops the business strategy for a customer's business.
  - *Technology strategist* – the Role played when a Person develops the technology strategy for a customer's business.
- **Systems Administrator** – the Role played when a Person administers a data center and its associated production environments.
- **Technical Leader** – a Person who takes decisions regarding technical aspects of the Project.
- **Technical Writer** – a Person who writes documentation.
- **Tester** – a Person who plans, designs, implements, executes and evaluates tests:
  - *Build tester* – a Tester who is responsible for the operational, performance, and stress testing of a build.
  - *Class tester* – a Tester who is responsible for the testing of a class.
  - *Component tester* – a Tester who is responsible for the testing of a Component.
  - *Integration tester* – a Tester who is responsible for performing integration testing of a build.
  - *Model tester* – a Tester who is responsible for the testing of a Model.
  - *Package tester* – a Tester who is responsible for the testing of a package.
  - *Regression tester* – a Tester who is responsible for performing regression testing of a Component.
  - Test participant – an external Person participating in the testing of the Application.
  - *Usability tester* – a Tester who is responsible for performing usability testing of a user-interface Component or Application.
- **Toolsmith** – a Role played by a Person who is responsible for the development environment of an Endeavor.

- **Trainer** – a Role played by a Person responsible for arranging training:
  - *Classroom trainer* – a Trainer who provides formal, classroom training (lectures).
  - *Mentor* – a Trainer who provides one-on-one, on-the-job advice.
- **Usability Engineer** – the Person responsible for implementing the human interfaces.
- **User Analyst** – the Person who analyzes users and user Organizations in order to determine the users' desires and needs.

4.1.3 Tools

The OPF comes with the following predefined classes of Tools:

- A *Documentation Tool*, such as a word processor, is used to generate Documents.
- A *Process Engineering Tool* is a Tool specifically designed to assist the process engineer in constructing process instances from the process components in the repository of a framework-based process approach.
- A *Database Management Tool* is a Tool for creating and maintaining databases, be they relational, object-oriented or object relational.
- A *Computer-aided Software Engineering (CASE) Tool* is a Tool specifically designed to support software engineering:
  - An *upperCASE Tool* is a CASE Tool that works above the code level. Examples are a Configuration Management Tool, a Documentation Management Tool, a Metrics Tool, a Modeling Tool and a Requirements Management Tool.
  - A *lowerCASE Tool* is a CASE Tool that works at the code level. Examples are compilers, browsers, debuggers and interpreters.

4.2 Indirect Producers

An *indirect Producer* is any Producer that indirectly produces Work Products. The OPF comes with the following predefined classes of indirect Producers:

- Team
- Organization.

4.2.1 Teams

Good teamwork is critical to the success of almost every modern-day software-intensive Application development. Teams consist of individual Persons (and sometimes other subTeams) playing Roles in a cohesive and holistic fashion such that a Team has emergent properties (the whole, the Team, is more than the sum of its parts, the individual Team members). The key to successful team-building is to identify complementary skills in its members – and also be aware of people's weaknesses.

A number of types of Team are predefined in the OPF repository, although others are of course feasible. These are described briefly here – for full details see Appendix D.

- **Architecture Team:**
  - *Business Architecture Team*: a Team responsible for producing the Architecture of the business.
  - *Software Architecture Team*: a Team responsible for the overall Architecture of the software.
  - *System Architecture Team*: a Team responsible for the overall Architecture of the system.
  - *Website Architecture Team*: a Team responsible for the overall Architecture of the Website.
- **Business Engineering Team:**
  - *Branding Strategy Team*: a Team responsible for developing the digital brand of the business Enterprise.
  - *Business Strategy Team*: a Team responsible for the business-related strategic aspects of the Endeavor (e.g. business and market analysis, business strategy development).
  - *Technology Strategy Team*: a Team responsible for strategic decision-making on all technological issues of the Endeavor.
- **Change Control Board:** a Team responsible for approving proposed changes to baselined work products.
- **Component Acquisition and Integration Team:** a Team responsible for identifying and procuring Components.
- **Configuration Management Team:** a Team responsible for all aspects of Configuration Management.
- **Database Team:** a Team responsible for all aspects of data and object storage via some kind of database product.
- **Deployment Team:** a Team responsible for deploying the Application into its production environments.
- **Development Environment Team:** a Team responsible for production environments as well as the data and contact centers.
- **Documentation Team:** a Team responsible for supporting all aspects of documentation.
- **Hardware Development Team:** a Team responsible for developing hardware.
- **Hardware Prototyping Team:** a Team responsible for testing and evaluation of hardware using a prototyping approach.
- **Integration Team:** a Team responsible for performing integration Tasks, either between existing and new Components or between a new Application and an existing "legacy" system.

- **Management Team:**
  - *Hardware Management Team*: a Team responsible for managing hardware aspects of the system.
  - *Software Management Team*: a Team responsible for managing software.
  - *System Management Team*: a Team responsible for managing all system aspects (hardware, software and, notably, their integration).
- **Metrics Team:** a Team responsible for collecting, analyzing and publishing measurements.
- **Package Team:** a Team responsible for the development of an individual package.
- **Peer Programmer Team:** a Team, usually of two class owners, responsible for a cohesive collection of classes.
- **Process Team:** a Team responsible for all process aspects.
- **Project Team:** a Team responsible for creating all Work Products.
- **Project Initiation Team:** a Team responsible for all initiation aspects.
- **Quality Team**: a Team responsible for providing an independent evaluation of all quality aspects of the system.
- **Requirements Team:**
  - *Hardware Requirements Team*: a Team responsible for determining all Hardware Requirements.
  - *Software Requirements Team*: a Team responsible for determining all Software Requirements.
  - *System Requirements Team*: a Team responsible for determining all System-level Requirements.
- **Reuse Team:** a Team responsible for both strategic and operational issues in reuse.
- **Security Team:** a Team responsible for all aspects of internal and external security, specially relevant to networked sites.
- **Software Development Team:** a Team responsible for developing Application software.
- **System Development Team:** a Team responsible for developing the system.
- **Test Team:**
  - *Hardware Test Team*: a Team responsible for testing hardware Components.
  - *Software Test Team*: a Team responsible for testing software Components.
  - *System Test Team*: a Team responsible for testing system and integration issues.
  - *Usability Test Team*: a Team responsible for testing all usability aspects of an Application.
- **Training Team:** a Team responsible for identifying skills deficiencies and rectifying this situation by organizing training.

- **Usage Phase Team:** a Team responsible for the period of time when the Application is in everyday use. There are three areas of responsibility that are often assigned to subTeams:
  - *Contact Center Team*: a Team that mans a contact center and provides user support.
  - *Operations Team*: a Team responsible for the operational deployment and use of the Application.
  - *Maintenance Team*: a Team responsible for "bug fixes" and further enhancements throughout the lifetime of the Application.
  - *Content Management Team*: a Team responsible for the content of Websites as they grow.
- **User Interface Team:** a Team responsible for designing and perhaps implementing the graphical user interface, with a focus on its usability characteristics.
- **Web Development Team:** a Team responsible for all the Web-related aspects of the Project.

4.2.2 Organizations

A large-scale Indirect Producer is the *Organization*, which consists of one or more Teams. A number of types of Organization have been identified and predefined in the OPF repository, although of course others are likely to be useful too.

- **Customer Organization** – An Organization that pays a development Organization to develop an Application.
- **Development Organization** – An Organization that develops and releases one or more Applications to either a customer Organization or user Organization.
- **Maintenance Organization** – An Organization that maintains Applications developed by the development Organization.
- **Marketing Organization** – An Organization that markets Applications to customer Organizations.
- **Reuse Organization** – The project-independent Organization that is responsible for Enterprise reuse including documentation, deliverable software, and test software.
- **Subcontractor Organization** – An Organization that is subcontracted by the development Organization to undertake a specific portion of the overall work.
- **Support Organization** – An Organization that supports customer and user Organizations.
- **User Organization** – An Organization that uses Applications developed by a development Organization.
- **Vendor Organization** – An Organization that sells Commercial-Off-The-Shelf (COTS) products to the development Organization.

4.2.3 Endeavors

Although not Producers, they are closely associated with them, being staffed by members of Organizations. An *Endeavor* is a business venture and the collective name for Projects, Programmes and Enterprises – each of these is related to the development and maintenance of one or more related Applications, but at different scales.

- *Project* – an atomic Endeavor typically associated with a single contract that is undertaken to either provide a service (e.g., re-engineer a business) or else to produce and deliver Versions of one or more major work products (e.g., Application or reusable Component).
- *Programme* – an Endeavor consisting of a set of related Projects that are managed as a group.
- *Enterprise* – an Endeavor consisting of all Programmes when managed as a group. An Enterprise could be at the level of an Organization or across several Organizations.

Summary

A major focus of building Applications is the people that produce the Applications and related Work Products, aided by automatic Tools or hardware devices that supply data or other control elements. Producers may create Work Products themselves (*direct Producers*) or via their collaboration in Teams and other higher-level groupings (*indirect Producers*).

Producers, whilst often ultimately people, should really be acknowledged in terms of the Role they are currently playing. One Person may play several Roles, either concurrently or sequentially. It is the Role that is important, not the Person's job title. Finally, Producers collaborate by performing Tasks in order to produce Versions of Work Products.

The OPEN Process Framework comes with a number of predefined classes of Producers that may be tailored, extended, and used by a process engineer to meet the specific needs of an Endeavor.

5 Work Units

This chapter outlines the various Work Units that are one of the core elements (see Figure 2.4) of the OPEN Process Framework (OPF). A Work Unit, as you might guess, describes some chunk or unit of work or effort expenditure. The kinds of process elements that fall into this category include Tasks, Activities, and Techniques.

A **Work Unit** models a *functionally* cohesive operation that is performed, either directly or indirectly, by one or more Producers during the execution of a process instantiated from the OPF. Although functional rather than object-oriented, the OPF reifies (i.e., models as an object) the "Work Unit" concept in order to:

- emphasize Work Units as a major class of process component;
- provide users of the OPF with the necessary flexibility during the construction and tailoring of a project-specific process (e.g., one can create swappable functions using the strategy pattern);
- allow process engineers to constrain the relationships between Work Units and thereby create appropriate development cycles using assertions (e.g., invariants, pre-conditions and post-conditions).

As illustrated in Figure 5.1, the OPF class library of reusable process Components includes the following classes of Work Units:

- *activities*, which are large-scale Work Units that model a cohesive collection of Tasks that achieve a related set of goals (e.g., the production of a related set of Work Products);
- *Tasks*, which are small-scale Work Units that model a single assigned job that may be performed by one or more Producers.
- *Techniques*, which are the smallest Work Units, and which model ways a Producer can perform a Task (i.e., an implementation of a Task).

Tasks are a major focus since they can be clearly and generally uniquely defined, can be allocated to a producer Role, can be measured, monitored, and controlled, and can be linked to appropriate Techniques. Tasks delineate *what* needs to be done; Techniques state *how* the Task is to be best accomplished.

Activities differ from Tasks in that they are much larger in scope and typically involve the performance of numerous Tasks by multiple Producers (i.e., they are cohesive but heterogeneous). Which Activities are used in an OPEN process instance depends on variables such as Project size and 'degree of ceremony' required (see fuller discussion below). Producers directly perform Tasks, whereas Producers only indirectly perform activities. In other words, the operations of Producer objects are Tasks, not activities.

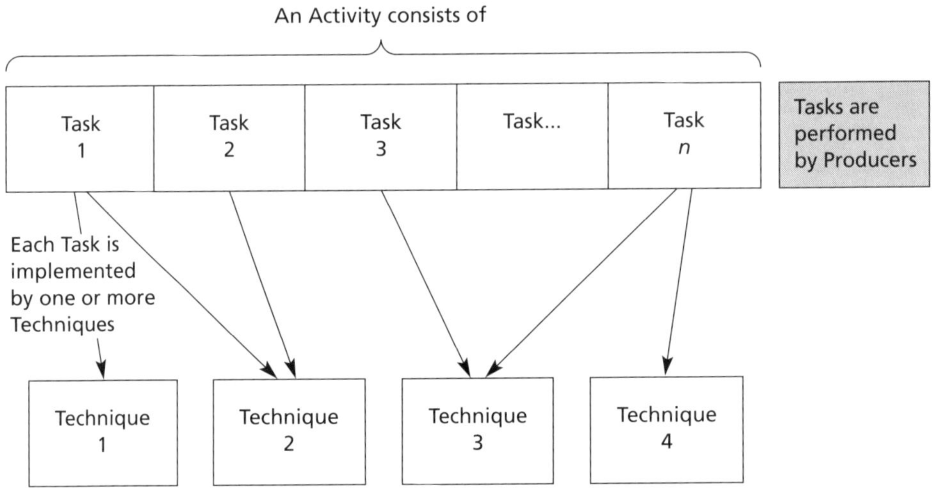

Figure 5.1 The relationship between Activities, Tasks and Techniques, which are all three kinds of Work Unit

Although not themselves Work Units, the OPF uses assertions (pre-conditions, post-conditions and invariants) to constrain the execution of Work Units and thereby ensure that Producers can collaborate successfully. OPF also uses Assertions to constrain development Stages and therefore produce specific Life Cycles.

Because this is an introductory book, this chapter merely identifies, but does not fully define, many of the predefined set of OPF Activities and Tasks.[1] For example, the complete documentation of an Activity would include its goals and objectives, its corresponding Tasks (including the Producers that perform them), its associated Work Products, the relationship between it and the Phases and Milestones, and its pre-conditions and post-conditions. Finally, because of their intimate association with Work Units in the OPF, we conclude this chapter with a brief discussion of assertions, which constrain the execution of Work Units.

5.1 Activities

The OPF defines an **Activity** as a major Work Unit that models a cohesive yet heterogeneous collection of Tasks that achieves a related set of goals. For example, the Requirements Engineering Activity would consist of all Producer Tasks (requirements elicitation, reuse, analysis, and specification) associated with the production of Requirements Work Products (e.g., System Requirements Specification and External API Specification).

1 Full details of OPEN's Activities and Tasks are given in the various books in the OPEN series, primarily in *The OPEN Process Specification* published in 1997 by Addison-Wesley. Appendix E in this book also provides more information on this topic. Further details are also found in various commercial websites, such as www.donald-firesmith.com.

Although Tasks are more clearly defined than Activities, they cannot be used to configure the life cycle process since they are far too granular. Instead, a set of appropriately selected, coarser-grained Activities is more useful. Typically 5–10 or so of these Activity objects are needed during the development life cycle. An overall life cycle plan is thus manageable. Further detail is then available in terms of the Tasks that are necessary to support the Activities that comprise the life cycle process and to add sufficient detail for high-quality Project Management.

Not all predefined Tasks are used in every OPEN process instance. Each particular instance is configured to very specific organizational requirements for that process. For example, for a high ceremony, multi-person-year project in a bureaucratic organization, extensive use of Project Management Tasks will be used and for high-quality, safety-critical systems a large emphasis would be placed on Testing Tasks. In such an instance (call it "OPEN Instance 1"), it is highly advisable to collect these like-minded Tasks together as an Activity – in this case, a Project Management Activity and a Testing Activity, respectively. In a second example ("OPEN Instance 2"), of a rapid e-business development well-integrated in a user environment perhaps using a "lightweight" OPEN process instance, having a separate Project Management Activity might be overkill. Instead, a small number of (lightweight) Project Management Tasks would be better integrated into other, appropriate Activities. For example, one common manifestation of such integration would be by having Testing Tasks spread across (possibly with minor duplication) most of the Activities, viewed perhaps as part of the Postconditions of those relevant Activities.

Since in "OPEN Instance 2", Project Management (for example) exists as integrated Tasks, i.e., no Project Management Activity exists, whereas in "OPEN Instance 1", there is a need for a Project Management Activity plus associated Team structures, it is less easy (than for Tasks) to list and define an orthogonal and unique set of useful Activities. Bearing that essential non-orthogonality in mind, we can now proceed to give you some indication of typical Task groupings (Activities) that can occur. We can divide these roughly into two groupings: Application-specific activities and Enterprise-level activities.

Application-specific activities are those activities that are performed on Projects producing a Version of a single Application, whereas Enterprise-level activities are not restricted to the development of a single Application, being instead appropriate to the development of multiple related Applications that often interoperate, for example by using the same database. The major Application-specific activities are those that have been identified and used by methodologists and developers for decades. Some of them therefore tend to correspond to the sequential Phases of the traditional waterfall development cycle although many other application-specific activities are typically performed concurrently. Thus, these do *not* correspond to the time-boxed Phases of a modern iterative, incremental, parallel development Life Cycle.

The OPF class library currently includes the following predefined instances of the Application-specific Activity class:

- **Project Management** Tasks in which knowledge, experience, Tools, and Techniques are applied in order to manage a Project so that stakeholder needs and expectations regarding the Project are met or exceeded.

- **Configuration Management**, which describes the management and baselining of configuration items.
- **Risk Management**, focussing on managing Project risks.
- **Metrics Management**, to ensure that Project estimates of performance, progress and quality are based on the analysis of solid data.
- **Quality Engineering**, the quality assurance and quality control Tasks used to ensure that the Project will satisfy the stakeholder's needs and expectations regarding quality.
- **Process Engineering**, to ensure the selection and use of a Project-appropriate process (a.k.a. method and methodology).
- **Environments Engineering**, for the installation and maintenance of the environments used on a Project.
- **Website Management**, which covers technical, graphical and business issues associated with creating and maintaining a serious Website (more than just a visual presence on the WWW).
- **Requirements Engineering**, eliciting, reusing, analyzing and specifying Requirements including operational requirements, quality requirements and design constraints.
- **Project Initiation**, developing business and strategic plans. [Not an Activity if a large-scale Project Management Activity is in use.]
- **Architecting**, producing the Architecture (i.e., strategic design decisions) of an Application or business.
- **Project Planning**, planning the Tasks, Phases, and Milestones of the Project. [Not an Activity if a large-scale Project Management Activity is in use.]
- **Design**, the set of Tasks that produces and maintains the tactical design of an Application. [Not used if a Build Activity is in use.]
- **Component Selection**, for a component-based solution, identifying, evaluating, and selecting the best-fit Components for inclusion.
- **Build** – Modeling and construction of the software Application:
  - *Evolutionary development* – Analysis, design and programming in an iterative, incremental and parallel fashion with integrated verification and validation.
  - *User review* – Involvement of the client during the development of the Application.
  - *Consolidation* – Final consolidation subsequent to iterative reviews.
- **Implementation**, the set of Tasks that actually produce the system Components. [Not used if a Build Activity is in use.]
- **Integration**, focussing on the integration of the system Components to form an executable Version of an Application.
- **Evaluation**, a wide-ranging formal review of system including post-implementation review (a.k.a. retrospective). It has strong links to the notions of Quality Assurance (QA).

- **Testing**, focussing on the execution of Work Products (e.g., Models, Software and the Application) in order to cause failures so that the underlying defects may be identified and eliminated. [Testing Tasks may be distributed among other Activity objects as a set of Tasks – or collected together as here in a single concurrent Activity.]
- **Deployment**, resulting in the placing of a tested Application into production (i.e., transfer of control to the client Organization and initiation of usage by the user Organizations).

Some typical instances of the Enterprise-level Activity class, currently described within the OPF library, include:

- **Business Modeling**, focussing on [re]engineering an Organization's business model regarding the Applications it develops and maintains. It also covers issues relevant to domain modeling.
- **Reuse Management**, which provides organizational-level support for reuse: important for both object technology (OT) and Component-based development (CBD).
- **Programme Management**, managing a Programme of related Projects.
- **Resource Planning**, Project management focus of allocation of resources: time, people, money, Tools. (May be a subject of Project or Programme Management.)
- **Training**, providing stakeholders (e.g., developers, maintainers and users) with the necessary knowledge and expertise to perform their assigned Tasks.

Programme-level activities may alternatively be grouped as Reuse Management plus, collectively:

- **Extra-Project Activities**, a grouping of resource allocation and Project Planning and Domain Modeling.

A new and interesting area of application of an instance of the OPF is in the area of organizational transition to object technology and the adoption of an OO/CBD process such as OPEN.[2] When used in this context, it is advised that the Change Management Strategy Task is replaced by two new Activities (Organization Assessment and Predevelopment Acceptance) together with a third called Technology Insertion. These can be described briefly as follows:

- **Organization Assessment** describes the current and desired situation and the "road map" between.
- **Predevelopment Acceptance** (a.k.a. Transition Acceptance) addresses all the issues of cultural change.
- **Technology Insertion** deals with the actual process of transitioning.

2 Henderson-Sellers, B. and Serour, M.K. (2000) Creating a process for transitioning to object technology, *Procs. 7th Asia-Pacific Software Engineering Conference (APSEC2000)*, IEEE Computer Society Press, 436–440.

Further details of these Activities are found in other books of the OPEN series and one summarized in Appendix E.

Finally, since the OPF is extensible, process engineers and methodologists in the future may easily add additional activities to support the specific needs of new Application domains or new styles of computing (e.g., agent-oriented and aspect-oriented computing or perhaps even complex adaptive systems).

5.2 Tasks

OPF defines a Task as a small-scale Work Unit that Models a single assigned job that may be performed by one or more Producers in order to create one (or several) Work Products (Figure 5.2). A Task describes *what* a Producer must do, but *not how* it should be done (which is the realm of the Technique – see below).

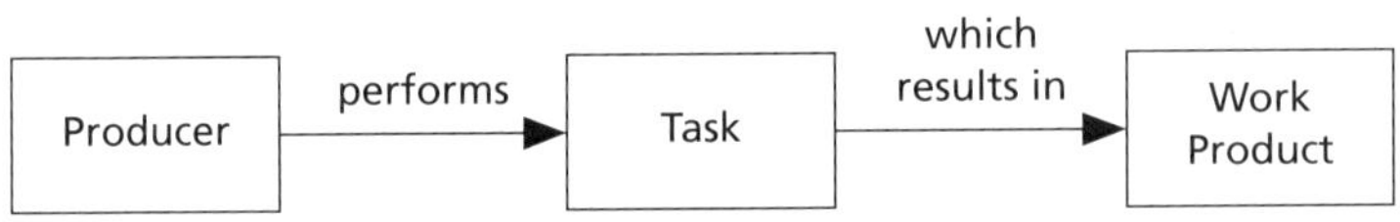

Figure 5.2 Producers perform Tasks in order to produce Work Products

Activities and Tasks are related in a one-to-many relationship. Some Tasks are management focussed, while others are engineering-focussed. In the OPF repository, there are many predefined Tasks, although it is perfectly possible to add more because of the extensible nature of the OPF.

This book is only intended to be an introduction to the OPF and other books in the series (for example, *The OPEN Process Specification*) document Tasks in more detail. This chapter, therefore, will only list the OPF Tasks (Table 5.1). For discussion on how to select appropriate Tasks, see Chapter 8. Readers should evaluate the following list of Tasks to better understand Tasks and to identify "missing" Tasks that are not currently being performed on their Projects (but should be!).[3]

Table 5.1 List of OPEN's current Tasks (in alphabetical order)

Acquire reusable Work Products
Act on Metrics report
Agree on the future
Analyze customer Organization(s)
Analyze market

3 If you identify missing elements in OPEN, please let all users know by sending an email to the OPEN public listserver facility at open@it.swin.edu.au (see OPEN Website at http://www.open.org.au for subscription information).

Table 5.1 List of OPEN's current Tasks (in alphabetical order) *continued*

Analyze metrics data
Analyze risks
Analyze technology
Analyze training needs
Analyze user requirements
Analyze users
Assess current state of organization
Assess metrics needs
Assess organization's resources for transition
Assess quality needs
Assess staff skills/knowledge
Assess transition paths
Build white site/wireframe prototype
Capture the design
Choose and install hardware
Choose appropriate component framework
Choose appropriate components
Choose project team
Choose toolset
Code
Code test suite
Collect metrics data
Communicate the brand identity
Communicate the process to stakeholders
Construct the object model
Control the configuration
Create and/or identify reusable components ("for reuse")
Create a software architecture
Create a system architecture

Table 5.1 List of OPEN's current Tasks (in alphabetical order) *continued*

Create content (on Website)
Create navigation map for website
Create SWAT team
Decompose programmes into projects
Define acceptance criteria for website
Define website testing strategy
Deliver Product to customer
Describe the past/identify important events
Design and implement content management strategy
Design and implement personalization strategy
Design and implement physical database
Design test suite
Design the database model
Design the data center
Design user interface
Design Web system architecture
Design Website standards
Develop a brand identity
Develop Business Object Model (BOM)
Develop data standard
Develop data standard
Develop education and training plan
Develop reusable Work Products
Develop training materials
Disseminate information regarding reuse opportunities
Document environments
Document risk potential
Document test suite
Document the architecture
Document the design
Document the process

Table 5.1 List of OPEN's current Tasks (in alphabetical order) *continued*

Effect rapid culture change
Elicit user requirements
Enforce the architecture
Enforce the process
Enhance teamwork
Ensure schedule management
Establish change management strategy
Establish data take-on strategy
Establish optimum development environment
Evaluate and select appropriate technologies
Evaluate quality
Establish policy on component acquisition
Establish policy on COTS
Establish policy on outsourcing
Establish risk avoidance strategy
Evaluate the architecture
Evaluate the design
Evaluate the potential component frameworks
Evaluate the potential components
Execute integration plans
Execute tests
Identify an appropriate configuration
Identify appropriate reusable work products ("for reuse")
Identify CIRTs (Class, Instance, Role, Type)
Identify client's vision
Identify context
Identify pilot project
Identify potential risks
Identify programme funding
Identify project roles and responsibilities

Table 5.1 List of OPEN's current Tasks (in alphabetical order) *continued*

Identify reusable Requirements
Identify source(s) of Requirements
Identify training vendor
Introduce and enforce new technology
Instantiate process framework
Integrate components
Integrate content with user interface
Integrate with existing, non-OO/CBD systems
Iteratively improve software components
Maintain development environment
Maintain process framework
Maintain trace between Requirements and design
Manage content
Manage contract(s)
Manage human resources
Manage library of reusable components
Manage resources
Manage subsystems
Manage the customer relationship
Map roles on to classes
Mitigate risks
Model and re-engineer business processes
Monitor configuration status
Obtain business approval
Optimize reuse ("with reuse")
Optimize the design
Plan integration
Plan testing strategy
Prototype the architecture
Prototype the human interface

Table 5.1 List of OPEN's current Tasks (in alphabetical order) *continued*

Provide training opportunities
Refactor
Report on metrics data
Report on Programme status
Report on status of integration
Report on status of process
Report on status of training
Report on test results
Report on training costs
Requirements elicitation
Requirements reuse
Requirements analysis
Requirements specifications
Research technology trends
Screen the candidate list of component frameworks
Screen the candidate list of components
Select partners and vendors
Set transition goals
Set up metrics collection programme
Specify quality goals
Specify user requirements
Tailor the process
Test
Train users
Undertake client analysis
Undertake configuration auditing
Undertake cost management
Undertake domain modeling
Undertake feasibility study
Undertake (formal) risk analysis

Table 5.1 List of OPEN's current Tasks (in alphabetical order) *continued*

Undertake in-process review
Undertake market analysis
Undertake post-implementation review
Undertake Programme cost reporting
Undertake Programme planning
Undertake project planning
Undertake testing of Website
Undertake usability design
Undertake user analysis
Write manual(s) and prepare other documentation

5.3 Techniques

The OPF defines a *Technique* as a small-scale Work Unit that Models a single way a Producer can perform a Task. Thus, OPF reifies Task implementations as Techniques in order to provide significant flexibility when it comes to instantiating and tailoring the OPF to produce a Project-specific process.

Tasks and Techniques are related by a many-to-many relationship. A Task may be implemented by one or more Techniques, and the same Technique can sometimes be used to implement more than one Task.

Numerous Techniques have been developed, used, tested and evaluated in industry settings over the last decade or so. Because approximately 150 Techniques are documented in *The OPEN Toolbox of Techniques*, it is inappropriate to Document them here (but they are listed by name in Appendix E). We will therefore restrict ourselves to providing a few examples to illustrate the idea of a Technique and its relationship to Tasks.

As one small example, Producers can use the following Techniques to perform the following Requirements Engineering Tasks:

- Requirements Elicitation Task. Useful Techniques are:
  - Interviewing
  - Workshops
  - Brainstorming
  - Questionnaires
- Requirements Analysis Task. Useful Techniques are:
  - Cost-benefit analysis
  - Impact analysis

- Prioritization
- Context Models
- Object Models
- Use Case Models
- Class, Responsibility, Collaborator (CRC) cards
- Use Case cards

5.4 Assertions

An **Assertion** is a Boolean expression that describes the state of something at a specific point in time. The OPF uses Assertions to describe the state of the process at the start or completion of a Work Unit (or Stage) to specify dependencies between Work Units. Assertions thereby constrain when Work Units can successfully begin and also define what successful completion means. The exact specification of pre-conditions is left to the process engineer in constructing (and tailoring) their Project-specific instance of the OPF. The use of assertions in process modeling is identical to their use in programming. They can specify the required:

- Entry conditions to work (pre-conditions),
- Exit conditions (post-conditions), or
- Consistent state conditions (invariants).

5.4.1 Pre-conditions

A **pre-condition** is an Assertion (i.e., Boolean condition) associated with a Work Unit that must be true before the Work Unit can successfully begin. The following are examples of Work Units with associated pre-conditions:

- Requirements Engineering Activity:
  - The Application Vision Statement has been stated.
  - Domain experts are available.
- Refactoring Task:
  - The Software Component is suboptimal, perhaps exhibited by inadequate performance.

5.4.2 Post-conditions

A **post-condition** is an assertion associated with a Work Unit that must be true at the successful completion of the Work Unit. The following are examples of Work Units with associated post-conditions:

- Requirements Engineering Activity:
  - The following Work Products have been completed, inspected, and baselined:
    - System Requirements specification.
    - External API (Application Programmer Interface) specification.
    - Domain Model Document.
  - The Project Glossary Documents all significant terms included in the Requirements Specifications and Domain Model Document.
- Refactoring Task:
  - The Software Component has been refactored to remedy its previous "poor design".

5.4.3 Invariants

An **invariant** is an assertion associated with a Work Unit that must be true both prior to and at the successful completion of the Work Unit. The following are examples of Work Units with associated invariants:

- Requirements Engineering Activity:
  - None.
- Refactoring Task:
  - Unit tests exist for the software Component to be refactored.
  - The Software Component has been implemented.
  - The Software Component passes its unit tests.

5.5 Work Performances

Work Units are static descriptors. In reality, they are performed by one or more Producers (playing a Role). This combination is called a "Work Performance". Two important kinds of Work Performance are Task Performance and Work Flow, the latter a sequenced collection of Task Performances (Figure 5.3).

5.5.1 Task Performances

A Task Performance is an atomic kind of Work Performance that brings together a specific Task and a specific Producer. It recognizes the importance of the interaction between these two process elements – rather than simply focussing on Tasks and ignoring Producers, as has been done previously.

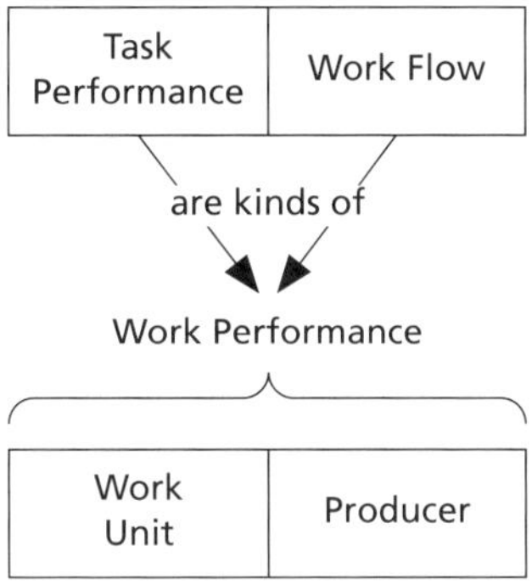

Figure 5.3 Work Performances

5.5.2 Work Flows

A *Work Flow* models a collection of Task Performances, sequenced by the assertions that must be performed in order to produce a single significant Work Product. Work Flows may cross Activity boundaries and can be linked to the delivery of certain Work Products. They can also be constructed for various business domains and can be project-managed by using a flexible Tool, such as eTrack™. While space prevents us from giving the full details of all the specific Work Flows suggested in the OPF, we have incorporated one example here (for the External Interface Specification Work Flow) in Appendix F.

Summary

A Work Unit is a kind of OPF Process Component that models a *functionally* cohesive operation that is performed by one or more Producers during the execution of a process instantiated from the OPF. Work Units are thus what Producers do when producing Work Products.

Work Units in the OPF are categorized as either Activities, Tasks or Techniques. This reification as objects then permits their use in creating a process that provides both extensibility and flexibility. Activities are used in creating and tailoring the process itself; Tasks provide smaller-scale "goals" within these Activities that provide a granularity which can now be actioned and project-managed.

Tasks are performed by Producers, often people. In order to perform the Task successfully, one or more Techniques will be found necessary which describe the "how". The result of each Task is the production of one or more related Work Products.

Sequencing (an important element of process construction) is assisted by the use of assertions, primarily pre-conditions and post-conditions, which determine the ordering of the Work Units and constrain a Work Unit at a specific point in time.

Finally, Task Performances and Work Flows express the necessary synergy between Work Units and the Producers responsible for using them in order to create one or more Work Products.

6 Stages

A *Stage* is a formally identified and managed interval of time (Stage With Duration) or a point in time (Instantaneous Stage) either during development or as part of an Enterprise level Endeavor. Stages provide a macro Organization to the Work Units. The OPF contains the following predefined classes of Stage:

- Stage With Duration:
  - Cycle:
    - Life Cycle
    - Development Cycle
  - Phase
  - Build
    - Release (a kind of Build)
- Milestone (Instantaneous Stage)

6.1 Cycles

Cycles describe either the large spans of time during which development and delivery occurs or the span of time which can be equated to the lifetime existence of an Endeavor or Application. A Cycle is therefore the largest of the development Stages. The OPF discriminates between elements of higher level Cycles and Cycles specific to individual software developments.

6.1.1 Life Cycles

A Life Cycle is the span of time associated with the existence of an Application to a business problem *in the business domain* i.e. it may encompass the Development Cycle (q.v.) and other business Phases related to a single Project (e.g. the Project Life Cycle) or may relate the temporal span associated with several developments of an Application suite or Programme (e.g. Programme Life Cycle) in which case it may additionally encompass several Project Life Cycles.

6.1.2 Development Cycles

A *Development Cycle* is the collection of all Development Cycles and Phases performed on a Project to develop the associated Application. Typically (see below) it might include the Initiation, Construction and Delivery Phases. It also follows a particular philosophy in terms of the Life Cycle Model it utilizes. Whilst not a kind of Stage, it thus seems appropriate to include a short discussion on Life Cycle Models here in this chapter.

6.1.3 Life Cycle Models

A *Life Cycle Model* describes the underlying philosophy underpinning the rules by which a development Life Cycle may be constructed.

The OPF contains the following predefined classes of Life Cycle Models:

- Waterfall
- Fountain
- Spiral
- Iterative, Incremental, Parallel
- Extreme Programming
- Contract-driven
- Web system.

Waterfall Life Cycle Model

The *Waterfall Life Cycle* was introduced to add some structure to the then *ad hoc* nature of software development. A number of Phases were identified and a sequence superimposed (Figure 6.1). This led to considerable rigidity in the process and the segregation of analysts from designers from coders. Later additions permitted some overlap of Phases (as shown here) and some reverse flow "up the waterfall" although in practice the existing segregation of Phases that had grown up would prove an obstacle. The Phases shown in Figure 6.1 are identical to the Activities discussed earlier in this book. In other words, in a Waterfall Model, Activities and Phases are unfortunately confused and merged together as a single concept whereas in OPEN these are separated into two distinctive concepts.

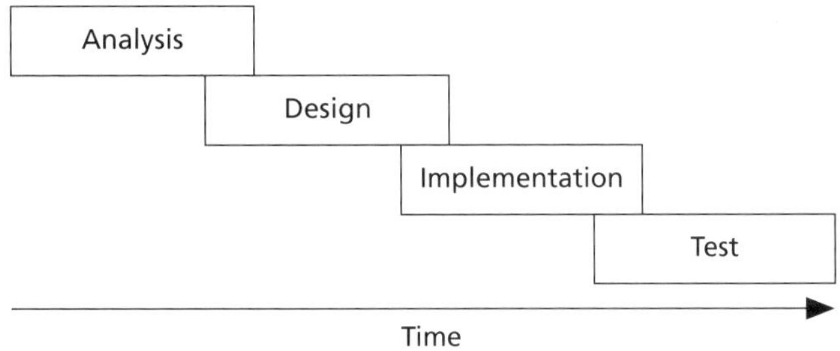

Figure 6.1 A traditional Waterfall Life Cycle Model

Fountain Life Cycle Model

The *Fountain Life Cycle Model* (Figure 6.2) was proposed in 1990 as a description of the more "fuzzy" nature of the OO development approach emphasizing the ability to support iteration and, particularly, explaining the role of reuse. It is now subsumed by the Contract-Driven Life Cycle Model (see below).

Spiral Life Cycle Model

In the *Spiral Life Cycle Model*, risk is an important element. At each turn of the spiral, the risks are re-evaluated. Interspersed with these risk analysis steps are the normal requirements, design, and coding etc. of a fairly traditional development approach.

Iterative, Incremental, Parallel Life Cycle Model

An *IIP* (*Iterative, Incremental and Parallel*) *Life Cycle Model* reflects the ideal that the Life Cycle should be (i) iterative and allow rework, (ii) deliver (new) Work Products in an incremental fashion; and (iii) permit decomposing the work so that individual Work Units can be allocated to a number of Teams working in parallel.

Extreme Programming (XP) Life Cycle Model

If a waterfall is pictured as a linear progression in time across a number of Phases (Figure 6.1) and an IIP Life Cycle as the repetition of this but over shorter periods (Figure 6.3) then the XP Life Cycle shortens the Life Cycle time so much that the various Phases are effectively superimposed (Figure 6.4).

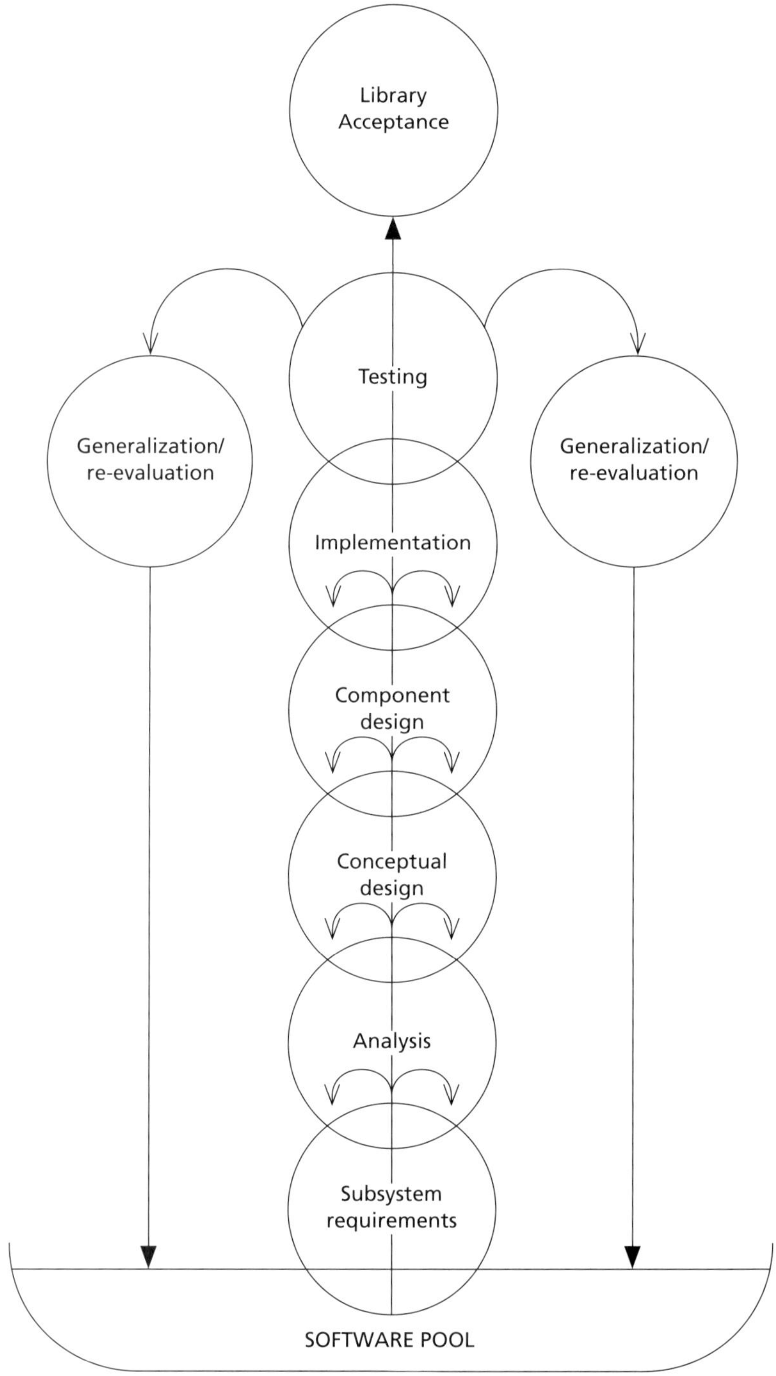

Figure 6.2 Cluster version of the Fountain Life Cycle Model

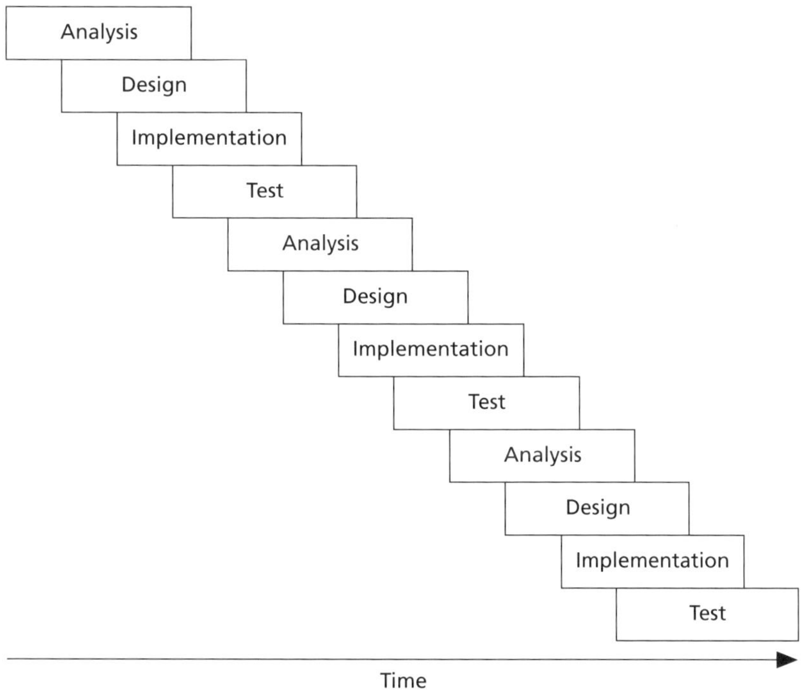

Figure 6.3 A Waterfall Life Cycle with a shortened timescale

Contract-Driven Life Cycle Model

A *Contract-Driven Life Cycle Model* is one in which the Phases (and Work Units) which comprise the Life Cycle interact using a contracting protocol. Developers can move from Work Unit to Work Unit only when the associated pre- and post-conditions are met. It is a generic description since, by varying the pre- and post-conditions, most of the other Life Cycle Models described here can be generated. Imposing strict assertions that prevent backtracking leads to a waterfall model, for instance.

Web System Life Cycle Model

Emerging as a distinctive Life Cycle Model, the Web System Life Cycle Model modifies the relationship between the Requirements and the Design Phases. Effectively, a lack of clarity (by both client and developer) in not only the desired solution but also the actual problem being addressed has led to the use of design prototypes to aid clients in understanding their needs and hence in formulating their problem. Consequently, Design Tasks become more tightly interwoven with the Requirements Engineering Tasks. This in turn leads to system specifications that utilize design artefacts to document requirements decisions. The implications of these changes are still being researched but are likely to lead to an increased consideration of approaches such as SSM (soft systems methodology).

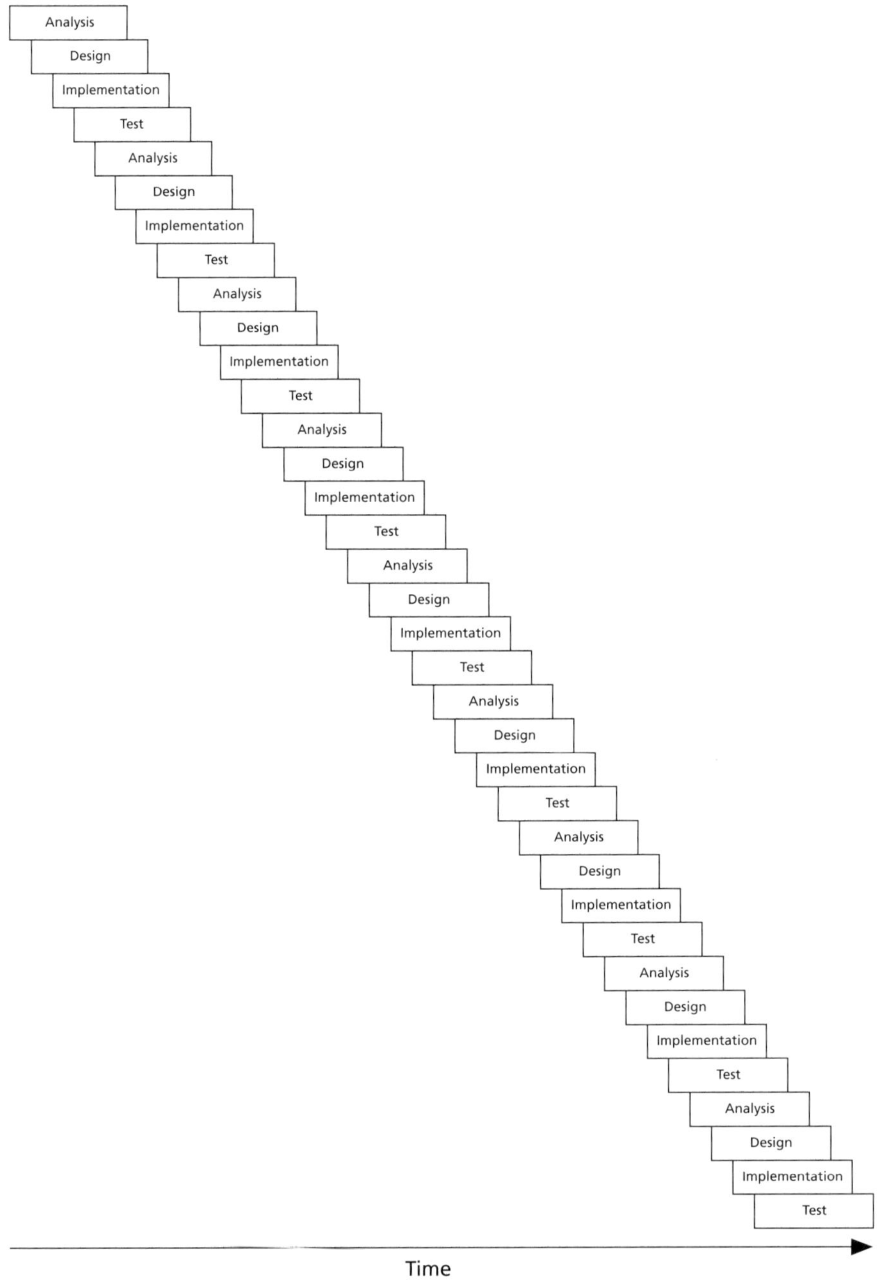

Figure 6.4 The XP Life Cycle Model

6.2 Phases

The OPF defines a *Phase* as a kind of Stage (With Duration) consisting of one or more related Builds, Releases, and Milestones (see below). The OPF recommends consideration of the following predefined instances of Phase:

- *Business Strategy* is the Phase during which the business is analyzed and a strategy for reengineering it is produced.
- *Business Optimization* is the Phase during which the business strategy is put into effect and the business is actually reengineered.
- *Initiation* is the Phase during which the Endeavor is started and initial Requirements Engineering and Architecting are performed.
- *Construction* is the Phase during which the Application is developed and prepared for release.
- *Delivery* is the Phase during which the Application is delivered, installed and tested at the production environments.
- *Usage* is the Phase during which the Application is used by the user Organization.
- *Retirement* is the Phase in which the use of the Application is terminated.

The first two Phases are used for Business Engineering Endeavors where as the last five Phases are used on Application Development Endeavors. Initiation is typically performed only once each at the beginning of an Endeavor, whereas Construction, Delivery and Usage are performed for each Release of the related Work Product (Model or Application). Retirement is also typically only performed once – at the end of the Endeavor, although in a Component-based Application, individual Components may be retired and replaced by newer Components at some time during the lifetime of the system itself.

6.2.1 Initiation

Initiation is the initial Phase of an Application Development Cycle during which sufficient Requirements and Architecture is produced to enable estimation of the remainder of development.

6.2.2 Construction

Construction is typically the second Phase of an Application Development Cycle during which the Work Products are developed and prepared for release.

6.2.3 Delivery

Delivery is typically the third Phase of an Application Development Cycle during which the Application is deployed into its production environments and accepted by the customer's Organization.

6.2.4 Usage

Usage is the penultimate Phase of the Application Life Cycle during which it is used over a period of months or years by the user Organization.

6.2.5 Retirement

When an Application reaches the end of its useful life, it must be gracefully retired. There are organizational and technical issues raised when it is withdrawn from service. These are considered in this Phase.

6.3 Builds

A Build is the smallest Endeavor-wide Stage of development, forming a scheduled part of a Phase. Depending on the duration of the Phase and the amount of iteration and incremental development, a Build may last from several months to several days. If the Build results in Work Products being delivered to the customer Organization, then the Build is called a Release.

6.4 Milestones

A *Milestone* is a scheduled point in time which occurs during a development when some set of significant objectives is to be achieved. For example, Milestones can occur when the Vision Statement is first baselined, a class passes unit testing or when a Version of the Application is released to the customer Organization. The OPF contains the following predefined types of Milestones:

- Management Milestones.
- Technical Milestones.

6.4.1 Management Milestones

A *Management Milestone* is a major Milestone that is scheduled by management for management purposes. Consequently, Management Milestones occur relatively infrequently, typically at the end of Phases when:

- major Endeavor objectives are to be met; or
- major Work Products are to be completed.

Management therefore has the information necessary to make major decisions regarding costs, schedule, Project goals and even whether or not to continue the Endeavor.

The OPF repository contains a number of predefined kinds of management Milestones including the following:

- Vision Statement baselined;
- Requirements Specification relatively complete and stable;
- Architecture Document relatively complete and stable;
- Operational testing relatively complete;
- Product released to Customer.

6.4.2 Technical Milestones

A *Technical Milestone* is a minor Milestone that is scheduled by the development staff for technical reasons. Consequently, technical Milestones occur relatively frequently (typically every few days or weeks) and are frequently associated with a single Work Product.

The OPF contains the following predefined subtypes of technical Milestones:

- a *Document Drop* which occurs when a Document is baselined and issued for evaluation;
- a *Code Drop* which occurs when the current deliverable and test software are baselined prior to integration and testing.

6.5 A Typical Life Cycle Configuration

Figure 6.5 illustrates a typical configuration of Phases and Life Cycle elements in an overall Application Development Endeavor. Projects typically focus on the development of a single Application, in contrast to Programmes, which organize several Projects. The Programme and Project Life Cycles are broken down into constituent parts (using a configurational whole-part symbol) such that each "branch" is a Phase. At a high level of granularity there is much seriality to this but inside, particularly in initiation and construction there are many incremental and iterative Builds within these Phases and the whole set of Phases, particularly construction, are applied in an incremental manner such that for each Increment achieved, a product Version is delivered to the client.

Application Development itself is the focus of the Application Development Cycle, as we noted above. In this Cycle we see the Initiation, Construction, Delivery Phases. When users are introduced into the equation, we need to consider usage of the Application followed by (after some years, we hope) a graceful retirement taking into account the replacement software, processes, strategies etc.

Each of the Phases can be divided into a number of Builds, Releases and Milestones (see, for example, Figure 6.6 for the Construction Phase). These divide up the timeline of the Phase (or, rather, the current Increment of that Phase) based initially on internally-focussed Work Products and, finally, externally delivered Work Products (those marked as Releases).

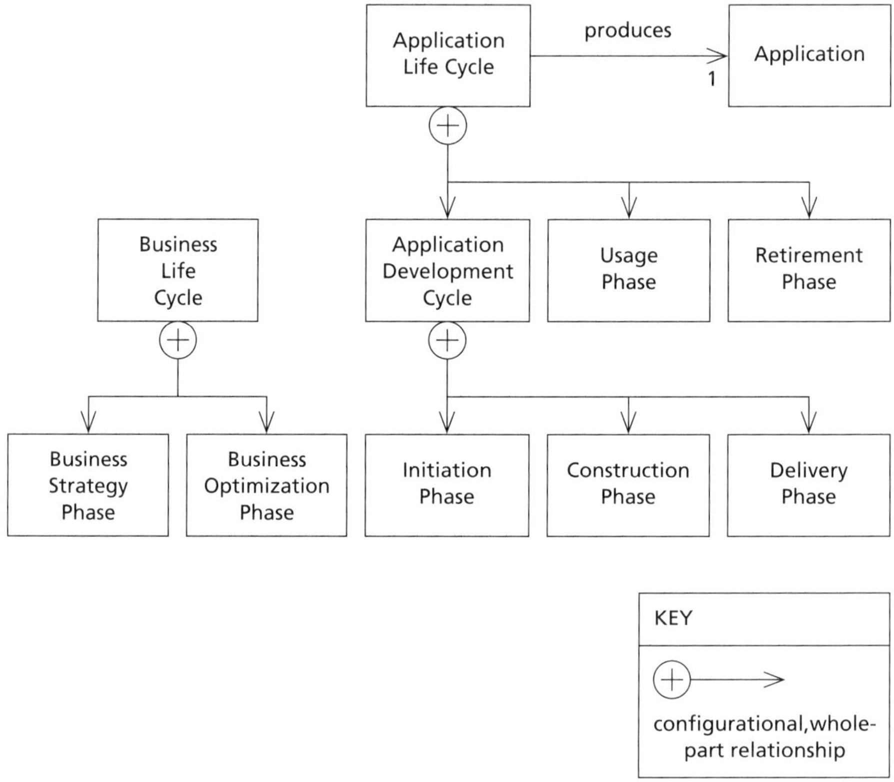

Figure 6.5 Life Cycles and Phases that make up a Programme and Project Life Cycle

6.6 Timeboxes

A timebox is a characteristic of a Work Unit or a Stage With Duration. It is specified as a "drop-dead" deadline for delivery that *never* slips. If anything has to give, it is the extent of the functionality being delivered. Other than imposing deadlines on developers, an additional (and important) advantage of timeboxing occurs for the client: they know exactly when the product will be delivered to them so that they allocate resources for acceptance testing and they know they can rely on the developer to deliver on time.

6.7 Relationship of Stages to Work Units

In the OPF, Stages provide the macro-organization to the Work Units and are themselves scheduled by the Milestones and Timeboxing. The duration of a Stage is usually expressed in calendar time (i.e. granularity of days, weeks or months). In contrast, Work Units focus on what is to be done and say nothing about *when* it is to be done. The fine-scale sequencing (but not calendar time) is done by assertions. Thus Activities often cut across Builds – although individual Tasks are often completed within a single Build. This is in contrast to the waterfall approach where Activities and Phases were strongly coupled, usually taken to be identical.

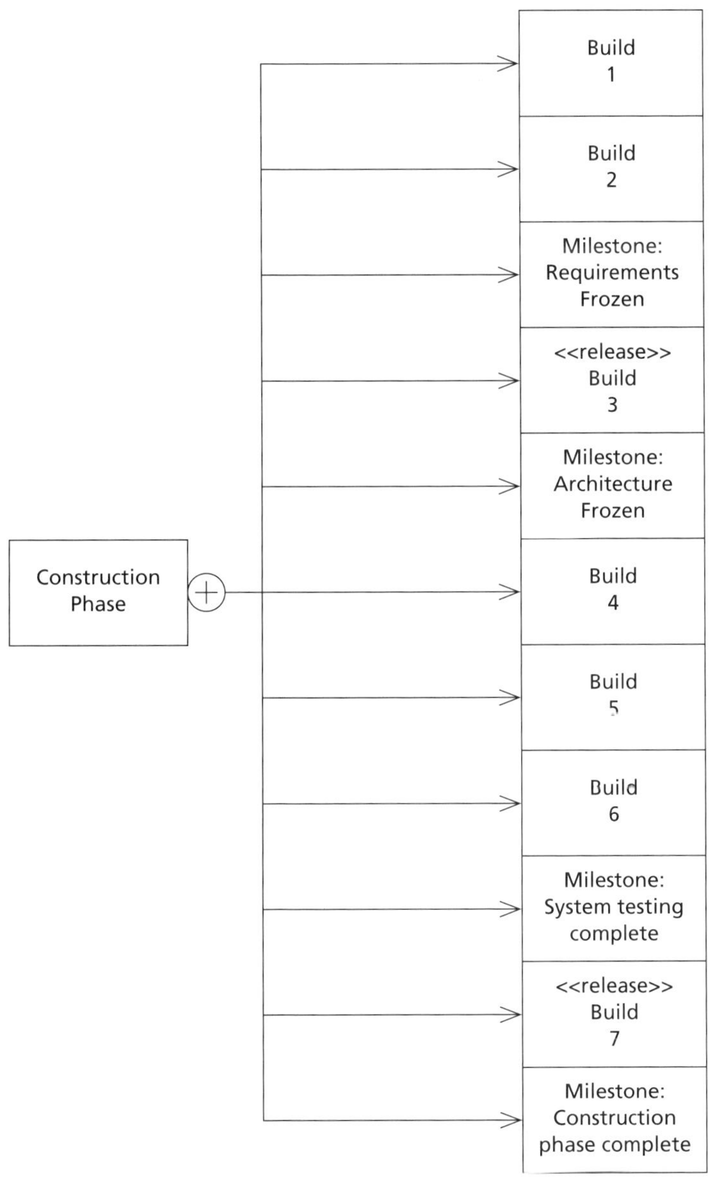

Figure 6.6 Details of the Builds, Releases and Milestones that might make up a typical Construction Phase

Summary

Stages relate to periods of time or points in time. There are various kinds of Stages with different granularities, including Cycles, Phases, Builds, and Milestones. Development Cycles focus on Application creation and are decomposed into Phases and then further into Builds and Releases, marked by Milestones.

To support the Development Cycle, the OPF offers a variety of Life Cycle philosophies, from waterfall to fountain and from XP to spiral. The Contract-Driven Life Cycle is a generic description encompassing these earlier approaches to a Life cycle Model and can be used to create each of them if this is desired. The Life Cycle style usually recommended in OO/CBD is one with strong elements of iteration, incremental and parallel (IIP) development and delivery. Timeboxing is also found to be highly useful by many companies.

7 Languages

7.1 Introduction

In the course of producing software-intensive systems, a wide variety of languages is encountered. During requirements elicitation and specification, a natural language such as English will typically be used, although some industries might use a formal mathematical language like Object-Z. Over the last few decades the trend has been to use a graphical language for modeling. In OO terms, these are usually called *Modeling Languages*. Ideally, they are a combination of a *notation* underpinned by a *metamodel* (Figure 7.1) and some additional semantics. Finally, and most well known, there are the Implementation Languages: Coding Languages such as Eiffel, Java and C++ and Database Languages such as SQL.

Each of these language groups is useful at different Stages in the Development Life Cycle. Languages are used to describe Work Product Versions in OPEN. The specific Languages to be used of course depends upon which of the Work Products we are considering. Within the language, there are then choices of several products, either conceptual or software. Language is therefore a small but important Component of the overall OPEN process architecture.

In this chapter, we take a brief look at some of the languages that might be encountered during the production of a software Application using OT and CBD. Because software Tools are used to support many of these Languages, there is a direct implication of choice of any particular Language on the resources needed for the Project. For example, choice of database environment may significantly affect the cost of the developmental environment.

7.2 Natural Languages

Natural Languages are used extensively for documenting almost all of the Work Products, either in textual Documents or as Natural Language annotations to graphical Documents like a UML Class Diagram. Similarly, the content of Websites is highly reliant on the use of Natural Language, as are a wide variety of Data Components. Finally, contemporary Applications (e.g. airline Websites) must also recognize the need to support multiple Natural Languages in order to support both a local and an international readership.

Although English is a widely accepted Natural Language, there are many others that are more likely to be used in non-English speaking countries. Some languages are more regular in their grammars and might therefore be more useful in creating a Requirements Document with a good structure. Indeed, the whole idea of use cases was to add some structure to writing Requirements. Other ideas that have been extensively used include the SVDPI[1] format for English Language sentence construction and more formal mathematical languages, often based on set theory or on some specified algebra.

One large problem with the English Language, and one loved by poets and novelists, is the rich vocabulary and the subtle use of tenses. Unfortunately, in using a Natural Language to document development, we are not writing a novel. We do not want the reader to have to interpret and delve deep into the nuances of the writing. Rather the opposite: we want our use of the Natural Language to be crystal clear and totally unambiguous. So, the use of a Natural Language in a stylized fashion is advocated, much like the use of Structured English in traditional systems analysis. Create an agreed glossary of words and their *precise* meanings (only in the context of the Endeavor of course). Always use these words, in writing and in conversation, with that agreed and documented meaning – and no other – and ensure that those meanings are compatible with or even derived from the user's domain. Since a major cause of failure of IT Projects is poor communication, this is an opportunity to increase your chances of success.

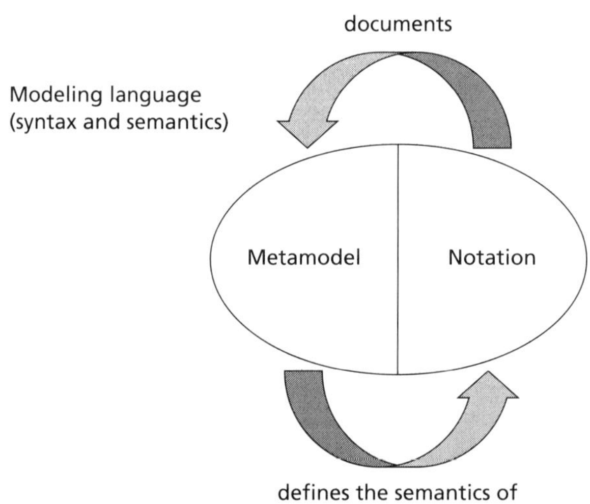

Figure 7.1 A modeling language consists of a metamodel plus a notation. It has syntax and semantics

1 SVDPI = Subject/Verb/Direct object/Preposition/Indirect object.

7.3 Modeling Languages

Modeling Languages, in contrast to Natural Languages, are more technically focussed. We like to use some formal Language, text or graphics, that helps us create, understand, and maintain our engineering Work Products. Since Modeling Languages are artificially created, they tend to be slightly less ambiguous than a Natural Language. The original intention of adopting the phrase "Modeling Language" by the OO community in around 1996 was to stress that a notation was not enough and that some formality underpinning the notation was needed. This followed from some studies begun in 1995[2] that identified inconsistencies in the OO "methods" then available. Of course, most of the methods were in fact what we now call Modeling Languages: notations enhanced by some minimal underpinning (but implicit) metamodeling concepts and a minimal amount of process thinking. Consequently, the term Modeling Language is intended to mean "a notation and its underlying semantics". The metamodel is essentially the set of rules that says what you can and cannot do with the language elements, which are themselves represented graphically or textually. Together, the metamodel and notation will be the Tools you use to depict the results of modeling and coding as you build Applications. Deep understanding of the metamodel is the realm of methodologists and CASE Tool builders; developers do not generally need to see the metamodel itself (although they do need to understand the basic semantics of the notation!). If the methodologists get the metamodel right and the CASE Tool vendors implement it correctly, then you have access to fine Tools to increase your quality and productivity.

Most of the methodology groups in the world chose to use metamodels to provide the formality to underpin the notation. In fact, the Object Management Group's intention in creating a modeling standard was focussed on the creation and adoption of a common metamodel. The notation was originally intended to be an adjunct and not the focus it later became. Once the OMG's UML standard was published, it fell under criticism from many formal methods users who stated that the so-called Semantics Document was no more than syntax and that what the UML lacked (and still lacks at the time of writing this book) is a full semantics. A group in Europe and North America, pUML, was formed in 1999 to address and correct this deficiency.

7.3.1 Metamodel

A metamodel is a model of a model. The model is the thing we are building to mimic the things in the real world. The software design documents normally produced during Application development are in fact a Model – of the world and of the software about to be built. Models contain (in OT) classes like Bank and Customer and show how the information system will sustain the business interaction between real banks and their customers. The Design Diagram will typically show classes, their

2 Later published as *Object-Oriented Metamethods*, by Henderson-Sellers and Bulthuis, Springer-Verlag, 1998.

associative relationships, perhaps some inheritance structures, possibly some aggregations. Each of these modeling concepts and relationships obey a number of rules. These rules are the same for all classes, all associations, all aggregations and so on. The rules belong to the metamodel. The metamodel, which itself can also be portrayed visually, defines those rules. It states whether an association joins together only two classes or whether three can be joined by the single association. It states whether or not an inheritance hierarchy may be cyclical; and whether an aggregation part can be the same thing as the whole. A metamodel also underpins all CASE Tools – in fact the rationale for the OMG effort in OO analysis and design Modeling Languages since 1995 has been the interchangeability of models between CASE/drawing Tools.

The metamodel (for UML, say) shows metalevel concepts such as Class, Relationship, Association, Dependency, and so on. It states the rules by which these may be used by a developer or by a CASE Tool implementer. It thus permits a CASE Tool to flag errors in usage and thus enhance the quality of the design being produced. It essentially introduces rigor and consistency into the modeling process.

Unfortunately, as noted above, the current UML metamodel is regarded by many as being somewhat weak on semantics and still, largely, as describing syntax. The meaning is largely indeterminate, which has meant that many parts of UML have been used in contradictory manners, thus thwarting the goal of a single universally practised and understood modeling approach for OT and CBD. On the other hand, for present purposes, many of these "disagreements" in the wider community are too detailed and small-scale for the typical developer or manager to worry about. This deliberation can be left to the OMG committees and will eventually lead to higher quality CASE and drawing Tools.

7.3.2 Constraint Language

While the original hope was that the metamodel would provide not only the syntax but also the full semantics, this turned out not to be the case. An additional, textual Language was invented as part of the OMG standard. This is called the Object Constraint Language or OCL.[3] It is a mathematical style of formal methods Language derived from the work done in the Syntropy method[4] but without the normal mathematical symbols short for "for every" (the universal quantifier) and "there exists" (the existential quantifier). This was done in order to make the OCL useful, not only as part of the UML definition but also to end-users. The OCL is used to add many of the constraints you would expect in a Modeling Language to ensure, for instance, the non-cyclic nature of inheritance, the irreflexive nature of aggregation at the instance level, and so on. It is also available at the modeling level as well as the metamodeling level to provide an additional Tool for adding business rules and other constraints into user-developed models.

3 Warmer and Kleppe (1999) *The Object Constraint Language. Precise Modeling with UML*, Addison-Wesley.

4 Cook and Daniels (1994) *Designing Object Systems*, Prentice Hall.

7.3.3 Notation

Once a metamodel and a Constraint Language have been devised, they need to be realized graphically and/or textually. Knowing what a Dependency Relationship is and how to use it is fine, but we need to know how to depict it in our diagrams. There are many ways to do this, ranging from formal to the informal, from the fully textual to the fully visual. UML takes an approach that is largely graphical, although there remains a significant amount of textual notation within it. There is a stated aim for UML to be turned into a fully graphical, Visual Programming Language, although this may, conversely, limit its use in Requirements Engineering.

The most straightforward approach is to take each concept in the metamodel and devise the very best notation for its realization. The very best here means that it should be readily understandable, unambiguous, easy to learn, easy to use, space saving, rotatable and so on. Ideally, it should embody the best elements of semiotic theory[5] by which the meaning of the sign is communicated to the user with the least effort and should undergo usability testing. For example, consider the two symbols in Figure 7.2. What would you guess they were meant to represent in terms of relationships available to you in object modeling?

Does the symbol at the left hand side have any semiotic meaning? Is it at all suggestive? The upper symbol can readily be seen as a plus sign in a circle. Or it might be seen as an image of the top of a Philips screw. Whichever of these you see first, you might immediately think of items being bound together in some way: plain addition (the sum is equal to the sum of the parts) or screwed together. So using this to represent the whole-part relationship in the OPEN modeling Language (OML) seems apposite. In addition, the whole-part relationship is inherently asymmetrical, as shown by the unidirectional arrow. Unfortunately, we have not been able to identify a similar argument for the lower symbol – which incidentally is also supposed to represent a style of whole-part called "composition" in UML (but which at the time of writing has ambiguous and contradictory semantics[6] and is on the agenda for UML2.0 for improvement).

Indeed, UML is based in pragmatism and purposefully uses signs and symbols from previous approaches e.g. the rectangle borrowed from structured analysis and design, some symbols such as those for inheritance and association borrowed from OMT and so on. This is argued to provide continuity. Certainly, if the new use is the

Figure 7.2 Two relationships

5 Semiotics is the study of signs and symbols.

6 Henderson-Sellers, B. and Barbier, F. (1999) Black and white diamonds, Procs «UML» 99, LNCS 1723, Springer-Verlag, 550–565.

same as (or at least not at odds with) the original usage, then this could be a good way forward. The danger comes if the use of a pre-existing symbol has a meaning different (especially if only subtly different) from previous usage.

7.3.4 Example Modeling Languages

In choosing a Modeling Language, you should consider current standards and their possible evolution, the fit of the language to your own thinking style and, afterwards, the availability of CASE Tools.

The Unified Modeling Language or UML is the Object Management Group (OMG) standard, although it will still evolve over the next few years. There is a wide range of software tools supporting UML although all to a different extent and quality. UML has a style well suited to those who are concentrating on implementation, particularly in C++ or Java, or to those familiar with relational databases. For those who have more empathy with an Eiffel or Smalltalk way of thinking, the variant of UML known as OML will be more suitable.

UML

UML or the Unified Modeling Language is the OMG standard Modeling Language created by the merger of six submissions to the OMG in 1997 (one of the submissions being the precursor of the OML variant discussed below). It is controlled by a Task Force committee of the OMG who have been evaluating the several hundred comments filed on the language during 1998/9. At the time of writing, the current Version is 1.3 but Version 1.4 already exists in draft form. In addition, a Request for Information (RFI) for Version 2.0 of UML was issued in 1999 with a deadline for responses of December 1999. The RFP (Request for Proposal) and the evaluation of the proposals in response to this is scheduled for mid to late 2001.

UML has a metamodel assisted by OCL to define its rules and a notation reminiscent of OMT and Database Modeling Languages. It uses stereotypes[7] widely which appear in the notation as labels bracketed in guillemets: «label». Bidirectionality is used on all associations but not on the subtypes of association. Directionality must therefore be decided immediately upon drawing an association since there is no way to defer this decision. A few identified weaknesses from the OPEN process viewpoint are the poor support for Responsibilities, Roles and Whole-Part Relationships.

OML

The OPEN Modeling Language or OML was originally devised to support the Work Products produced from the OPEN process. It too has an extensive metamodel but one in which consistency was placed higher in the priority list than some of the more esoteric aspects of UML. Its notation is semiotically influenced and more congruent

7 Defined as "user-defined virtual sub-metatypes".

with pure OO thinking as embodied in responsibility-driven design, contract-driven design, Smalltalk, Eiffel and pure object databases. While also using stereotypes, it prefers to iconify the commonest of these, as does Objectory. Unidirectionality is the default for associations, aggregations and dependencies as well as the obvious inheritance relationships. Since it has been demonstrated that bidirectional associations destroy encapsulation and information hiding,[8] OPEN chose to adopt unidirectionality for all its relationships, this having the additional benefit of providing a way of showing TBD (to be decided) connections between classes.

7.4 Implementation Languages

At the "end" of the software development cycle, many aspects of the design have to be implemented in some way. This may be by programming (a.k.a. coding), or by using a Database Language or, in a distributed environment, by the use of an Interface Definition Language.

7.4.1 Coding Languages

In coding an object-oriented design, there is a wide variety of choice. Indeed, while the obvious choice may be an Object-Oriented Programming Language such as C++, Eiffel, Smalltalk or Java, there is no necessity for this. It is perfectly possible to implement an OO design in a traditional, third-generation Procedural Language such as COBOL or FORTRAN.

There are many ways of categorizing Programming Languages. Here are some characteristics that might help you decide between the various OO Programming Languages. You might choose between a strongly typed language such as C++, Java or Eiffel or an untyped (or dynamically typed) language such as Smalltalk. You might wish to have a language upwardly compatible with a standard 3GL, or third-generation language. You might think of C++ if you have existing C code, for example. While this might seem to be an obvious logical progression, it is often a poor choice. The compatibility is not perfect and the fact that C++ embodies a procedural programming style as well as an OO style means that less well skilled developers may not use the OO features correctly. Another upward compatibility would be between COBOL and OO COBOL. In contrast to C++ for which there is extensive industrial experience, OO COBOL has not yet (as of early 2001) taken off but is tipped to do so later this year.[9] It is not clear whether moving from COBOL to OO COBOL will be any more successful than the similar move from C to C++. If such a migration does turn out to be smooth, then OO COBOL, too, is a candidate for consideration.

8 Graham, I. *et al.* (1997), *Journal of Object-Oriented Programming*, **9**(9), 41–48.

9 See the whole of the special issue of *IEEE Software*, March/April 2000.

Eiffel is a pure OO Language that enforces and fully supports an OO style of programming. In addition, it can interface to C++ and Java code. It enforces a contracting style of programming as well as many other aspects of good software engineering. Smalltalk is also a pure OO Language but is contrasted to Eiffel because it is dynamically typed which some developers see as a potential problem. It comes with exceptionally good software libraries and its own environment. However, its use seems to be declining since, as we move towards a Component-Based Development world, all its classes are stored in the single image rather than in single files as in Eiffel (or split across two files as in C++).

Java is a Language that has rapidly gained a large user base. It is statically typed like Eiffel and C++, appears to be a cross between C++ and Smalltalk, with some of the good Eiffel features and, most of all, is Web-enabled. It works with a virtual runtime machine to make it hardware platform-independent and thus highly compatible with a distributed style of computing. Although it does not have explicit pointers as does C++, it still has many of the lower-level features of C++ that were originally designed for small real-time control situations particularly intelligent consumer electronic devices. Whilst being clearly the favorite for distributed and Web-based environments which use Java applets and Components using Java Beans and similar libraries, there is less evidence that Java can scale up to large-scale mainstream commercial "data processing" problems.

Some Languages highly relevant to modern Web systems are Javascript, HTML, XML, CSS and WML. Javascript is a scripting Language that is supported by Web browsers, running on the client. It works with HTML to add interactivity to Websites. In turn, HTML (HyperText Markup Language) is the standard Language for writing Web pages that allows the programmer to control both content and format. XML (Extensible Markup Language) is a markup Language for documenting Web page (and other) content separately from format. CSS (Cascading Style Sheets) is a Language for formatting Web pages and WML (Wireless Markup Language) is the standard Web Language for mobile devices where screen space is at a premium.

7.4.2 Database Languages

Database Languages are targetted towards identifying data stored in the database based on multiple criteria. A Database Language should contain sophisticated means of retrieving data as well as archiving it correctly. The best known Database Language is probably SQL, which is based on relational calculus (others are based on relational algebra), but using English words rather than quantifiers and logical connectives. Dating back to the 1970s, it was designed to interrogate relational databases but more recent versions also take into account the structure of objectbases.

7.4.3 Interface Languages

A Language that is used in the implementation area, not for programming, but for definition or specification of an interface, is called an Interface Language. One of the best known of these is IDL (Interface Definition Language), an ISO standard (ISO 14750) created by the Object Management Group. IDL is a declarative language useful for describing the interfaces that client objects call and that object implementations provide. The IDL specifications of the interfaces are then mapped to the coding language used by the component/object.

Summary

There is a need to depict and document Work Products using some sort of Language, technical or natural. The most obvious Languages used in computing are Programming Languages such as C++, Java or Eiffel and Modeling Languages such as UML and OML. Other technical Languages are those specifically designed for interaction with databases and for interface definition. More mathematical languages, although not discussed here, are also evident in terms of Formal Languages but much more so in the research community than in practice. However, we would note here the incursion of a Formal Language like OCL into everyday use because of its usefulness in defining, modifying and constraining a Modeling Language such as UML. Finally, we must not forget the valuable use of Natural Language. This also occurs in the labeling on Class Diagrams, as Structured English or pseudocode associated with, for instance, Sequence Diagrams. The most use of a natural Language is, of course, in the extensive set of planning and management Documents.

8 Framework Usage Guidelines

8.1 Framework usage

The OPEN Process Framework (OPF) is primarily, as we have seen, a metamodel plus a library of process components (e.g. Work Units, Work Products, Producers) together with a set of process construction and tailoring guidelines (Figure 8.1). An OPEN process instance (i.e. an actual process) is created for a specific Endeavor (e.g. Project) by creating and/or selecting process components generated as instances of elements in the metamodel.

The OPF contains usage guidelines for:

- Instantiating the framework and choosing the process components to be instantiated or to be selected from those already in the process component library in order to meet the needs of a specific Endeavor. Instantiation and selection are collectively called *process construction*. Process construction also includes
  - Allocating Tasks to Producers.
  - Allocating Techniques to Tasks.
  - Obtaining the desired Development Cycle by setting the Assertions (pre-conditions, post-conditions) of the Work Units and Phases.
- Tailoring selected compounds at the detailed level.
- Extending the existing class library of process components.

When starting a new Endeavor, the process Team uses its understanding of the Endeavor and the above set of guidelines to construct the (business engineering or Application development) process from its framework elements and document the resulting Project-specific process. As with any other object-oriented analysis and design model, the process will be iterated (tailored) as lessons are learned during the course of the Project.

One useful Technique here is the application of process patterns. These are collections, or more strictly collaborations, of elements from the process framework library which occur together commonly and frequently enough to be identified as such and given a name. They are, as Christopher Alexander says, a solution to a

Figure 8.1 Creating an instance of the OPF

problem in a context. The use of process patterns is still in its infancy, although work is now beginning to emerge on this topic.[1]

8.2 Process construction guidelines

A *process construction guideline* is a usage guideline intended to help process engineers instantiate process components from the framework (metamodel) and select the best process components in order to create the process itself (Figure 1.2). Specifically, it will provide guidance concerning how to:

- Identify the scope of the problem.
- Identify the quality levels required.
- Identify the available skills sets in the people.
- Identify the organizational CMM/SPICE/OOSPICE level.
- Select the Work Products to develop.
- Select the Producers (e.g., Roles, Teams, and Tools) to develop these Work Products.
- Select the Work Units to perform:
  - How to allocate Tasks and associated Techniques to the Producers.
  - How to group the Tasks into Activities and/or Work Flows.
- Select the Stages of development that will provide an overall organization to these Work Units.
- Determine the Languages to be used.
- Choose Tools to be used.
- Provide training.

Although there are many process component instances available in the OPF repository, in this chapter we will describe these process construction guidelines

1 See, for example, Ambler, S.W. (1998) *Process Patterns*, CUP; D'Souza, D.F. and Wills, A.C. (1999) *Objects, Components, and Frameworks with UML. The Catalysis Approach*, Addison-Wesley.

only in the context of Work Units: Activities, Tasks and Techniques, as one specific approach to process engineering.

Activities are the large-scale "things that need to be done" – goals to be achieved. The appropriate Activities will depend upon many factors including project scope, extent of requirements formality required, degree of outsourcing and use of third-party components, level of quality required, constraints such as hard-real-time and so on. Using Activities from the OPF repository, an overall Life Cycle can be constructed, perhaps using as a template one of the published examples.[2]

Having identified appropriate Activities, the most useful OPEN Tasks are now sought. Tasks are like Activities in the sense that they describe things that have to be done (but not how to do them). However, while Activities are conceptual in nature, Tasks are linked to a Project Management mindset being the smallest unit of work that results in a deliverable and that can be Project-managed.

As with Activities, Tasks are selected from the OPF repository. The currently available selection is given in Table 5.1 – but the list is user-extensible. To assist you in Task selection, we introduce here the idea of a deontic or possibility matrix. An example is shown in Figure 8.2 for a process with 5 activities and 11 Tasks. For each Activity/Task pairing, we identify one of five levels of possibility that might apply to this specific pair. Some pairs are mandatory (labeled M), other recommended (R), some optional (O), some discouraged (D) while others are forbidden (F). Of course, if you find one of these rows is full of "F"s, then that Task should be deleted from the matrix (Task 8 in our example of Figure 8.2).

Initially, you may prefer to use only two levels of possibility (M and F) and mandate the pairings. While this initial approach is more authoritarian, it provides less room for misunderstanding and consequent error in a novice, learning organization. Later the developers may be given the freedom to choose between alternatives (R, O and D values now permitted). For a more sophisticated Team, the values in this matrix (Figure 8.2) will vary depending upon a number of things – such as Project size, organizational culture, domain of the Application to be developed, skills and likes/dislikes of the development Team.

The relationship between Activity and Task is many to many; in other words, there are likely to be several Tasks associated with any one Activity, and, conversely, one Task may be useful in more than one Activity. Process construction using this matrix approach is one of the strengths of OPEN that makes it suitable for a wide range of Project types. This is why we call OPEN a process *framework* rather than a process.

Tasks also have pre- and post-conditions associated with them which are used to configure the sequencing of the process itself. One way to visualize the relationship between Activities and their sequencing is shown in Figure 8.3 which shows a medium-scale process used across a suite of Projects. Here the ellipses represent Activities (using a Catalysis style of extended UML notation), many of which are timeboxed (indicated by the black squares). The existence of the lines connecting

2 For example, in Henderson-Sellers, B. and Unhelkar, B. (2000) *OPEN Modeling with UML*, Addison-Wesley.

Activities

Tasks	A	B	C	D	E
1	M	D	F	F	F
2	D	D	F	F	D
3	D	D	O	O	D
4	F	O	O	O	F
5	F	M	O	D	F
6	R	R	M	R	O
7	D	R	F	M	O
8	F	F	F	F	F
9	R	R	D	R	R
10	O	D	O	O	R
11	F	M	O	F	D

For each Activity/Task combination, one of the five levels of possibility (from Always to Never) may be chosen as appropriate

5 levels of possibility
M = mandatory R = recommended O = optional D = discouraged F = forbidden

Figure 8.2 Activity/Task matrix

Activities indicates a likely path, as governed by the pre- and post-conditions – these are on the Tasks although the Tasks themselves are not shown in this low granular visualization. Project planning is shown as a "wrap-around" as are the Activities associated with the Programme aspects of development (labeled Extra-Project Activities) and with reuse – which is only feasible when multiple Projects occur. An alternative depiction is given in Figure 8.4 in which a full-scale Project Management Activity is in use together with explicit Design, Implementation, Integration and Testing Activities (rather than the compound Build Activity as shown in Figure 8.3). This Life Cycle Model has been used successfully for slightly larger Projects than that of Figure 8.3.

Together, the Activities and Tasks say what is to be done. They do not suggest any ways of accomplishing them. This is the role of the OPEN Techniques. These Techniques, documented separately and in detail in *The OPEN Toolbox of Techniques* (see Bibliography), bring together all the well-tested OO Techniques that have been used worldwide over the past decades. Users of the process are able to choose the one(s) most likely to be successful for their particular Task.

Linking together Techniques and Tasks follows the same argument as for Tasks and Activities. OPEN represents these links by a many-to-many fuzzy relationship represented again as a two-dimensional matrix (Figure 8.5). Again, the values in this matrix must be tailored to your own requirements. Indeed, this matrix is much more likely to reflect the individualistic needs of your developers and your Project than the first matrix in Figure 8.2. This is because there are, in fact, many "duplicates" in OPEN's toolbox.[3] For example, there are several Techniques for finding objects. Some OO software developers start by a textual analysis, some use simulation, some use CRC cards and yet others prefer a use-case driven approach. It is your choice. Indeed a master craftsman (and by analogy a master OO developer) is often recognized by the size of their toolbox and the skills they possess to both select and use those Tools.

3 A full list of Techniques is given in Appendix E.

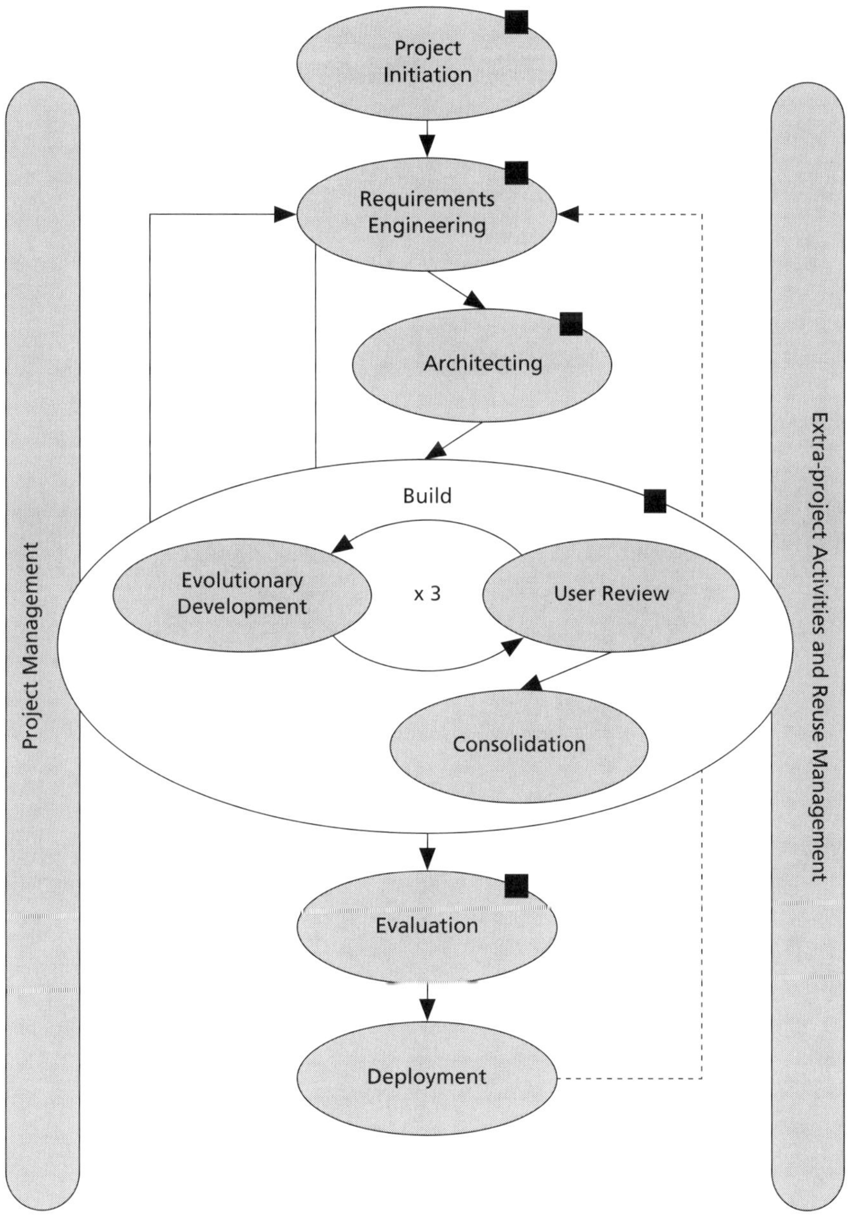

Figure 8.3 An example of an OPEN process instance for a medium-sized project with integrated project management and testing

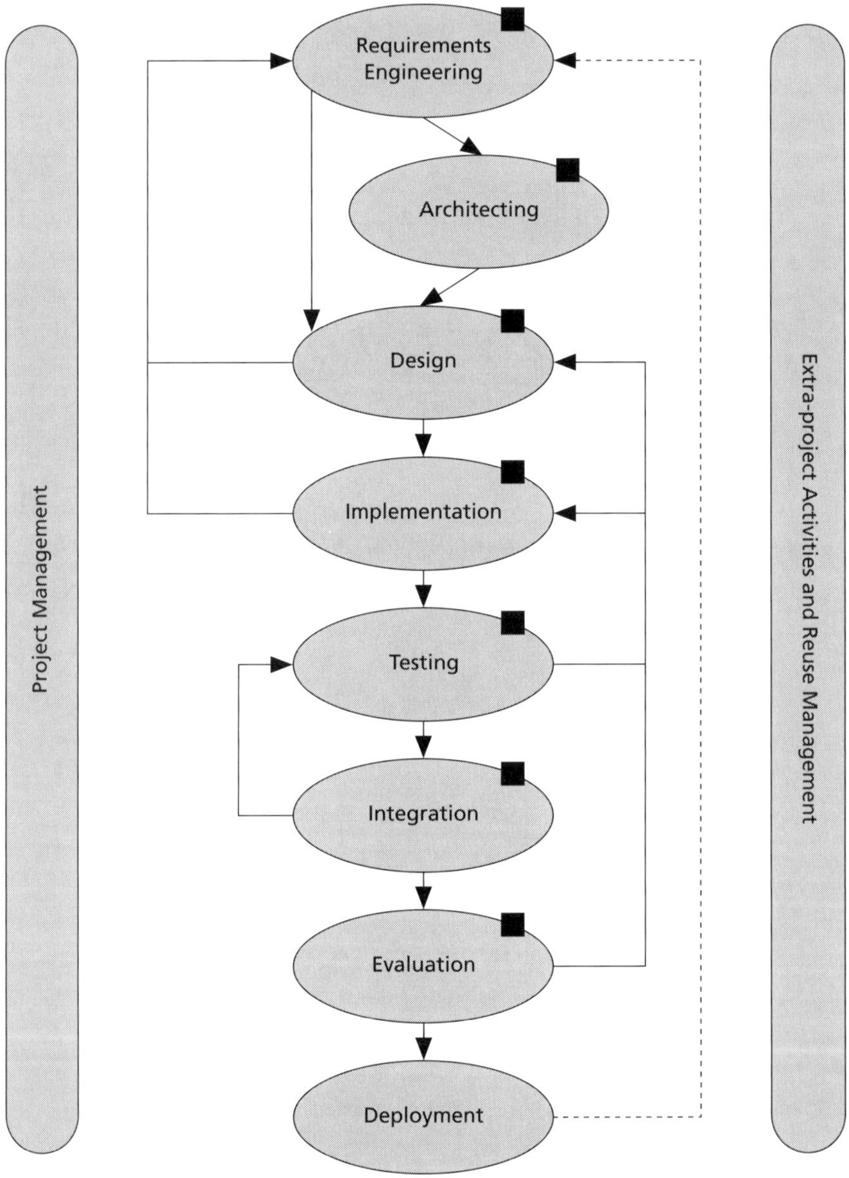

Figure 8.4 An example of an OPEN process instance for a larger-sized project with explicit project management and testing

In the next few sections, we outline the process construction appropriate for three cases: for small Research & Development Projects, for business-critical systems and for Programmes of multiple Projects.

Tasks

Techniques	A	B	C	D	E	F
1	R	D	F	M	F	F
2	O	D	F	F	D	F
3	D	F	D	O	D	O
4	F	O	O	F	F	D
5	M	M	F	D	F	D
6	R	R	M	R	O	R
7	D	R	F	M	O	M
8	D	F	M	D	D	D
9	R	R	F	R	R	R
10	F	D	F	O	R	F
11	F	M	O	F	D	F
12	D	F	R	F	D	F
13	F	M	R	F	F	F
14	F	F	F	R	O	O
15	F	M	F	F	F	F

For each Task/Technique combination, one of the five levels of possibility (from Always to Never) may be chosen as appropriate

5 levels of possibility
M = mandatory R = recommended O = optional D = discouraged F = forbidden

Figure 8.5 Task/Technique matrix

8.2.1 Small, simple, research and development projects

Small Projects, perhaps in a Research & Development (R&D) environment or when the product has been outsourced, may not require a formal Requirements Engineering Activity (as shown in Figure 8.3, for example). Project Planning might also be much reduced and the main focus might simply be on the Build Activity (Figure 8.6). To create such a process is simple: only those depicted activities are instantiated and some tailoring of the Tasks and Techniques within the main Build Activity is also likely. It might be called a "low ceremony" process.

8.2.2 Large, complex, business-critical projects

Here both process construction and tailoring become important and extensive because there is more need for formal Project Management, for extensive Version Control and Configuration Management and for high levels of quality. In this case, a larger number of the OPF's elements will be found useful. Those common with other smaller Projects will be emphasized more and the process becomes a "high ceremony" one.

8.2.3 Programmes (suites of projects)

When organizations repeatedly work in the same domain, as do most in-house information systems development Teams, then there are advantages that can be gained from operating with a Programme of Projects rather than considering each Project as if it were stand-alone. Programmes are represented in Figure 8.3, for

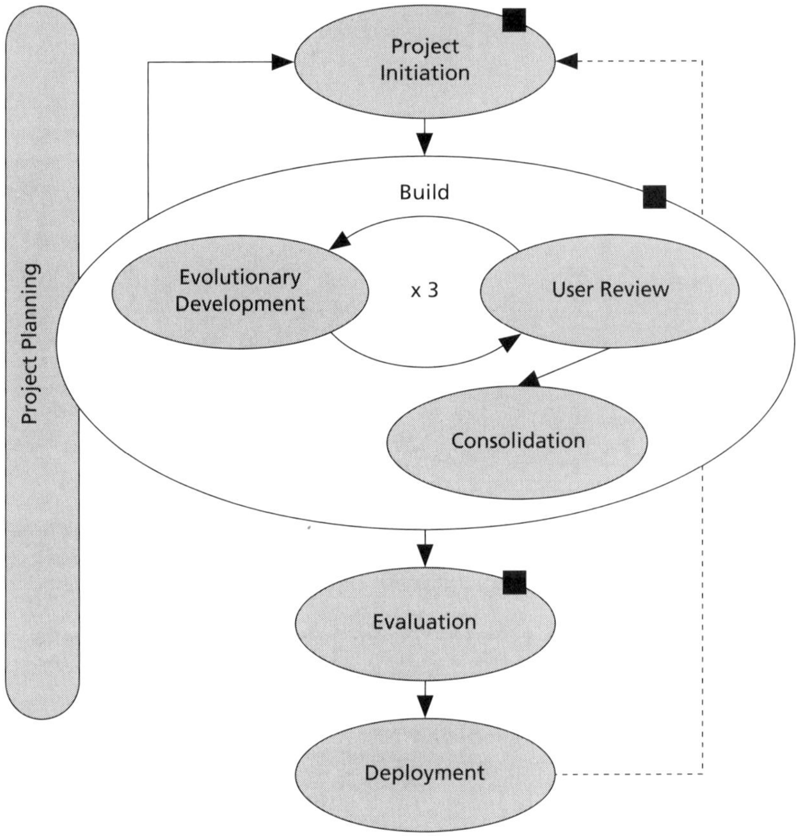

Figure 8.6 Example of an OPEN instance suitable for a small, R&D or outsourced project

example, by the ellipses labelled "Extra-Project Activities and Reuse Management". Metrics can be derived from one Project and applied to future Projects; Components that are reusable across several Projects can be built because the effort to do so becomes worthwhile; robust Architectures can be produced that remain valid across multiple Projects; resources can be invested in with a payback schedule longer than the timeline of an individual Project. Generally, the focus is on benefitting the organization through a "product line" rather than focussing on a single Project.

8.3 Tailoring guidelines

Once the process has been constructed from the process framework components, it typically will be necessary to perform some fine-tuning by tailoring the instantiated process Components to meet the specific needs of the Project as well as when lessons are learned during development. *Tailoring guidelines* are usage guidelines intended to help process engineers tailor the instantiated process components. Tailoring involves making minor modifications, at the detail level, to Tasks, Roles,

Techniques etc. and, particularly, to Work Products by adding, modifying or removing unnecessary parts of Documents.

Tailoring overlaps to some degree with the process construction described above, although they have different foci. The engineered process already contains constraints imposed by the specific choices in the bottom-up process of selection of process components from the OPF library of process components (Figure 8.1). Further tailoring is feasible in terms of the careful determination of the pre- and post-conditions that govern the sequencing. Iterative and incremental process strategies need to be identified. Is timeboxing to be used? Which of the Work Products will be used, when and to what extent? How many versions of these Work Products will be required? Do we use organizational standards or industry or international standards for these Work Products? Are templates available either from third-party vendors or in-house? Should all intricacies of chosen Tasks and Techniques be used or could a "simpler version" be created that is more appropriate locally?

8.4 Extension guidelines

No repository or class library can ever be totally complete. Because of the large differences between development projects, new classes of process components will eventually be needed. Also, software and system engineering are evolving disciplines and new process components will need to be added as the field advances. (Witness the recent advent of Component-based and Web-based development approaches.)

A process framework should therefore come with *extension guidelines*. An extension guideline is a usage guideline intended to help the process engineer extend the existing process framework by adding new process components. For example, by:

- adding a new instance of an existing class such as Activity, Task, or Technique. This can be done easily by creating the instance and adding it to the repository and by adding the associated process component descriptions into the repository.
- adding new metalevel classes to the metamodel, either directly or by subclassing. This is also feasible but less likely to be needed.

Since the OPF is fully componentized, it is extremely easy to add other components to the process framework library. A case in point was the advent of Component-based development (CBD) – which we have discussed throughout this book – which was not "in vogue" when the original OPEN framework was constructed. The extensions undertaken in 2000/1[4] to incorporate support for CBD was simple. All that was needed was the identification of a small number of Activities, Tasks, and Techniques which were then added to the matrix. Similar extensions have been developed in the context of Web-based development,[5] including the addition of business strategy and digital branding.

4 Henderson-Sellers, B. (2001) An OPEN process for component-based development. Chapter 18 in *Component-Based Software Engineering: Putting the Pieces Together* (eds G.T. Heinman and W. Councill), Addison-Wesley, Reading, MA.

5 Haire, B. *et al.* (2001) Supporting Web development in the OPEN process: additional tasks. Procs. COMPSAC 2001, Chicago, October 2001.

Similarly, although less likely, since the OPF is defined by a metamodel, if at some future date it was determined that a new metaclass was needed, it would be acceptable and relatively easy to extend this metamodel (see Appendix G) by the addition of new classes and subclasses.

As an interesting postscript, we also note from Figure 8.7 that there is an additional opportunity not yet realized by the OPEN community: to engineer an OPF-derived process *specifically* for a generic domain such as finance or real time and consequently "productize" that OPF-compliant process for that particular context.

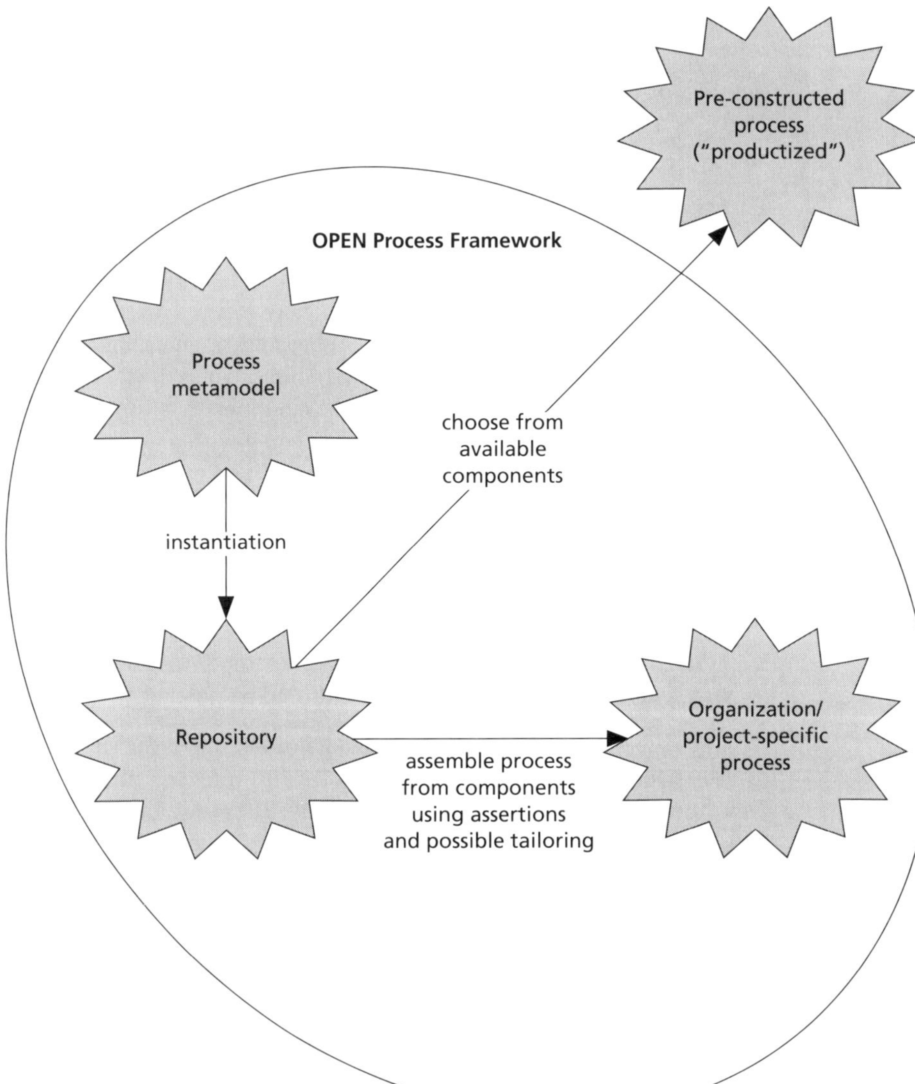

Figure 8.7 An opportunity to create a "productized" instance of OPEN

Summary

Using a framework approach such as the OPF supports a strong degree of flexibility (at all levels) in creating an organizationally-specific process. The metaclasses in the framework (Appendix G) are instantiated only on an "as-needs" basis and further tailoring is possible through the incorporation of Assertions.

As software engineering advances, it is clear that new ideas will emerge – as exemplified by the recent rise in Web-based development and Component-based development. Future advances in Agent-oriented technology (and others as yet unheard of) are readily accommodated in the OPF by creation of new process components in the repository, perhaps supplemented by additional elements in the OPF metamodel itself.

Appendices

This section contains the following appendices:

A List of acronyms

B Glossary

C Work Products

D Producers

E Work Units

F Example Work Flow

G Metamodel Diagrams

A List of acronyms

a.k.a.	also known as
API	Application Programmer Interface
BOM	Business Object model
BPR	Business Process Re-engineering
CASE	Computer-Aided Software Engineering
CBD	Component-Based Development
CCB	Change Control Board
CD	Compact Disk
CDLC	Contract-Driven Life Cycle
CIRT	Class, Instance, role or Type
CMM	Capability Maturity model
CPM	Critical Path Method
CRC	Class, Responsibility and Collaborator
DBMS	Database Management System
DCS	Distributed Computing System
DVD	Digital Video Disk
EIS	External Interface Specification
GQM	Goal-Question-Metric
GUI	Graphical User Interface
HCI	Human–Computer Interaction
IDE	Integrated Development Environment
IIP	Iterative, Incremental and Parallel
JAD	Joint application Development
OCL	Object Constraint language
OMG	Object Management Group
OML	OPEN Modeling Language

OMT	Object Modeling Technique
OO	object-oriented
OPEN	Object-oriented Process, Environment and Notation
OPF	OPEN Process Framework
OT	Object Technology
PERT	Program Evaluation and Review Technique
QESTA	Quantification, Examination, Specification, Transformation, Aggregation
RAD	Rapid Application Development
RUP	Rational Unified Process
SEI	Software Engineering Institute
SMART	Specific, Measurable, Attainable, Relevant, Trackable
SPICE	Software Process Improvement and Capability dEtermination
SVDPI	Subject/Verb/Direct object/Preposition/Indirect object
SWOT	Strengths, Weaknesses, Opportunities, Threats
TBD	To Be Decided
TOM	Task Object Model
TQM	Total Quality Management
UI	User Interface
UML	Unified Modeling Language
WBS	Work Breakdown Structure
XP	eXtreme Programming

B Glossary

abstraction A model of something that captures all of its essential characteristics while ignoring all of its diversionary details. Different abstractions can be distinguished by having different definitions and thus different relevant characteristics.

Acceptance Testing The testing to determine whether the Application is acceptable to the customer and thus completing the contract (or a contract Stage).

Activity A major Work Unit consisting of a cohesive collection of Tasks that produce a related set of Work Products.

Application A major, fully-functional, standalone Work Product that is developed by a development Organization for use by one or more user Organizations. See also *system Application* and *Software Application*.

Application Tester The Role played by a Person when testing an Application.

Architect The Role played by a Person who is responsible for an Architecture.

Architecting The Activity associated with creating an Architecture.

architectural style An architecture-level pattern that describes the overall structure and type of Architecture. For example, architectural styles include layers, pipes and filters, transaction, etc.

Architecture The strategic "design" of an Application, Business Model or set of reusable Components. Thus, an Architecture is an abstraction, capturing only the most important decisions and mechanisms, i.e. those that significantly influence the design and implementation.

Architecture Document A Document describing some aspect of the Architecture.

Architecture Team The Team that is responsible for an Architecture. *See Software Architecture Team* and *System Architecture Team*.

Architecture Work Product Documents and prototypes produced during the architecturing. These include Business Architecture Documents, System Architecture Documents and Software Architecture Documents.

Assertion (1) A Boolean condition used to control the sequencing of Work Units or Phases in a Contract-Driven Life Cycle. (2) A Boolean condition used to specify a condition that must be true at a specific point during the execution of an operation (e.g., method, use case). See also *pre-condition, post-condition*, and *invariant*.

baseline A formally identified collection of Work Product Versions that has been placed under configuration control and that is to be established by a certain Milestone.

beta testing The testing of an Application in its production environment by a few key users prior to acceptance testing and its release to the entire user community.

browser A Tool that permits a client machine to access a server across the Internet/Web.

Build The smallest Endeavor-wide Stage of development, forming a scheduled part of a Phase. Depending on the duration of the Phase and the amount of iteration and incremental development, a Build may last from several months to several days. If the Build results in Work Products being delivered to the Customer Organization, then the Build is called a Release.

Build Integrator The Role played by a Person who integrates packages into the growing Build.

Build Testing Testing related to the Build Phase.

Business Model A Model focussing on the business objects or processes. Independent of any software Applications being considered or being deployed.

Business Architect An architect who is responsible for the architecture of the business.

C++ Coding Standard A Coding Standard for C++ software.

CASE Tool A computer-aided software engineering Application used by a Role in the production of work products. *See lowerCASE Tool* and *upperCASE Tool.*

Change Control Board The Team that evaluates and approves/rejects proposed changes to a baselined configuration item.

class description A Work Product that describes an individual class.

Class Designer A designer who designs a single class.

class library A repository of reusable classes and their associated Documentation and test software.

Class Owner The Role played by a Person who designs, implements and maintains an individual class.

Class Tester The Role played by a Person who tests individual classes.

Class Testing Unit testing focussed at the granularity of a single class.

Code A Work Product consisting solely of software.

Code Drop A Drop consisting of the current Versions of software Work Products (i.e., deliverable and test software) that are issued for integration and testing purposes.

Coding Standard A Standard for a particular Coding Language.

Collaboration Diagram An Interaction Diagram that documents the potential interactions that occur between related classes of objects.

Compiler Software that transforms higher-level Languages into machine understandable code.

Component An architecturally-significant Work Product (e.g. software, hardware) with the following properties:

- It is a major part of an Application or Framework.
- It is therefore a configuration item.
- It is cohesive in the sense of having a well-defined set of related Responsibilities.
- It is accessible via a well-defined set of Interfaces and associated protocol.
- These Interfaces allow it to be replaceable within the context of a well-defined Architecture.

compound technique A Technique that is composed of Techniques.

Computer A Hardware Component that possesses both processing and memory capability.

Configuration Auditing The auditing of a baseline to verify if it is complete, correctly identified and properly versioned.

Configuration Control The management of changes to baselined configuration items including requesting, evaluating the impact of, approving/rejecting and implementing changes.

Configuration Identification The identification and designation of Components as configuration items and the identification of baselines.

Configuration Item A Work Product that is baselined and placed under configuration control.

Configuration Management The management of configuration items and baselines. Configuration Management consists of the following Tasks:

- configuration identification.
- configuration control.
- configuration status accounting.
- configuration auditing.

Configuration Management Plan The Work Product that documents the plans for performing Configuration Management.

Configuration Management Team A Team that is responsible for Configuration Management.

Configuration Management Tool An upperCASE Tool that supports Configuration Management Tasks.

Configuration Manager The Role played by a Person who leads the Configuration Management Team.

Configuration Status Accounting The recording and reporting of information needed to effectively manage a configuration including the:

- status of proposed changes, deviations and waivers to the configuration.
- implementation status of approved changes.

Constraint Language A Formal Language for describing rules.

Construction Guideline A Guideline that supports the instantiation of a process from the Framework (metamodel) together with advice on how to select the best process component instances.

Construction Phase An intermediate Phase of a development Cycle during which the Work Products are created (or developed) and prepared for Delivery.

context The relevant components of the external environment of an Application or business.

Context Diagram A Diagram that documents the context of an Application or business in terms of its externals and the relationships between it and its externals.

Convention A process Document that captures standards, procedures, guidelines, templates and inspection checklists.

Customer Organization An Organization that pays a Development Organization to develop an Application.

Customer Representative The Role played by a Person who represents the Customer Organization in dealings with the Development Organization.

Cycle A large-scale Stage consisting of several Phases. Cycles may be Development Cycles or Life Cycles.

Database A means of retaining information from computer memory in a permanent form. Databases are built using one of various models, including relational and object models. These models are necessary to optimize database access and information retrieval.

Database Designer A designer of the various parts of the database to be used.

Debugger/Debugging Tool A lowerCASE Tool that assists in finding defects ("bugs") in an Application.

Deliverable The attribute of a Work Product that indicates whether it is to be released to the Customer Organization.

Delivery The final Phase of the Development Cycle during which the Work Products are released to the Customer Organization and placed into usage by the User Organization.

Delivery Cycle A Cycle relating to product delivery to the client.

Deployment Diagram A Diagram that documents the deployment of software to hardware in a distributed Application.

Deployment Work Product Work Products related to deployment include installation guides, release notes and user manuals as well as the Application itself.

Designer (also known as modeler). A Role for a Person who creates, documents and maintains the design of an element of the Application.

Design Work Product The set of Work Products related to design.

Development Cycle The collection of all Phases performed on a Project to develop the associated Application.

Development Environment A collection of Hardware and Software Tools used to develop an Application.

Development Environment Team A Team that establishes and maintains the development environment.

development method A synonym for development process.

Development Organization An Organization that develops and releases one or more Applications to either a Customer Organization or User Organization.

development process A process, the objective of which is to develop a Model or an Application. See *process.*

development process framework A framework for creating development processes. See *process framework.*

Development Stage A formally identified and managed interval or period of development. See *Development Cycle, Phase* and *Build.*

Development Team The Team that develops the software.

Device A Hardware Component that has neither significant processing nor memory capability.

Diagram A graphical Work Product that represents a part of a Model or Application. It may describe the static or the dynamic/behavioral characteristics of the Model. A Diagram typically consisting of a directed graph of nodes connected by arcs representing relationships between the nodes.

Direct Producer A Producer that directly produces Work Products.

Document An electronic or printed Work Product consisting of official written (and possibly graphical) information about one or more related Work Products.

Documentation Standard A convention that documents content and format Requirements for a Document.

Documentation Team A Team that helps developers document an Application.

Documentation Tool A Natural Language Tool for creating and maintaining Documents.

Document Drop A Drop consisting of a Version of a Document, typically issued for purposes of evaluation.

Document Management Tool An upperCASE Tool that assists the developer in managing his/her suite of Documents.

Domain Expert The Role played by someone who provides authoritative information about a given domain.

Drop A minor technical Milestone consisting of a Version of a Work Product that is scheduled and released by a technical Team. Drops therefore tend to be relatively small (only a part of an Application) and frequent (e.g., daily, weekly, monthly).

Dynamic Behavior Diagram A Diagram that captures the dynamics or behavioral aspects of an Application or business.

Endeavor A high-level venture undertaken to develop and maintain one or more related Applications. See also *Programme, Project* and *Enterprise.*

Enterprise An Endeavor consisting of all Programmes within a business.

Extension Guideline A guideline to assist in extending the process framework and its repository of process component instances.

External Interface Specification A Requirements Specification specifying the external Application Programmer Interfaces of an Application.

External Interface Specification Standard A Documentation Standard specifying the content and format for External Interface Specifications.

External Interface Specification Template A template that can be filled in to produce an External Interface Specification.

Framework A reusable class library of collaborating classes.

Framework Component A predefined class in the class library of the Framework.

Framework instantiation The instantiation of the classes in a framework to form a collection of collaborating objects.

Glossary A Document that defines all significant terms and abbreviations used on an Endeavor.

Guideline (1) A Document that provides guidance on how to perform one or more related Work Units. (2) Assistance for construction or tailoring a process or for extending the OPF itself. See also *construction guidelines, extension guidelines, tailoring guidelines.*

Hardware Component A Component consisting essentially of hardware. These include Devices, Computers, Networks, and Stages.

Hardware Development Team A Team that is responsible for procuring or fabricating the necessary Hardware Components.

Hardware Management Team A Team that is responsible for managing hardware aspects of the system.

Hardware Prototyping Team A Team that is responsible for testing and evaluation of hardware using a prototyping approach.

Hardware Requirements Specification Standard A Documentation Standard specifying the content and format for Hardware Requirements Specifications.

Hardware Requirements Team A Team that is responsible for determining all Hardware Requirements.

Hardware Team A Team responsible for the development of hardware.

Hardware Test Team A Team that is responsible for testing Hardware Components.

implementation Changing a design into reality, usually in terms of code.

Implementation Work Product A Work Product created during the Implementation Activity. These can be categorized as Software Components, Hardware Components, Data Components, or Business Components.

Increment A collection of the Work Product Versions that is transferred as a unit by their developers to a receiving Team or Organization at a specific point in time.

incremental Describing a process that produces large Work Products (e.g., Documents, Applications) in successively more complete Versions called Increments.

independent Test Team A test Team comprising of members from outside the Development Team.

Indirect Producer A Producer that indirectly produces Work Products via its associated Direct Producers.

Inheritance Diagram A Diagram showing the inheritance hierarchy of the system or a part of the system.

Initiation Phase The initial Phase of a Project Development Cycle during which the Endeavor is started and preparation for Development is made.

Inspection Checklist A Document to guide the inspection of one or more Work Products.

Instantaneous Stage A Stage corresponding to a point in time.

Integrated Development Environment A collection of Tools that interoperate, used to develop an Application.

integration Combining elements of an Application prepared separately.

Integration Work Product A Work Product created during the Integration Activity.

interaction Interchanges of information between Objects or Components are represented by interactions on Static Architectural Diagrams or Dynamic Diagrams.

Interaction Diagram A Diagram that documents the interactions between Model elements. See also *collaboration Diagram, sequence Diagram.*

interpreter A lowerCASE Tool that transforms a higher-level Language to a machine understandable format in real time.

Invariant (1) An Assertion associated with a Producer that must be true both before and after the successful execution of all associated Work Units. (2) An Assertion associated with a class that must be true both before and after the successful execution of all public operations. Contrast with *pre-condition* and *post-condition*.

iterative Describing a process, the Work Units of which are repeated on existing Work Products in order to improve them (e.g., by fixing defects or to meet changing Requirements).

Java Coding Standard A Coding Standard for Java software.

JavaDoc Class-level HTML Documentation that is automatically generated from Java code by an industry-standard lowerCASE Tool.

Language Syntax and semantics used for documentation. Languages may be Natural Languages (e.g. English), Modeling Languages (e.g. UML, OML) or Implementation Languages – including Coding Languages, Database Languages, Constraint Languages and Interface Languages.

Life Cycle A Cycle describing the underlying process philosophy such as waterfall, spiral or contract-driven.

lowerCASE Tool A code-level CASE Tool for creating, compiling, debugging, testing, and managing software.

Management Milestone A major Milestone that is critical from a business standpoint. A Management Milestone occurs relatively infrequently, typically at the end of a Phase.

Management Team A Team responsible for various aspects of managing the Project.

Management Work Product A Work Product produced and managed by the management Team. See *planning Work Product, staffing Work Product*, and *scheduling Work Product*.

Manager The Role played by a Person who administers a Project.

Marketing Organization An Organization that markets an Application to Customer and User Organizations.

Marketing Requirements Specification A detailed specification of the marketing (as opposed to engineering) requirements of the Application, organized by release to the Customer/User Organization.

Marketing Team The Team that markets an Application to Customer and User Organizations.

Marketing Vision Statement A brief, very high-level specification of the customer/user base, the customer/user needs, a description of the Application and its required characteristics.

Mentor The Role played by a Person who provides on-the-job training.

Metric A Work Product measuring some aspect of something (e.g., progress of a process, quality of a Work Product).

Metrics Analyst The Role played by a Person who collects, analyzes, and publishes Project progress and Metrics.

Metrics Team A Team that collects, analyzes, and publishes Project progress and quality Metrics.

Metrics Tool An upperCASE Tool that collects and/or analyzes Metrics for the software.

Milestone A scheduled point in time during a development when some set of significant objectives is to be achieved. See *Management Milestone* and *Technical Milestone*.

Model A Work Product representing some part of an Application or Application domain. As a representation of reality, a Model is less complex and less complete than the thing being modeled.

Modeler See Designer.

Model Tester A Tester responsible for the testing of the Model.

Modeling Language A combination of the semantics and an (often graphical) notation, possibly supplemented by a Constraint Language that documents Models.

Modeling Tool An upperCASE Tool that assists the developer in creating the Model. Typically these Tools are focussed around a particular notational set and are very sophisticated drawing Tools.

Network A set of connected computers and the network connectivity devices and communication pathways that connect them.

Notation An element of a Modeling Language that communicates concepts to the reader by a form of a set of graphic symbols and textual annotations.

Object Modeling Guideline A Guideline to assist the developer in creating an object-oriented Model.

OO Modeler A Modeler specializing in OO Requirements Engineering, Architecting, and Design.

Operational Requirement (a.k.a. Functional Requirement) A Requirement that specifies a required blackbox stimulus/response behavior of an Application or business. An Operational Requirement therefore specifies a function or action that the Application or business must be able to perform.

Operational Testing A kind of Testing, the purpose of which is to identify defects with regard to the fulfilment of Operational Requirements.

Organization A cohesive aggregation of Teams that carry out some overall process.

Organization Chart A Diagram that documents the structure of an Organization or Teams in terms of its component Organizations and Teams.

Package A cohesive collection of design elements or code used to break a large system into smaller, more manageable pieces.

Package Description A Document that describes an individual package.

Package Design Document A Design Document that captures the package-level design of an Application.

Package Design Document Standard A content and format standard for Package Design Documents.

Package Design Document Template A Template that can be filled in to produce a Package Design Document.

Package Designer A Designer responsible for a single Package.

Package Diagram A Diagram that describes how Packages interact with *no* internal details of any particular Package. Sometimes also used to describe a single Package and its contents.

Package Team A Team that produces a specific Package of software and its related Documentation.

Package Tester The Role played by a Person who tests Packages.

Package Testing Testing undertaken at the Package level of granularity.

parallel Describing a Development Cycle, the Work Units of which occur concurrently.

Peer Programmer Team A Team consisting of two Programmers who work closely together to develop software.

Performance Testing Testing the performance characteristics of the Application.

Person A human being who plays one or more Roles in a process.

Phase A Development Stage in which Builds and Releases occur. See *Initiation Phase, Construction Phase, Delivery Phase, Usage Phase* and *Retirement Phase.*

Plan A Document that encapsulates forward-looking decisions.

Planning Work Product A Management Work Product associated with planning. See *system development plan, software development plan, risk management plan, configuration management plan,* and *training plan.*

Post-condition (1) An Assertion associated with a Work Unit that must be true after the successful execution of that Work Unit. (2) An Assertion associated with an operation that must be true after the successful execution of that operation.

Pre-condition (1) An Assertion associated with a Work Unit that must be true before that Work Unit can be successfully executed. (2) An Assertion associated with an operation that must be true before that operation can be successfully executed.

Procedure A Document that specifies the Work Products, Producers and Tasks for a specific Activity.

process (1) The Project-specific cohesive collection of process components (i.e., Work Products, their Producers and the Work Units performed by the Producers as they collaborate to produce the Work Products). (2) An instance of a develop ment process framework. A process is also often known (loosely) as a method or methodology.

Process Engineer A Person responsible for creating and maintaining a process.

process framework A cohesive collection of predefined classes of process components (i.e., Work Products, Producers and Work Units) and a set of associated instantiation, extension and tailoring guidelines. A process framework is intended to be extended and instantiated by process engineers to generate an Endeavor process.

Process Metric A Metric that captures some aspect of process.

Process Team A Team that produces and inculcates the process for an Endeavor.

Process Work Product A Work Product primarily developed by the Process Team during the process engineering Activity. These include Procedures, Guidelines, Standards, Templates and Inspection Checklists.

Producer Any process component that produces (i.e., creates, evaluates, iterates, or maintains), either directly or indirectly, versions of one or more Work Products.

production code Code that has been verified to the degree that it can be considered to have moved from being tentative and experimental into being commercial strength and ready for deployment on a production environment.

Programme A collection of related Projects managed as a single Endeavor.

Project The enactment of a development process (i.e., execution over time) to produce one or more versions of a major Work Product (typically an Application).

Project Initiation Team A Team that performs the initial Project activities.

Project Manager A Person responsible for all management aspects of a Project.

Project Team The overall Team that is responsible for creating all Project Work Products.

Prototype A kind of Work Product that describes a partial design or implementation used to elicit further Requirements or to test Architecture, design, or implementation decisions, possibly with user involvement.

quality A characteristic and level of acceptability which can be benchmarked using an objective measure. Acceptable quality depends strongly upon customer Requirements.

Quality Engineer The Person responsible for all quality aspects of the development.

Quality Metric A Metric that captures one or more quality characteristics of the thing being measured.

Quality Requirement (a.k.a. Non-Functional Requirement, quality factor) A Requirement that specifies a required property of an Application (e.g., correctness, operational availability, portability, reliability, robustness, safety, security etc.).

Quality Team The Project subTeam that is responsible for independently evaluating and reporting the quality of the Application Work Products.

Release A Build during which major Work Products are released (i.e., delivered) to a Customer or User Organization. Similar to the internal Build but focussed externally.

Requirement A capability or condition to which an Application or business must conform. A Requirement is thus a formalized need of a customer, user or other stakeholder.

Requirements Analysis The subActivity of Requirements Engineering during which Requirements are modeled in order to ensure that they are complete, consistent, understandable etc.

Requirements Elicitation The subActivity of Requirements Engineering during which Requirements are identified by eliciting them from customers, domain experts, marketing and users.

Requirements Engineer The Role played by a Person who performs Requirements Engineering Tasks.

Requirements Engineering The Activity that results in Work Products in the Requirements Set.

Requirements Evaluation The subTask of Quality Control during which a Requirements Specification is evaluated to ensure that its specified Requirements are complete, consistent, testable, traceable, and understandable.

Requirements Management Tool An upperCASE Tool that assists the Requirements Engineer in their Role.

Requirements Specification (1) The subActivity of Requirements Engineering during which Requirements are specified in a Requirements Document. (2) A Document that formally specifies the Requirements of all or part of an Application.

Requirements Team The Team that engineers the Requirements of an Application.

Requirements Work Product A Work Product produced during the Requirements Engineering Activity.

Responsibility Card An index card that documents the responsibilities of some thing (e.g., class, package).

Retirement Phase The final Phase wherein the Application is decommissioned.

Reuse Librarian A Person responsible for adding reusable Components to a library or repository, maintaining the library quality and making developers aware of what Components are available in the library.

Reuse Team The project-independent Team that is responsible for Enterprise reuse.

Risk Management Plan The planning work Document that identifies major Project risks, documents steps to be taken to avoid and mitigate them, as well as assigning responsibilities for these steps to Roles and Teams.

Risk Management Plan Standard A content and format standard for Risk Management Plans.

Risk Management Plan Template A template that can be filled in to produce a Risk Management Plan.

Role A cohesive part that is played by a Person during the production of one or more Versions of Work Products.

Schedule A scheduling Work Product that captures the estimated and actual dates and time utilization associated with a Role, Team, Task, or Work Product.

Scheduling Work Product A Management Work Product dealing with scheduling of Producers, Work Units, and Work Products.

Sequence Diagram An Interaction Diagram that documents the actual sequence of interactions. The nodes are timelines.

Smalltalk Coding Standard A Coding Standard for Smalltalk software.

Software Ideas represented in computer momory.

Software Application A piece of Software which constitutes a computer program which is useful to an end-user.

Software Architect An Architect who is responsible for the Architecture of the Application software.

Software Architecture Document An Architecture document that Documents the overall Architecture of a Software Application.

Software Architecture Document Standard A content and format Standard for Software Architecture Documents.

Software Architecture Document Template A Template that can be filled in to produce a standard-compliant Software Architecture Document.

Software Architecture Team A Team that produces and maintains the overall Software Architecture.

Software Component A Component consisting of Software.

Software Development Plan A planning Work Product that documents the plans for performing Software Development.

Software Development Plan Standard A content and format Standard for Software Development Plans.

Software Development Plan Template A Template that can be filled in to produce a standard-compliant Software Development Plan.

Software Development Procedure A Procedure for undertaking Software Development.

Software Development Team A Team that is responsible for developing Application Software.

Software External Interface Specification A Requirements Specification for Application Programmer Interfaces (APIs) or Graphical User Interfaces (GUIs).

Software Management Team A Team that is responsible for managing software development.

Software Requirements Specification A specification of the Requirements that need to be met by the evolving software Application.

Software Requirements Specification Standard A Standard specifying the content and format of a software Requirements Specification.

Software Requirements Team A Team that performs Software Requirements Engineering.

Software Test Team A Team that tests Software.

Staffing Work Product A Management Work Product dealing with staffing issues.

Stage A formally identified and managed interval of time (Stage With Duration) or a point in time (Instantaneous Stage). See also *Stage With Duration, Instantaneous Stage.*

Stage With Duration A Stage lasting a discrete amount of time i.e. a Stage which has a measurable duration.

Stakeholder A Stakeholder is the Role played by any Person who is significantly impacted by an Application.

Standard A Document that specifies the required content and format for a Work Product.

State Machine A Model of how something changes state. A state machine is typically represented by a State Transition Diagram with nodes representing states and directed arcs representing transitions between states.

Static Architectural Diagram A Diagram that describes one or more of the static, architectural aspects of the system.

Storage A Hardware Component that relates to permanent recording of otherwise ephemeral digital representations in computer memory.

Support Organization An Organization that provides technical support customer and user Organizations.

System Application An individual Application which includes not only software but Hardware and Data Components.

System Architect An Architect who is responsible for the overall Architecture of the System Application.

System Architecture Team A Team that produces the system Architecture.

System Development Plan A planning Work Product that documents the plans for performing System Development.

System Development Plan Standard A content and format Standard for System Development Plans.

System Development Plan Template A Template that can be filled in to produce a System Development Plan.

System Development Team A Team that is responsible for developing the Application software.

System Management Team A Team that manages system development.

System Requirements Specification A detailed specification of the Requirements of the Application from a systems-engineering perspective specifying hardware, software, wetware (Personnel) and paperware (e.g., user Documentation) Requirements.

System Requirements Team A Team that performs system-level Requirements Engineering.

System Test Team A Team that tests an integrated system.

tailoring The fine-tuning of a development process or process element to make it more appropriate for the needs of the Project.

Tailoring Guideline A Guideline that supports the fine-tuning of a process to an Organization or Project.

Task A functionally cohesive operation (reified as a Work Unit) that is performed by a Direct Producer. A single responsibility of a Producer will be fulfilled by the execution of one or more Tasks. A Task results in the creation, modification, or evaluation of a Version of one or more Work Products.

Task Performance A kind of Work Performance consisting of the execution of a Task (usually via a Technique) performed by a Direct Producer.

Team A cohesive group of Roles (or aggregation of Component Teams) that collaborate to perform the Tasks comprising the Work Flows that produce a cohesive collection of Work Products.

Technical leader The Role played by a Person who provides technical leadership of a Team.

Technical Milestone A minor Milestone that is scheduled by the development staff for technical reasons.

Technique The reified implementation (i.e., way of performing) of a Task using the Strategy Pattern. In order to provide flexibility during instantiation and tailoring, Direct Producers may delegate the performance of their own Tasks to Techniques.

Template A partial prototypical Document.

Test Code Code written specifically to operate on the software or Application under test in order to cause failures to enable the detection of any possible defects.

Tester The Role played by a Person who tests a Work Product Version.

Test Metrics Metrics about the test process.

Test Plan A Plan documenting all aspects of testing.

Test Procedure The Procedure by which testing will be undertaken.

Test Report A report of failures produced during testing.

Test Work Product A Work Product related to testing. These include test harnesses, test procedures, test reports, and defect reports.

Timebox Describing a Stage or Work Unit for which a hard deadline is set for deliverables. The deadline is immutable, the functionality delivered possibly being less than 100%.

Tool A Software Application (or device) that is used to create, modify, evaluate, and manage Versions of Work Products. See also *Documentation Tool, lowerCASE Tool*, and *upperCASE Tool*.

Toolsmith A Role responsible for developing and maintaining software Tools.

Training Plan A Document formalizing plans for ensuring adequate training.

upperCASE Tool A model-level CASE Tool for creating, compiling, debugging, testing and managing Models.

Usage Phase A Phase in which the software is in daily use at the client site.

Use Case Model A Model which focusses on describing the use cases of an Application or business, i.e., its functionality.

Use Case Modeler A Modeler who specializes in use case analysis Techniques.

Use Case Modeling Standard A standard for documenting a use case Model.

Use Case Path Specification A Document specifying a path through a use case.

Use Case Specification A Document specifying a single use case.

User-Interface Designer A Designer who designs, prototypes, and leads the evaluation of User Interfaces.

User Organization An Organization that uses Applications developed by a Development Organization.

Vision Statement A Document that defines the customer's vision of one or more related Applications in terms of the associated Stakeholders and their needs.

Work Flow A kind of Work Performance consisting of a sequence of contiguous Task Performances whereby Producers collaborate to produce a single, significant Work Product.

Work Performance The performance of one or more Work Units by one or more Producers.

Work Product Anything of value (e.g., Document, Diagram, Application, class) produced during the performance of one or more Tasks. During the evolution of a Work Product, Work Product Versions are created. Therefore, each Work Product has an associated time-ordered set of Work Product Versions.

Work Product Version A uniquely identified and dated occurrence of a Work Product that is produced by a direct Producer during iterative or incremental development. A Version of a Work Product may be deliverable or produced only for internal use.

Work Unit A functionally-cohesive operation that is performed by a Producer during a process and which is reified as an object to provide flexibility during the construction and tailoring of a development process. See also *Activity, Stage, Task, Technique* and *Work Flow*.

C Work Products

This appendix expands on some of the OPF Work Products, focussing on the classes of Document and Component. The Process Team can use the following tables to identify the Work Products that are cost-effective and appropriate to produce for any specific Endeavor.

In the first section we describe Management Work Products, including two sections relating specifically to Staffing and Scheduling Work Products. These are then followed by sections for Process, Requirements, Architecting, Design, Implementation, Integration, Test and Deployment, which describe Work Products that can collectively be called Engineering Work Products.

Management Set of Work Products

In this category we can include Plans and Organization-specific Conventions. Both are kinds of Document. Also under this heading are the Staffing and Scheduling Work Products and a number of other Documents.

Plans

The OPEN process framework repository contains a number of predefined kinds of planning Work Products including the following:

- Management Plan
- Build Plan
- Conversion Plan
- Configuration Management Plan
- Quality Plan
- Metrics Plan
- Risk Management Plan
- Security Plan
- Test Plans
- Training Plan
- Disaster Recovery Plan
- Change Request Form.

The format of each of these Documents commences in the same way (see Table C.1) and then adds specialized sections as detailed below.

Table C.1 Front matter and first section for *all* Plans

Title Page
Table of Contents
Executive Overview
Change History
Introduction
– Document objectives
– Intended audience
– References
– Organization of Document

Management Plan

The overarching *Management Plan* is a Document that formalizes the plans for managing an Endeavor. A typical table of contents for a Management Plan is shown in Table C.2 which should also incorporate the "boiler plate" of Table C.1. Keeping the Management Plan up to date is usually the responsibility of the management Team with significant input from the Process Team. The Management Plan is typically developed at the beginning of the Project and maintained during the life of the system.

Table C.2 Typical contents of a System Development Plan in addition to those in Table C.1

Endeavor Goals
Endeavor Organization
Cycle, Phases, and Milestones
Overall Project Schedule
Development Environment[1]

In using a Management Plan, the following usage guidelines are relevant:

- Modify the existing Management Plan and associated Template and Inspection Checklist to meet the specific needs of the Endeavor.
- Include the process Work Products by reference rather than repeating them in the Plan.

1 Possibly by reference to a separate Environments Description Document.

- Keep the schedule at a high level of abstraction; keep the detailed schedules in the Build Plan and the Component and Team schedules.

Build Plan

The *Build Plan* is a Document that formalizes the Plans for developing Builds. For example, the Build Plan could have the following contents – composed of the generic initial contents (Table C.1) followed by the specifics as delineated in Table C.3. The Build Plan is developed and maintained by the Development Team with significant input from the Management and Process Teams. The Build Plan is typically developed at the beginning of the Project and maintained during the life of the system.

Table C.3 Typical contents of a Build Plan in addition to those in Table C.1

Development Cycle
Build Schedule. For each Phase, we then document:
Major Builds
Major Milestones
Major Deliverables

The following usage guidelines are relevant to the Build Plan:

- Plan for a specific number of iterative Builds particularly between the developers and the users so that feedback can be incorporated and fed back into necessary rework.
- Plan the overall number of Increments and what size of Increment will be "delivered" at each Increment Milestone.
- Identify "natural breaks", probably corresponding to packages or Large-scale Components within the Application, which can be developed by development Teams working in parallel.
- Identify success measures, perhaps in the form of the major Milestones.
- Put in place a measurement Programme and determine how the results of the Metrics analysis will be fed back into the control of later Builds and Increments.

Conversion Plan

The *Conversion Plan* is only relevant when the OO/CBD system is to interface to or incorporate so-called legacy or heritage systems, i.e., those constructed on principles other than those being used for the new part of the developing system.

There are several strategies which include Techniques such as wrappers which protect investments while permitting them to participate in the OO/CBD system, but there are also concerns for migrating data from these systems into the new one. Data might be split between the older databases and the new Objects/Components. Four strategies[2] are:

- **handshake strategy** – a duplicate, live copy of common data and keeping both copies up to date. This works well when there is little or no overlap between old and new.
- **borrowing strategy** – keep the data in the old system and only make available to the new as and when required
- **take-over strategy** – copy the data to the new objects and let the old go out of date.
- **translation strategy** – a true migration of data from old to new incorporating the use of Reverse Engineering Techniques and a solid OO analysis.

Risk Management Plan

The *Risk Management Plan* is a Document (e.g. Table C.4) that formalizes the plans for risk assessment and risk management.

Table C.4 Contents of Risk Management Plan in addition to four introductory sections listed in Table C.1

Risk assessment by category (risk identification)
Ranking of risks via risk evaluation
Decision on acceptable risk level cutoff
Risk problem identification
Contingencies for each risk above cutoff (a.k.a. risk mitigation or risk avoidance)

The Risk Management Plan is developed and maintained by the Management Team with significant input from the Quality Team. The Risk Management Plan is typically developed at the beginning of the Project and maintained during the life of the system.

The following usage guidelines are relevant to the Risk Management Plan:

- Risk management is at the core of Project Management and of ensuring the chances of success are optimized. Therefore, do not skimp on this plan.
- Divide risks into groups: technical, management, marketing, and users.
- Elicit risks under these four separate headings from the Organizations most affected.
- Merge together these separately identified "candidate risks" then circulate to all reviewers and only then trim down the list.

2 Graham, I. (1995) *Migrating to Object Technology*, Addison-Wesley, p. 69.

- Risks vary in both likelihood and impact. A rare risk with little impact should be neglected but risks that are either common or rare but with high impact should all be considered seriously.
- Risks outside all control, however catastrophic, may not be able to be considered. Here we are thinking of extreme events such as your headquarters being hit by a meteorite three days before delivery date.
- Consider the impacts on your business and identify an acceptable level of risk.
- Risk management should be performed continuously during an Endeavor, not just once.
- Remember, risk management is there for the same reason as you pay insurance premiums.

Security Plan

The *Security Plan* may be a separate Document or may be part of the Risk Management Plan. It describes how access to the system should be controlled and how an individual's data are to be isolated from others'; in other words, who has access to what. The Security Plan will also suggest a policy for regular system backups, including the location (possibly off-site) for backup copies. It will address logical security and physical security. In today's computing environments, network security has a high profile so the security policy of the Organization on whether to introduce firewalls for additional security on their network server should be addressed in this Document.

Disaster Recovery Plan

The *Disaster Recovery Plan* documents the management of the preparation for and recovery from a foreseen (sometime unforeseen) disaster. This may be a loss of data or software or a calamitous event to the hardware or the site itself. It describes exactly what should happen following this event and consequently may sometimes be part of a Risk Management Plan rather than a standalone Document. It is also often aligned closely with the Deployment Plan.

Staffing Work Products

One of the most important, yet often most easily overlooked, aspects of developing Applications and, in particular, software-intensive systems are people. Two of the necessary Work Products associated with human resource allocation and development relate to their individual goal plans and job descriptions and, secondly, to the Organization *in toto*.

Especially in a new development using OO and/or CBD for perhaps the first time, job descriptions need to be clear and may need to be generated as part of the Project itself. There are many Roles that people can play in an Organization or Project Team. While the Roles themselves are described elsewhere in this book, here we draw the reader's attention to the need to generate specific job descriptions as *Work Products* for each Team member.

Secondly, an Enterprise-level Model of the Organization, in terms of a Work Product such as an Organizational chart, is also recommended.

Job Description

A Work Product which documents and delineates the job description of each individual in the Endeavor. It should state responsibilities and expectations, the reporting structure within the Organization, and required expertise and training.

Organization Chart

Figure C.1 shows an example of a typical Organizational chart drawn using object-oriented modeling notation.

Scheduling Work Products

Work Products are "delivered" to someone in the Development and/or Management Team or to the customer/end-user. Some Work Products may be delivered to yourself in the sense of being aides-memoires. Scheduling these "deliveries" demands time management skills and, to some extent, effort estimation ability. There are two approaches to scheduling Work Products: by Work Product and within timeboxes.

The most obvious way to deliver a Work Product is at a time when it is complete and therefore ready to be handed over to another party. Software Components are, however, notorious for their exponential decrease in readiness with time – the last 5% may take a significant proportion of the overall time budget! This has often led to slippage in scheduled delivery dates; so much so that on-time delivery can be a (happy) surprise to the customer. In scheduling the delivery of Work Products in this way, careful estimation is needed. Contingencies need to be allowed so that an "emergency" time allowance or "buffer" is *always* built in to the schedule. This should be done explicitly, not surreptitiously as is often the case at present. Never allow the management or the client to decrease your estimates *if they are professionally and carefully done in the first place.*

The alternative approach to scheduling is to use a series of timeboxes, which can be applied to both Stages and Activities. In a timebox approach, *the deadline never slips.* Work Products are always made available on the stated date. What might slip, if anything, is the degree of functionality of the delivered system (or Component). This is possible using OT/CBD because of the high degree of modularization and Componentization that is used. The element can be delivered but with a reduced functionality. The system works and so can be tested by the end-user and feedback obtained. Delivery dates are never altered so the recipient of the Work Product is 100% certain that they will have it at that time which means that they can allocate valuable resources *on that date* to validate and evaluate it immediately after receipt.

Project Schedule

A master schedule is needed for each Endeavor, usually at the Project level. This depicts (calendar) timing for all Phases, and Milestones etc. within the overall estimated duration of the Project. This plan is of course subject to continual revision during the lifetime of the Project. Planning Techniques such as Gantt charts, CPM and PERT charts may be found useful in preparing this plan.

Component Schedule

Since the main aim of a software-intensive system development is to develop the system and deliver this to the client, scheduling delivery of Work Products, probably in a componentized framework, needs to be accomplished. We can consider major Work Units, software versions etc. as Components, and schedule the delivery of these (e.g. to testing the customer). Thus Component delivery is typically externally focussed. Scheduling can be done as for internal "deliveries" (as discussed above).

Team Schedule

Since Teams and individuals are all playing Roles, it is highly unlikely that a uniquely composed Team will operate *throughout* the whole of the Life Cycle. Rather, individuals and individual Teams will exist in specific Roles for discrete time periods. This will mean overlapping demands on Teams and Team members. The trick with Team scheduling is to avoid any "downtime" so that Teams form, split and rebuild in such a way that Teams, and particularly their members, are always assigned to some Task. Scheduling Tools, such as Gantt charts coupled with lists of Roles and actual Persons, may be helpful here.

Other Documentary Work Products

There are a number of other Work Products which are part of the Management Set but are not strictly Plans (of what might be), but rather reports of what is or has been.

Contract

The contract is the management Work Product consisting of a mutually binding agreement that formally specifies the obligations of the development and customer Organizations. The objective of the contract is to formally obligate the development Organization to provide the specified Work Products and services to the customer Organization within the agreed schedule and budget, and the Customer Organization to pay the Development Organization for the specified Work Products and services, if properly delivered.

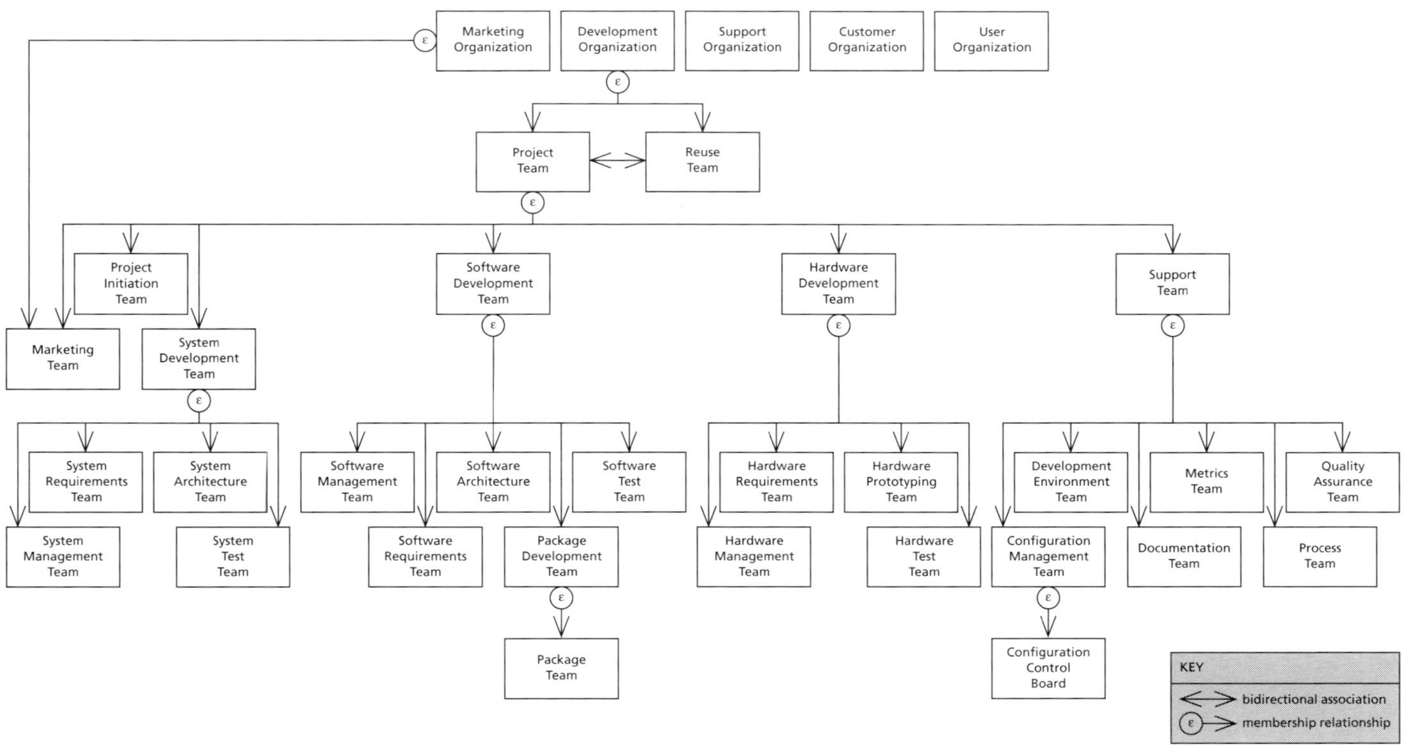

Figure C.1 Example organization chart

Statement of Work (SOW)

The statement of work is the management Work Product consisting of a detailed narrative description of the Work Products and services to be delivered by the Development Organization to the Customer Organization under the contract. It is used to formally summarize the Work Products and/or services to be delivered.

Work Breakdown Structure (WBS)

The work breakdown structure (WBS) is the Management Work Product that Documents the decomposition of the work in terms of Activities and Tasks to be performed on the Project. The objectives of the WBS are to document the work to be performed on the Project as well as the scope of the Project.

Budget

The budget is a Management Work Product that highlights the financial aspects of the Endeavor. Although created prior to the Project Initiation, it should also be regularly updated with respect to any variances that might have arisen as the Endeavor has been proceeding.

Status Report

A status report is a management Work Product that regularly reports the status of the Endeavor. It is subject to frequent updates and should therefore always be a reflection of the current progress of the Endeavor.

Project Debrief Report

The Project debrief report is the management Work Product that documents the analysis and lessons learned resulting from the end of Project "post mortem" walkthrough (the retrospective). The main foci of the Project debrief report are to capture lessons learned and thus to improve the process for future Projects.

Configuration Management Set of Work Products

Work Products associated with Configuration Management include *inter alia* the Configuration Management Plan (outlined below), Change Request Form, Configuration Status Report and Configuration Audit Report.

Configuration Management Plan

The *Configuration Management Plan* is a Document that formalizes the plans for performing configuration management and Version control. The contents typically follow those depicted in Table C.5.

Table C.5 Typical contents of a Configuration Management Plan in addition to those in Table C.1

Configuration Management Roles and Responsibilities
Configuration Manager
Configuration Management Team
Change Control Board (CCB)
Configuration Management Tasks
Configuration Identification
identifying configuration items
identifying baselines
Configuration Control
baselining [parts of] configuration items
requesting changes to baselined configuration items
evaluating proposed changes to baselined configuration items
approving/rejecting proposed changes to baselined configuration items
implementing approved changes to baselined configuration items
tracking and controlling versions and deltas
Configuration Status Accounting
status of configuration items
status of proposed changes
status of approved changes
Configuration Auditing
ensuring baseline completeness
ensuring proper versioning
Configuration Management Tools
Version control
Change control
Status reporting
Appendices

The Configuration Management Plan is developed and maintained by the Configuration Management Team with significant input from the Process Team. The Configuration Management Plan is typically developed at the beginning of the Endeavor and maintained during its life.

The following usage guidelines are relevant to the Configuration Management Plan:

- On small Projects requiring little formal configuration management, consider implementing the Configuration Management Plans as a section in the System Development Plan or the Software Development Plan.
- The Configuration Management Plan should document how the parts of Work Products smaller than a file (e.g., a part of a Document, a method in a class) can be baselined if an iterative, incremental Development Cycle is used.
- The Configuration Management Plan should document if multiple Tools are used to support change control (e.g., ENVY for Smalltalk and ClearCase for C++ and Documents).

Change Request Form

A *Change Request Form* is a Configuration Management Document that formalizes a request for a change to a baselined work product. It outlines not only the change required but also the rationale for the desired change and the source of the request, which may be the Development Team, the Test Team, the Quality Team or may come from an end-user evaluation.

Business Modeling Set of Work Products

Business modeling Work Products are targetted at either business strategy, branding strategy, or technology strategy.

Business Strategy Work Products

Business Strategy Work Products are aimed at the analysis of existing market conditions and developing appropriate strategies to create a winning commercial situation. For example, an Analysis Report documents the Customer Organization's current business, thus providing a solid foundation on which to make recommendations for improving the Customer Organization and customer relationships. A Market Analysis Report documents the marketplace(s) in which the customer Organization currently competes and plans to compete. For each marketplace, the Customer Organization's competitors and their competing Applications are fully documented.

The User Analysis Report is the Work Product produced during business (re)engineering that documents the results of the analysis of the user Organization(s)) that use the Customer Organization's Applications. The future is addressed in the Proposed Applications List and for each a business case is proposed in the Application Business Case. Finally, recommendations are made in a Work Product for each Programme and Project.

Branding Strategy Work Products

The Brand Strategy Document outlines the strategic decisions taken to ensure that a new digital brand can be established and how that establishment will be best effected. The Brand Communication Plan discusses how the brand can be established in the minds of customers. The Brand Style Guide is the Work Product that documents guidelines for ensuring that the user interfaces and user Documentation of Applications conform to the brand strategy of the customer. Its objectives are to document brand strategy guidelines for user interfaces and for user Documentation.

Technology Strategy Work Products

The main Work Product focussing on technology strategy is the Technology Strategy Document which documents the decision made for the introduction of new technologies into the Organization, along with the costs and timelines associated with this introduction.

Quality Set of Work Products

Quality Plan

The *Quality Plan* describes how quality is to be assured and controlled. It is likely to describe how quality reviews are to be undertaken, and when, and to list critical success factors, major Milestones, Metrics to be collected and how these factors are to be evaluated. It will discuss and delineate how the client is defining quality (i.e. which "ilities" are important to them), and what are the Requirements for reliability and mean time between failure (if appropriate). The depth of detail in this Plan depends critically on Project size, the Quality Plan being more appropriate as a separate Planning Document only for relatively large Projects.

The Quality Plan will also discuss auditing responsibilities and requirements.

Metrics

Appropriate *Metrics* need to be selected from those available. These are described at the technical level. Their purpose should be recorded, as should the warning levels to be used. These warning levels relate to whether a "watch" is put on a Component (a "medium-range" value for the Metric in question) or whether the value is high enough to lead to immediate investigation of that Component as being likely to be of poor quality.

Metrics Plan

The *Metrics Plan* is a Document (e.g. Table C.6) that formalizes the plans for performing Metrics collection, analysis, and reporting.

Table C.6 Typical contents of a Metrics Plan in addition to those in Table C.1

Metrics Goals	Teams, Roles, and Responsibilities
Metrics:	Tools
– Process Metrics	Metrics Tasks:
– Quality Metrics	– Collection
– Reuse Metrics	– Analysis
– Test Metrics	– Reporting

The Metrics Plan is developed and maintained by the Metrics Team with significant input from the Process Team. The Metrics Plan is typically developed at the beginning of the Project and maintained during the life of the system.

The following usage guidelines are relevant to the Metrics Plan:

- The reason for Metrics collection needs to be identified. This could be as a baseline for future maintainence cost estimation, for control, or for process improvement, for example.
- The number of Metrics to be collected need to be identified and listed.
- If possible, automated Tools for Metrics collection should be acquired.
- Determine how the results of the Metrics analysis will be reported and to whom.

Metrics Report

A Metrics report is the management Work Product that regularly reports Project Metrics including data on Quality Metrics, Design Metrics, Productivity Metrics, Reuse Metrics, and so on.

Training Set of Work Products

The most obvious training Work Product is the Training Plan. Others include participants surveys and tendering procedures for third-party training vendors.

Training Plan

The *Training Plan* is a Document (e.g. Table C.7) that formalizes the plans for ensuring adequate training is available to members of the various Teams.

Table C.7 Contents of Training Plan in addition to the standard listed in Table C.1

Matrix of subjects/topics and Roles showing what level of expertise each Role requires for that particular topic
Recommended mix of lecture/classroom style training versus workshops versus on-the-job
Recommended timescales e.g. one day a week or "sheepdip" intensive training
Team, Roles, and Responsibilities

The Training Plan is developed and maintained by the Training Team with significant input from the Process Team. The Training Plan is typically developed at the beginning of the Endeavor and maintained during its life.

The following usage guidelines are relevant to the Training Plan:

- Training for different Roles is different. CIOs, managers, developers, and end-users all require different foci in their training. The Training Plan should comprehensively address all Roles.
- All Roles should have a basic understanding of Project management[4] and process so they can relate to other Roles.
- Adult learning approaches should be considered. This often means experiential learning is better.
- Not all individuals have the same learning style, even for the same Role and seniority/level of experience. Some prefer to acquire knowledge by studying books, while for some a topic only comes alive when they "get their hands dirty". Some prefer to study alone, others in Teams.

4 Goldberg, A. and Rubin, K. (1995) *Succeeding with Objects*, Addison-Wesley, p. 413.

Process Set of Work Products

The Process Set of Work Products is our first example of engineering work products. These Work Products focus on Conventions, which can be subdivided into five categories.

Conventions

As well as Plans, the OPEN Process Framework contains a number of *Conventions*. Conventions describe how "we do it this way here". They are the local, possibly idiosyncratic, ways in which business is conducted *at that particular business or on that specific Endeavor*. They relate to the company's (or sometimes Project Team's) set of procedures and guidelines, enhanced by local or international standards, locally obtainable templates etc. Conventions also are likely to cover the local standard for Inspection Checklists. The various kinds of Convention in the OPF include:

- Procedures
- Guidelines
- Standards
- Templates
- Inspection Checklists.

Procedures

A *Procedure* is a Document that specifies the Work Products, Producers, and Tasks of the Work Flows for a specific Activity. The OPEN Process Framework comes with the following predefined instances of procedures in its repository.

- Configuration Management Procedure:
  - Configuration Management Plan Work Flow
  - Change Request Work Flow
- Metrics Procedure:
  - Metrics Plan Work Flow
  - Metrics Report Work Flow
- Requirements Procedure:
  - Vision Statement Work Flow
  - System Requirements Specification Work Flow
  - External Interface Specification Work Flow
  - Software Requirements Specification Work Flow

- Architecture Procedure:
  - System Architecture Document Work Flow
  - Software Architecture Document Work Flow
- Design Procedure:
  - Database Design Document Work Flow
  - GUI Design Document Work Flow
  - Package Design Document Work Flow
- Implementation Procedure
- Integration Procedure
  - Build Work Flow
- Testing Procedure
  - Test Procedure Work Flow
  - Test Report Work Flow
- Delivery Procedure
- Deployment Procedure

The following usage guidelines are relevant to procedures:

- To be useful and followed, procedures need to be understandable to those carrying out the procedure.
- Procedures should aim to be parsimonious. They are to help the system development, not hinder it by insisting on steps considered unnecessary by the Development Team.

Guidelines

A *Guideline* is a Document that provides advice on how to perform one or more related Work Units. The OPF contains the following predefined kinds of Guidelines in the repository:

- Use Case Modeling Guidelines
- OO Modeling Guidelines
- GUI Design Guidelines
- OPF Usage Guidelines (for Construction, Tailoring and Extension).

The following usage guidelines are relevant to guidelines:

- Guidelines offer only heuristic support. Remember that and do not treat them as the one and only way forward.
- Add to the guidelines from your own experience as you gain it.

Standards

A *Standard* is a Document that specifies the required content and format for a Work Product. The OPEN Process Framework contains a number of predefined kinds of content and format standards, one for each major engineering Work Product. These major Work Products to which standards (and later, as we shall see, templates and inspection checklists) apply are listed in Table C.8.

The following usage guidelines are relevant to standards:

- Use (and tailor!) international standards (e.g. OMG, ISO, IEEE) if at all possible.
- If international standards are not available, create, adopt and stick to a set of organizational standards.
- Some standards may need aligning with the chosen Implementation Language. For example, if you are using Smalltalk, you may choose to use a Smalltalk style of naming convention in your UML Diagrams rather than the standard recommended in the OMG Documents.
- Create your own Templates for the many Plans, Guides and other Documents you will find useful (see below).

Templates

A *Template* is a Document that can be used as a skeleton for creating an associated Document. The OPEN Process Framework contains a predefined Template for each of the engineering Document Work Products listed in Table C.8.

The following usage guidelines are relevant to Templates:

- Only instantiate a Template if the associated Work Product is to be produced.

Table C.8 List of example Work Products for Standards, Templates and Inspection Checklists

Requirements Set	Vision Statement
	Glossary
	Executive Requirements Summary
	System Requirements Specification
	External Interface Specification
	Software Requirements Specification
	Use Case Specification
Architecture Set	Enterprise Architecture Document
	Programme Architecture Document
	System Architecture Document
	Software Architecture Document

	Website Architecture Document
Design Set	Class Responsibility Collaborator Card
	Database Design Document
	Package Design Document
	Reusable Components Manual
	Framework User's Manual
	UI Design Document
	Modeling Language Document
	JavaDoc
	GUI Prototype
	White Site/Wireframe Prototype
Implementation Set	C++ Coding Standards
	Eiffel Coding Standards
	Java Coding Standards
	Smalltalk Coding Standards
Test Set	Test Harness
	Testing Procedures
	Test Reports
	Defect Report
Deployment Set	Application
	– Website
	Deployment Plan
	Installation Guide
	Release Notes
	User's Manual

Inspection Checklists

An *Inspection Checklist* is a Document that can be used to guide the inspection of a set of one or more related Work Products. The OPF repository contains a predefined Checklist for each engineering Document Work Product listed in Table C.8.

The following usage guidelines are relevant to Inspection Checklists:

- Check for quality, not merely existence.
- Tailor the Inspection Checklists to concentrate on the most critical defects as the Producers learn.

- Keep the Checklists relatively complete, yet concise.
- Provide training to the inspectors in the proper use of the Checklists and the meaning of the questions.

Requirements Set of Work Products

The OPF repository contains the following predefined example Requirements Specifications:

- Vision Statement
- Glossary
- Executive Requirements Summary
- System Requirements Specification
- External Interface Specification
- Software Requirements Specification
- Use Case Specification.

Note that when OPEN is being used in the business modeling mode, there are different Requirements. These relate to customer stakeholder profiles, customer analysis report, user task matrix, competitor analysis report, technology analysis report, market analysis report, user analysis report and so on.

Vision Statement

The *Vision Statement* is a Document that specifies the customer's vision of one or more related Applications. It must not only communicate the customer's vision of the Application(s) but also document the stakeholders of the Application(s) and communicate the business goals, constraints and required Components of the Application(s) to their stakeholders. It is sometimes referred to as the "Project proposal".

The contents of the Vision Statement, in addition to those shown in Table C.1, are

- Application Description – a top-level description of the Application(s).
- Stakeholders – a description of the Stakeholders of the Application(s) especially the sponsor.
  - Definition – a definition of the Stakeholder.
  - Needs – a listing of the key needs of the Stakeholder.
  - Environment – the environment in which the Stakeholder would use/interact with the Application(s).
- Business Goals – a business-level listing of the business goals of the Application (i.e., how the Application fulfills the needs of its Stakeholders).
  - Operational Goals – a business-level listing of the needed capabilities (features) of the Application(s).
  - Quality Goals – a business-level listing of the needed quality factors of the Application(s).

- Constraints:
  - Rules and Regulations – a list of references to and brief description of any business rules and regulations to which the Application(s) must comply.
  - Technology constraints – a description of each technical constraint (e.g., interoperability with legacy systems, required reuse of existing frameworks or products) on the Application.
- Components – a high-level description of each major envisioned hardware, software, personnel, and Documentation Component of the Application(s).

The Vision Statement is developed and maintained by the Customer Organization with significant inputs from the Marketing Organization, Domain Experts, and the Requirements Team. It is typically developed at the beginning of the Endeavor and maintained during the life of the associated Application(s).

The following usage guidelines are relevant to the Vision Statement:

- Assign development of the Vision Statement to the Requirements Team if not developed by the customer Organization.
- Modify the existing vision statement and associated Template and Inspection Checklist to meet the specific needs of the Endeavor.
- Instantiate the Vision Statement by using the Vision Statement Work Flow documented in the Requirements procedure.

Glossary

The *Glossary* is a Document that defines all significant terms and abbreviations used on an Endeavor.

The Glossary needs to promote communication by promoting the use of a well-defined standard terminology; document a standard terminology of the Application; and provide both a source of key business abstractions for modeling and also the official source of the text for the class comments of the associated classes. An agreed glossary of terms, drawn from the user's domain as far as possible, can be critical to the success of the Endeavor since ubiquitous use of the same "Language" avoids ambiguity and misunderstandings.

The Glossary has the following contents added to those of Table C.1.

- Abbreviations – the definitions of all abbreviations used on the Endeavor.
- Terms – the definition of all major terms used on the Endeavor.

The Glossary is developed and maintained by the Requirements Team with significant inputs from the Domain Experts and the Architecture Team. It is developed concurrently with the Vision Statement and maintained during the life of the Endeavor.

The following usage guidelines are relevant to the Glossary:

- Assign development and maintenance of the Glossary to the Architecture Team if not developed by the Requirements Team.
- Modify the existing Glossary and associated Template and Inspection Checklist to meet the specific needs of the Endeavor.
- Instantiate the Glossary by using the Glossary Work Flow documented in the Requirements Procedure.

System Requirements Specification

The *System Requirements Specification* is a Document that formally specifies all Requirements of a system Application. It is used to communicate the system's operational and Quality Requirements to their Stakeholders and also communicate the system's design constraints.

The System Requirements Specification has the following contents, which follow the first four main sections listed in Table C.1:

- System Description – a brief description of the system.
- System Context – a brief description of the context of the system, including all of its externals and how they relate to the system.
- Operational Requirements – the Functional Requirements of the system, in the form of a Use Case Model:
  - External Type W (Hardware, Software, Role)
    - External X – A specification of a specific external including all of its use cases
      - Use Case Y – A specification of a specific use case of the external including all of its paths.
        - Use Case Path Z – A specification of a specific path through the use case.
- Data/Content Requirements – The specification of all required data and content.
- Quality Requirements – The specification of all required system-level quality factors.
- Design Constraints – The specification of all system-level design constraints including required Hardware and Programming Languages.

The System Requirements Specification is developed and maintained by the System Requirements Team with significant inputs from the Domain Experts Team. It can be started once the Vision Statement is relatively complete and stable and is maintained during the life of the Application.

The following usage guidelines are relevant to the System Requirements Specification:

- Only instantiate the System Requirements Specification if the Application contains significant non-software Components. Otherwise, just use the Software Requirements Specification.
- Modify the existing System Requirements Specification and associated Template and Inspection Checklist to meet the specific needs of the Application.
- Consider including the contents of the external interface specification instead of producing a separate external interface specification if the size of the System Requirements Specification is small enough and there are few external interfaces.
- Instantiate the System Requirements Specification by using the System Requirements Specification Work Flow Documented in the Requirements Procedure.

Executive Requirements Summary

The Executive Requirements Summary summarizes the major Requirements on Endeavors with so many requirements that the System Requirements Specification is overwhelming to executive management.

External Interface Specification

The *External Interface Specification* is a Document that specifies the Requirements for all external Application Programmer Interfaces (APIs) of an Application. It communicates the system's external interfaces to their Stakeholders. It has one major section in addition to those listed in Table C.1:

- Application Programmer Interfaces – A specification of each API.
  - API X – A specification of a specific API.
    - Purpose – The purpose of the API.
    - Externals – The externals that use the API.
    - Interaction Y – The specification of a specific interaction across the API.
      - Semantics – The informal meaning of the interaction.
      - Syntax – The format of the interaction.
      - Protocol – The pre-conditions and post-conditions that formalize the semantics.

The External Interface Specification is developed and maintained by the Systems Requirements Team with significant inputs from the Domain Experts and sometimes the Software Architecture Team and/or Development Environment Team. It can be started once the context part of the system Requirements Specification is relatively stable, and needs to be maintained during the life of the Application.

The following usage guidelines are relevant to the External Interface Specification:

- Consider incorporating the External Interface Specification into the system Requirements Specification if there are few APIs to specify, each API is relatively simple, and the System Requirements Specification is also small and relatively simple.
- Do not develop the External Interface Specification if there are no external APIs.
- Modify the existing External Interface Specification and associated Template and Inspection Checklist to meet the specific needs of the Application.
- Instantiate the External Interface Specification by using the external interface specification Work Flow documented in the Requirements procedure.

Software Requirements Specification

The *Software Requirements Specification* is a Document that specifies all Requirements of the software Components of a system Application. It is useful for communicating the software's operational and quality Requirements to their stakeholders as well as communicating the software's design constraints. It has the following contents:

- Four introductory sections from Table C.1.
- Software Components.
- Operational Requirements – The Functional Requirements of the system, in the form of a Use Case Model:
  - External Type W (Hardware, Software, Role).
    - External X – A specification of a specific external including all of its use cases.
      - Use Case Y – A specification of a specific use case of the external including all of its paths.
        - Use Case Path Z – A specification of a specific path through the use case.
- Data Requirements – The specification of all required data and content.
- Quality Requirements – The specification of all required system-level quality factors.
- Design Constraints – The specification of all software-focussed design constraints.

The Software Requirements Specification is developed and maintained by the Software Requirements Team with significant inputs from the Domain Experts Team. It can be started as soon as the software-specific parts of the System Requirements Specification and system Architecture specification are relatively stable. It is maintained during the life of the Application to remain relevant as new Requirements are added and existing Requirements are changed.

The following usage guidelines are relevant to the Software Requirements Specification:

- Consider not producing a separate Software Requirements Specification if a System Requirements Specification was developed because its contents are likely to be redundant.
- Consider removing the Quality Requirements from this Document if a System Requirements Specification is developed because most Quality Requirements are really at the system level rather than at the software level.
- Consider including the contents of the External Interface Specification here instead of producing a separate External Interface Specification Document if there is no System Requirements Specification, the size of the Software Requirements Specification is small enough and there are few external interfaces.
- Modify the existing Software Requirements Specification and associated Template and Inspection Checklist to meet the specific needs of the Application.
- Instantiate the Software Requirements Specification by using the Software Requirements Specification Work Flow documented in the Requirements procedure.

Use Case Specification

The *Use Case Specification* (UCS) is a Document that specifies a single use case. It is used for documenting the Requirements of the use case and for specifying the Requirements of each associated use case path.

The UCS typically has the following content:

- Use Case Specific Information:
  - Use Case Name – The unique name of the use case.
  - Use Case Requirement – A uniquely identified high-level *Requirement* stated in the form of a brief narrative English specification of the use case.
  - Superclass – The parent use case from which the use case inherits.
  - Business Justification – The business reasons for the use case. Only required for externally visible top-level use cases.
  - Use Case Diagram – Optional Diagram showing subordinate use cases (if any).
  - Use Case Paths – This subsection shall list and specify a basis set[5] of normal and exceptional paths through the use case in accordance with the following:

5 Because a use case may have an indefinitely large number of paths due to branching and looping logic, only a minimal set of basis paths will be specified. All path segments shall be executed by at least one path in the basis set of paths.

- For each basis path, the Use Case Path Specification:
  - Path Requirement – A uniquely identified mid-level *Requirement* stated in the form of a brief narrative English specification of the path through the use case.
  - Externals – A list of all externals involved with the use case path.
  - Pre-conditions – Any pre-conditions that must be satisfied before the use case path can execute.
  - Interactions – An English pseudocode[6] listing of interactions between the Application (or software Component) and its externals. The interaction specifies the initiator of the interaction, the receiver of the interaction and the information (if any) that is passed between the two as part of the interaction. The interactions initiated by the Application are *Requirements* and are thus individually identified.
  - Blackbox Sequence Diagram[7] – Optionally, a blackbox Diagram capturing the statements and assertions of the use case path.
  - Post-conditions – Individually identified *Requirements* in the form of post-conditions that shall be satisfied by the correct execution of the use case path. Only those post-conditions not explicitly implied by the statements (e.g., hidden state changes) are listed.
  - Requirements Trace – The source of the use case path. Required only for externally visible use cases.
  - Categorization – Each use case path is categorized as follows to support prioritization and scheduling of analysis, development and testing:
    - Stability – The probability that the Requirement will change before delivery. Values may be high, medium or low.

      Frequency Whether the frequency of the path is high, medium or low.
    - Criticality – How important the correct functioning of the path is to the user. Values are high, medium, or low. High means that the Application will fail to meet the user's critical operational needs. Medium means that the Application can still satisfy the user's operational needs, but requires the user to use less convenient alternative mechanisms to get the work done. Low means that failure will cause a minor inconvenience to the user.
    - Probability of Defects – Whether the probability of defects is high, medium or low.
    - Risk – Whether the risk associated with the failure of the path is high, medium or low.

6 Includes logic such as branches and looping as well as classes to lower-level use cases.

7 Not supported explicitly in UML. In the OML variant of UML, it is defined as a sequence diagram that documents interactions between externals and the system or application viewed as a blackbox.

The UCS is developed and maintained by the Requirements Team with significant inputs from the Domain Experts Team. It can be started as soon as the associated external has been identified and Documented. It is maintained during the life of the Application to remain relevant as new Requirements are added and existing Requirements are changed.

The following usage guidelines are relevant to the UCS:

- Consider incorporating the specification into the System and Software Requirements Specification.
- Modify the existing UCS standard and associated Template and Inspection Checklist to meet the specific needs of the Application.
- Instantiate the UCS by using the Use Case Specification Work Flow documented in the Requirements procedure.

Architecture Set of Work Products

The OPF contains the following predefined classes of Architecture Work Products in the repository:

- Enterprise Architecture Document
- Programme Architecture Document
- Business Architecture Document
- System Architecture Document
- Software Architecture Document
- Website Architecture Document.

Note when using OPEN for business modeling, there is need of a Business Architecture Document which should include, *inter alia*, Application Strategy, Relationship Strategy, Business Transition Plan, Security Policy, Application Business Cases, the Business Process Model and Organizational Chart. Digital Branding is also of relevance in Web-focussed businesses.

Enterprise Architecture Document

The *Enterprise Architecture Document* depicts the overall architecture of the Enterprise depicted as a Model using OO Techniques. In addition to the information of Table C.1, this Document contains details of:

- essential Enterprise abstractions (Enterprise Object Model)
- Enterprise Process Model.

The Enterprise Architecture Document is primarily developed and maintained by the Business Architect.

Programme Architecture Document

The *Programme Architecture Document* (PAD) depicts the overall architecture of the Programme or suite of Projects. The PAD contains (in addition to the headings of Table C.1) information regarding resource allocation across Projects, a strategy for domain analysis, maintenance strategy, a reuse strategy and approaches to capital investment for infrastructure, software Tools etc.

Business Architecture Document

The *Business Architecture Document* depicts the overall architecture of the business depicted as a Model using OO Techniques.

Table C.9 Contents of Business Architecture Document in addition to the four introductory sections listed in Table C.1

Essential business abstractions (Business Object Model)
(optional) Task Model (Business Process Model)
Business rules
Business goals

The Business Architecture Document (Table C.9) is primarily developed and maintained by the Business Requirements Engineer. The following usage guideline is relevant to the Business Architecture Document:

- When using OT to Model the business, ensure the business is the focus, *not* the system.

System Architecture Document

The *System Architecture Document* depicts the overall architecture (strategic design) of the associated system (Table C.10). The System Architecture Document has the following specific aims: to communicate the overall architecture of the system to its stakeholders and to help ensure the integrity of the architecture by guiding the tactical design of the system.

The System Architecture Document is primarily developed and maintained by the Systems Architecture Team. It can be started as soon as architecturally significant parts of the System Requirements Specification are documented and relatively stable. The System Architecture Document is maintained during the life of the Application to remain relevant by reflecting additions and changes to the system Architecture.

The following usage guidelines are relevant to the System Architecture Document:

- Only instantiate the System Architecture Document if the Application contains significant non-software Components.
- Modify the existing System Architecture Document and associated Template and Inspection Checklist to meet the specific needs of the Application.
- Instantiate the System Architecture Document by using the system Architecture Document Work Flow documented in Architecture Procedure.

Table C.10 Contents of System Architecture Document in addition to the four introductory sections listed in Table C.1

Overview – A general description of the system and its architectural style.
Major Drivers – A description of the essential requirements and design constraints driving the system architecture.
Logical Design Essential Abstractions – A description of the essential application abstractions (objects and functions), their responsibilities, how they are related, their interfaces, and the associated strategic design decisions and their rationales.
Physical Architecture – A description of the major system components, their responsibilities, their internal interfaces, and how they are related, including: • Hardware components such as clients, servers, devices, and networks. • Software components (distribution units) such as subsystems, layers, frameworks, and key packages. • Personnel components such as system-supplied roles (e.g., operator). • Documentation components such as user guides.
Major Architectural Mechanisms.
Technology and Product Selection.

Software Architecture Document

The *Software Architecture Document* is a Document (Table C.11) that details the overall architecture of the software of an Application and communicates this information to its stakeholders, thus helping to ensure the integrity of the Architecture by guiding the tactical design of the software.

The Software Architecture Document is developed and maintained by the Software Architecture Team. It can be started as soon as the significant parts of the Software Requirements Specification are relatively stable and is maintained during the life of the Application.

The following usage guidelines are relevant to the Software Architecture Document:

- Communicate the overall architecture of the system to its stakeholders.
- Help ensure the integrity of the architecture by guiding the tactical design of the system.
- Modify the existing Software Architecture Document and associated Template and Inspection Checklist to meet the specific needs of the Application.

Instantiate the Software Architecture Document by using the Software Architecture Document Work Flow documented in the Requirements Procedure.

Table C.11 Contents of Software Architecture Document in addition to the four introductory sections listed in Table C.1

Major Drivers – A description of the essential requirements and design constraints driving the software architecture.
Essential Abstractions – The application architecture of the software in terms of the definition, responsibilities, interfaces, and strategic design decisions (and their rationales) of architecturally-significant: • classes and packages • layers • frameworks.
Infrastructure Architecture – The infrastructure architecture of the software in terms of: • Concurrency • Distribution • Persistence • Exception Handling • Startup and Shutdown.
Requirements Verification – A description of how the software architecture fulfills the architecturally significant software: • Operational requirements • Quality requirements.

Website Architecture Document

The *Website Architecture Document* is a Document that delineates the overall Website structure. In particular, it links the Information Architecture of the system (i.e. the content models, information viewpoints, site map navigation paths, etc.) to the Functional Architecture (content process, functional models, backend Work Flows and transaction handling, etc.) in a way that is consistent with the business Model underpinning the system. This Document is maintained by the Web Development Team.

Design Set of Work Products

The OPF comes with the following Work Product instances relevant to design. All except the last two are instances of Document, the last two being instances of Prototype.

- Class Responsibility Collaborator Card
- Database Design Document
- Package Design Document
- Framework User's Manual
- GUI Design Document
- Brand Style Document
- JavaDoc [in a Java coding environment only]
- GUI Prototype
- White Site/Wireframe Prototype.

Class Responsibility Collaborator Card

The *Class Responsibility Collaborator (or CRC) Card* approach is well-established in OO circles. Using CRC cards is a kind of brainstorming and role-playing Technique which has many benefits. It can track specific collaborations, refining them and often identifying missing objects/classes; it can create group think, particularly in terminology and definitions of concepts in the problem domain; and it can form the basis for advanced object-oriented design.

A CRC card is an index card upon which is written the class name, together with a small list of all its responsibilities and the collaborating objects/classes which are needed in order for this target class to be able to fulfill its own responsibilities. An index card is used because its size limits the number of responsibilities and collaborators that can be written thereon. Thus the guideline that a class has only a relatively small number of both responsibilities and collaborators is encouraged through use of this Technique.

Database Design Document

The *Database Design Document* is a Document that documents the design of the databases used by an Application. It has the following incremental contents (in addition to those in Table C.1):

- Logical database schema.
- Physical database schema.
- Stored procedures (if any).

The Database Design Document is developed and maintained by the Database Team for the life of the Application.

The following usage guidelines are relevant to the Database Design Document:

- Do not develop a Database Design Document unless the Application uses a database.
- Start with the Database Design Document Template.

Package Design Document

The *Package Design Document* describes the design of the software packages of an Application. It has the following contents (in addition to those listed in Table C.1):

- Package Design – The design of all packages.
  - Package X – The design of a specific package; for example, using various Diagrams using UML or OML (both Static Architecture and Dynamic Behavior Diagrams). If Components are used, then this Design Document must include formal descriptions of all Component Interfaces.

The Package Design Document is developed by the Package Team and maintained during the life of the Application.

The following usage guidelines are relevant to the Package Design Document:

- Ensure packages encapsulate a domain or a subdomain within the problem space.
- Ensure all packages have clearly specified interfaces with protocols for their inter-package collaboration.

Reusable Components Manual

For Components to be reusable, the designers and developers need to be aware of their existence. The *Reusable Components Manual* provides full documentation on reusable Components along with all their characteristics. It also differentiates between two types of "reusable Components": those that have been fully tested (either in-house or by the trusted vendor) and those that are only potentially reusable.

There are many models for reuse at the technical level. One which has had some success is where no effort is put into making Classes/Components reusable at the end of the project for which they were developed – as an investment for the future. Rather, they are labeled, and documented briefly in this Reusable Components Manual as being of potential reuse. The list of potentially reusable Components is thus created incrementally at the end of identifiable Milestones in the process. The list is then examined at the beginning of new Projects or new iterations in order to ascertain whether the embryonic "reusable Class/Component" really is worth investing the additional effort in so that it can be eventually reclassified (after full testing and several actual reuses) as a fully reusable entity.

Framework User's Manual

A *Framework User's Manual* is a Document that describes a Framework and how it is to be used. In addition to the "boilerplate" of Table C.1 it contains:

- framework description.
- framework usage.

UI Design Document

Table C.12 Contents of UI Design Document in addition to the four introductory sections listed in Table C.1

Contents
UI Overview – An overview of the user interface.
GUI – The design of the graphical user interface including all screens at all sites.
• Site – The design of the graphical user interface for each site including a sitemap, GUI Navigation Diagram and a listing of all screen Webpages.
Screen Design – For each site, the design of each associated screen including representative screenshots, content, behavior, etc.
Input Devices – The user interface design of each input device (e.g., keypad, keyboard, barcode reader, etc.).
Output Devices – The user interface design of each output device (e.g., printer, barcode writer, etc.).
Requirements Verification – How the UI meets its essential Requirements:
• Operational Requirements – Screenshots implementing essential use case paths
• Quality Requirements – Descriptions of how the UI meets its quality Requirements for usability, security, etc.

The *User Interface Design Document* encapsulates the design of the user interfaces of an Application. Its incremental contents (over and above Table C.1) are shown in Table C.12. The User Interface Design Document is developed by the Software Development Team with help from the Quality and Requirements Engineering Teams and maintained during the life of the Application.

The following usage guidelines are relevant to the UIDD:

- The user interface should relate easily to the end-user, not to the developer.
- External assessments are therefore vital.

JavaDoc

JavaDoc is automatically generated Documentation, in HTML format, specialized for the Java Language environment. It is included here as both an example of the many other similar automated generation packages for various other programming environments and because the increasing usage of Java as a language of choice recommends it (for that environment).

GUI Prototype

The *GUI prototype* is an exploratory version of the (yet to be built) final GUI. It should be used to pose questions and evaluate options *from the end-user viewpoint*. Usability[8] should be the key criterion here.

The GUI prototype is developed and maintained by the User Interface Team during the lifetime of the Application.

The following usage guideline is relevant:

- Explore questions and evaluate options.

White Site/Wireframe Prototype

A *White Site* (a.k.a. Wireframe Prototype in some countries) is a kind of Prototype, extremely useful for Websites. A White Site is a Website (usually a partial Website) which has no rich graphical content. It is used to:

- provide valuable client confirmation that the developer has understood the user Requirements;
- integrate change management strategy, usage and site navigation in a single visible working solution;
- provide a communication Tool between Website architect and customer.

8 See Constantine, L.L. and Lockwood, L.A.D. (1999) *Software for Use*, Addison-Wesley.

Implementation Set of Work Products

There are a number of Work Products defined in the OPF metamodel (see Appendix G) specifically aligned with the needs of implementation. These focus on both hardware and software.

Component

A *Component* is an implementation Work Product with the following properties:

- It is cohesive in the sense of having a well-defined set of related responsibilities.
- It is accessible via a well-defined set of interfaces. These interfaces allow it to be replaceable within the context of a well-defined Architecture.

Data Component

A *Data Component* is a Component that represents a cohesive set of data of any kind that is used by or stored in the system. One important type is the content of a Website.

Hardware Component

A *Hardware Component* is a Component that represents a physical computational resource such as a device, a computer or a network.

Device

A *Device* is a Hardware Component that has neither significant processing nor significant memory capabilities.[9] The OPF comes with the following predefined classes of devices in the repository:

- Converter (Analog to Digital and Digital to Analog).
- Input Devices (such as Barcode Reader, Card Reader, Keyboard, Sensor).
- Input-Output Device (e.g. Disk Drive, Tape Drive, DVD drive).
- Output Device (e.g. Actuator, Display, Printer).
- Network Connectivity (e.g. bridge, cable, firewall, hub, receiver, transmitter, router, switcher).

9 Some devices, such as modern printers, also have some (but, in this context, not significant) memory or processing capability.

Computer

A *Computer* is a Hardware Component having both significant processing and memory capabilities. The OPF comes with the following predefined classes of Computers:

- **Client.** A *client* is a Computer (in the context of a client/server Architecture).
- **Firewall**. A *firewall* is a Computer used to create a physical barrier to electronic messages passing between the Organization and the external world.
- **Router**. A *router* is a Computer used to pass on electronic communication by selecting appropriate routes along which the messages can travel most expeditiously.
- **Server.** A *server* is a Computer with one or more processors and shared memory to support multiple clients.[10] The OPF comes with the following predefined classes of servers:
  - Application Server. An *Application server* is a server that is used to provide Application-level computing.
  - Database Server. A *database server* is a server that is used to run database management systems.
  - Web Server. A *Web server* is a server that is used to provide Web access.
  - Other servers that may be useful include: e-mail, file, gateway, load balancer, media, presentation, print, security, Web accelerator servers.

Network

A *Network* is a hardware-connected collection of nodes which are usually PCs, UNIX boxes, servers etc. The OPF contains the following predefined classes of Networks in the repository:

- Internet – The *Internet* is a network that crosses organizational boundaries. Usually "The Internet" refers to the totality of all the computers in the world that are interconnected and which can therefore communicate with each other, e.g., by e-mail or remote logon.
- Intranet – An *intranet* is a network that is internal to a single Organization. Functionally it is identical to the Internet. However, because it is totally internal, it may be disconnected from the Internet behind a firewall with a high level of security. DMZ is one such product that provides a secure service for Internet and public services separate from the intranet.

10 The categorization of client and server can be fuzzy since it is relative, not absolute. A computer may play the role of client when running one piece of software, yet the role of a server when executing some other application.

Storage Unit

Storage Unit is a Hardware Component that provides permanent storage of otherwise ephemeral digital representations in the computer memory. Storage may be accomplished using a variety of different physical media. The most common Storage Units are:

- Disk library, in which storage is accomplished using hard disks, CDs or DVDs.
- Tape library, in which storage is accomplished using magnetic tapes or tape cartridges.

Software Component

A *Software Component* is a Component consisting totally of software. A Component must be cohesive in the sense of having a well-defined set of related responsibilities; it must be accessible via a well-defined set of interfaces, which allow it to be replaceable within the context of a well-defined Architecture. A Component is also a configuration item.

A Software Component may have one of the following types of instance:

- Deliverable Software
- Framework
- Test Software
- Package
- Class
- Stored Procedure
- Web Script.

Integration Set of Work Products

The following are only two kinds of Work Product of value in the context of system integration: the Increment and the Integration Test Results. The focus here is on melding together disparate pieces (third-party and in-house developed) into the desired Application.

Increment

An Increment is a composite Work Product that brings together in a single entity all the Components being developed in the period of time since the last incremental delivery.

Integration Test Results

When Components are integrated, it is important that tests, including regression and integration tests, are undertaken. The results from these tests need to be documented and then analyzed.

Test Set of Work Products

There are a number of Work Products specifically oriented towards the needs of testing. A selection of these are outlined below. Others, not described, include summary reports, test scripts, test suites and, specifically in the area of usability testing, screening questionnaires, orientation scripts, observation forms, pre-test questionnaires and post-test questionaires.

Test Plan

There may be one or more *Test Plans* covering areas such as the extent of testing to be undertaken. How are the integration tests to be undertaken (Integration Test Plan)? What is the proposal for customer acceptance (Acceptance Test Plan)? What is to be the strategy for unit testing (Unit Test Plan)? And so on. The technical details of the tests themselves and the test harness code etc. are separate Work Products in this Test Set.

Test Harness

A *Test Harness* is the software (e.g. set of classes) that constitute, essentially, a framework into which the Application awaiting test is placed. It is thus an example of a Software Component (see above). The Test Harness provides means for both whitebox and blackbox testing of the evolving Application. It should itself be evolved in parallel and *not* be deferred until after the software has been nearly completed. The features of the Test Harness are constructed such that they exercise the functionality of the Application using whatever test procedure (see below) is considered to be appropriate.

Application Testing Procedure

There are many approaches to testing Classes and Components. Underlying these are various strategies or procedures (see earlier in this appendix). While there is much research into the "best" strategy, at present the Development/Test Teams have choices. For instance, for safety-critical software, it may be worthwhile undertaking extensive testing of *all* paths through the system. For less critical software, a basis set may be identified and for low quality software only major pieces of functionality may be thoroughly tested. However, if reliability and exception handling are important, these less frequently utilized control flows must also be carefully examined.

Website Testing Procedure

Testing a Website can be accomplished in a similar fashion to Application Testing when the functionality of the Website in terms of transaction support is to be evaluated. However, many Websites, particularly the earlier ones or those that are "eye candy", are primarily evaluated by users in terms of how fast they respond, the acceptability of the graphics and their overall "interest" to the casual browser. For these sites, both commercial and non-commercial, aimed at providing a service, there are many other considerations. Navigability is always a major issue, as is the ability to acquire the service in a way that makes sense to the customer. Various metaphors are used, such as the shopping cart and the boutique. Due opportunity must be offered for the customer to change their mind and make an alternative purchase, and to see at a glance the various options available under each category. Reliability and perceived security are clearly important, as are unambiguous indications of whether a purchase has been successful or not.[11] These aspects of Websites must be tested as thoroughly as any other, more traditional characteristic of a system. A Website that does not pass these sorts of unique tests will be avoided by potential customers and there is thus a danger of the host Organization losing customers and, eventually, going out of business.

Test Report

When the software has been examined using the Test Procedure of choice, a Report is needed of any flaws found.

Defect Report

All defects that are found are documented in a Defect Report, usually using a number of categories of criticality e.g. those that *must* be fixed, those that cause a catastrophic problem etc. These are usually submitted to the Change Control Board (CCB) for the recommended action (see Appendix D).

Deployment Set of Work Products

When the Application is ready to be passed to the client and then the end-user, it is put into use on an external site. There are specific Work Products associated with this deployment, ranging from the Application itself (software is a Work Product too!), the Planning Document for the deployment itself and Documents to explain the software's functioning. Other Work Products, such as the Deployment Plan and the Disaster Recovery Plan, have already been discussed.

11 Some sites are so slow that it is not clear whether the Internet link might have failed. A second exploratory click (on the assumption that the first wasn't actioned) may lead to an unintended and unwanted duplicate purchase.

Application

A critical Work Product in deploying the software-intensive system is the Application itself.

Website

For Web-based situations, this specialized form of Application is a critical Work Product.

Deployment Plan

The *Deployment Plan* is a Document (e.g. Table C.13) that formalizes the plans for deploying the software-intensive system in the Organization, on-site and in a real business situation.

Table C.13 Contents of Deployment Plan in addition to four introductory sections listed in Table C.1

Recommended timeline for deployment, particularly if incremental
Style of deployment compared to existing system e.g. big bang, Phased parallel
Recommended training for end-users
Metrics for successful deployment

The Deployment Plan is developed and maintained by the Environments Team[12] with significant input from the Management, Test and Metrics Teams. The Deployment Plan is typically developed at the beginning of the Project and maintained during the life of the system.

The following usage guidelines are relevant to the Deployment Plan:

- Get buy-in from the future users *before* the system goes live on-site.
- Don't be afraid to "recant" if the first trial is an abysmal failure.
- Be very clear what are your measures of success.

Installation Guide

The actual installation of the Hardware, Software, and Data Components into the production environments is likely to need advice. Whilst "wizards" are becoming the norm for installation, there will still likely be notes of guidance for the installation that the user (or more particularly the Systems Person of the User Organization) will need to be aware of. The installation guide may be hard copy or electronic.

12 For domains such as embedded software, the skills and experience of this team will need to be enhanced by individuals expert in both the domain and specific deployment strategies.

Release Notes

A Document that is more important for subsequent Versions, the Release Notes document changes since the previous Version. Users of software typically upgrade regularly with new releases and do not need full user's manuals for each release but rather want to see the "deltas" i.e. what has changed since the last release.

User's Manual

Although much software today is intended to be "intuitive", this claimed attribute is seldom realized in actuality and a User's Manual is needed. This may be a hard copy manual that can be taken home and read; or may be an extensive (and hopefully intelligent) Help system created as part of the Application itself. The idea of the User's Manual is to have some Documentation *written in the language understandable by the user*, not by the development Team. That being so, the worst people to write this manual are members of the Development Team, and a Technical Writer would be more usefully employed to undertake the preparation of this Document. A User's Manual may be *User Task-oriented* (how do I ...?) or *Product-oriented* (e.g. description of menus and dialogues) or both. The former is important for efficient use of the software product and should describe frequent user actions. The product-oriented part of the manual can describe less frequent operations and allows more advanced users to exploit the product more fully.

D Producers

Producers are People, Roles or Tools that produce a Work Product. Here "produce" includes not only creation, but evaluation, iteration and maintenance. Producers may be Direct Producers or Indirect Producers. The OPF repository describes many Roles for both Direct and Indirect Producers. Remember that on any one Project only a small subset of these will be required.

Direct Producers

Direct Producers are generally People or Roles being played by direct creators of the Work Products. Thus, this category can include other software Tools. Here are some typical examples of Direct Producers under these two headings of Roles and Tools.

Roles

An alphabetical list of Roles is given in Table D.1. A brief description of each follows.

Table D.1 Alphabetical list of Roles and subRoles

Roles	Subtypes
Application Conscript	
Architect	Business Architect
	Database Architect
	Hardware Architect
	Information Architect
	Security Architect
	Software Architect
	System Architect
Class Owner	
Configuration Manager	
Content Worker	Content Approver
	Content Creator
	Content Editor
	Content Publisher
	Content Writer
	Content Translator

Table D.1 Alphabetical list of Roles and subRoles *continued*

Roles	Subtypes
Database Administrator	
Database Engineer	
Designer	Class Designer
	Component Designer
	Database Designer
	Package Designer
	User-Interface Designer
	Website Designer
	Graphic Designer
Domain Expert	
Hardware Engineer	
Integrator	Component Integrator
	Software Integrator
	Systems Integrator
Methodologist (OO and/or CBD)	
Metrics Analyst	
Modeler	OO Modeler
	Use Case Modeler
Network Administrator	
Process Engineer	
Programme Manager	
Programmer	Peer Programmer
Project Manager	
Prototype Developer	
Quality Engineer	
Requirements Engineer	Business Requirements Engineer
	Software Requirements Engineer
	Systems Requirements Engineer
Reuse Librarian	
Scheduler	
Security Analyst	

Table D.1 Alphabetical list of Roles and subRoles *continued*

Roles	Subtypes
Security Engineer	
Stakeholder	Administrator
	Customer/client
	Operator
	Developer
	Manager
	Subcontractor representative
	User
	Vendor representative
Strategist	Brand Strategist
	Business Strategist
	Technology Strategist
Systems Administrator	
Technical Leader	
Technical Writer	
Tester	Build Tester
	Class Tester
	Component Tester
	Integration Tester
	Model Tester
	Package Tester
	Regression Tester
	Test Participant
	Usability Tester
	Website Tester
Toolsmith	
Trainer	Classroom Trainer
	Mentor
Usability Engineer	
User Analyst	

Application Conscript

An *Application Conscript* is a developer (Designer, Programmer or Modeler) who is assigned a temporary Role on the Reuse Team.[1] This link is beneficial by keeping the developers and the reuse engineers in touch both with each other and with reality.

Architect

An *Architect* is the Role played by a Person when producing for an Architecture. Specifically, an Architect has many responsibilities. These include the responsibility for producing and maintaining the Architecture. To do this, the Architect needs to (i) identify the architecturally significant abstractions, components and patterns; their responsibilities, relationships, and interfaces; and how they collaborate; (ii) identify architectural mechanisms; (iii) select technologies and products; and (iv) ensure that these components meet their associated operational and quality requirements. This Person also documents the Architecture in the associated Architecture Document and enforces the integrity of the overall Architecture by collaborating with and mentoring the development staff. He or she is also responsible for reviewing the associated Requirements Specifications and Design and acting as a member of the Change Control Board to ensure that changes do not adversely impact the Architecture.

To fulfill these responsibilities, an Architect should be an abstract thinker (a "big-picture" Person) who can work at the high levels of abstraction. He or she must be able to manage and (re)prioritize the multiple concurrent issues, ambiguities, and contradictions that occur during the development of the Architecture. An Architect should be an excellent communicator who can explain and document the Architecture as well as being able to understand both the application domain and the major technologies used to implement the Architecture. They should also have had significant previous experience, although not necessarily at the architect's level of responsibility, in similar Endeavors.

The OPF repository comes with the following predefined kinds of architects:

- **Business Architect**. A *Business Architect* is an Architect who is responsible for the Architecture of a business.
- **Database Architect**. A *Database Architect* is an Architect who is responsible for the Architecture of one or more databases.
- **Hardware Architect**. A *Hardware Architect* is an Architect who is responsible for the overall Architecture of all hardware aspects of the system and its environments.
- **Information Architect**. An *Information Architect* is an Architect who is responsible for the information content of the system or Website.
- **Security Architect**. A *Security Architect* is an Architect who is responsible for the security mechanisms implement the security Requirements.
- **Software Architect**. A *Software Architect* is an Architect who is responsible for the Architecture of the Application software.

- **System Architect**. A *System Architect* is an Architect who is responsible for the Architecture of the overall Application including hardware, software, personnel and documentation.

Class Owner

A *Class Owner* is the Role played by a Person responsible for the production of an individual Class (here we are using the word Class to also encompass Component). Specifically, a Class Owner designs, codes, unit tests and debugs an individual class and related test software.

The idea behind "owning" a Class is (a) to avoid the possible fractures between analysis, design and code when multiple Roles (i.e. several People) are involved over the Life Cycle of the Class/Component and (b) to assign to an individual Person a sense of ownership and personal responsibility. It is well known that if people feel "ownership" in a process or product, they are more likely to invest personal effort in ensuring higher quality. Software developers like to feel proud of what they produce. Then, adopting a full Life Cycle responsibility for each Class permits not only enforcement of the ownership but also permits proper support for seamless development of the Class/Component. (Note that in a light methodology such as XP or a light version of OPEN adopting an XP mindset, class ownership is anathema.)

The Class Owner thus has many responsibilities. At the class level, he or she has responsibility for ensuring the class's integrity and semantic cohesion as well as being sure it will offer an interface of value to other Components in the system being developed. He/she is responsible for the design of the class and its implementation – thus transcending the role of programming. He/she is also responsible for its testing and quality evaluation, which should be an integrated part of the class development in any case, not an add-on "extra".

The skills required are thus of a "complete" OO/CBD developer. Both design skills and coding skills are required, as is an understanding of testing procedures and their value.

Configuration Manager

A *Configuration Manager* is the person responsible for the Configuration Management Activity including Configuration Identification, Configuration Control, Configuration Status Accounting and Configuration Auditing.

Configuration Managers therefore have the following responsibilities. They must produce and maintain the Configuration Management Plan or the associated section of the System or Software Development Plan as well as the Configuration Management Procedure. The Configuration Manager must also maintain an effective Configuration Management Activity including Configuration Identification (needing to identify configuration items and baselines); Configuration Control; Configuration Status

1 The "hairies and conscript" model of reuse is discussed in more detail in Graham, I. *et al.* (1997) *The Open Process Specification*, Addison-Wesley.

Accounting and Configuration Auditing (auditing the baseline to verify it is complete, correctly identified and versioned). Configuration Control includes the need to manage the baseline itself by placing the configuration items under Configuration Control as well as the need to manage the changes to the baselined configuration items including requesting, evaluating the impact of, approving/rejecting and implementing changes. On the other hand, Configuration Status Accounting describes the need to record and report the status of proposed changes, deviations and waivers to the configuration as well as to record and report the implementation status of approved changes. Effective leadership is to be provided by the configuration manager to the Configuration Management Team. He or she also interfaces with the Change Control Board (CCB), procures the configuration management environment and oversees the configuration management programmes of suppliers and subcontractors.

To fulfill his or her responsibilities, the skills possessed by a Configuration Manager should include training in configuration management theory and experience in performing configuration management "on the job" as well as excellent communication skills for interfacing with developers, testers and the members of the CCB.

Content Worker

Content Workers are those Persons playing Roles focussed on aspects of the Application content (user visable data), often most appropriate for Website Applications.

The OPF repository supplies the following predefined classes of Content Worker:

- **Content Creator**. A *Content Creator* is the Role that is played when a Person creates or obtains new content for one or more Applications. Content creators come in the following four types: Audio Artist, Content Author, Graphic Artist and Video Artist.
- **Content Translator**. A *Content Translator* is the Role that is played when a Person translates the content of one or more Applications: either from a foreign language into a native language or vice versa.
- **Content Writer**. A *Content Writer* is the Role that is played when a Person enters content for one or more Applications into a content management system. Typical responsibilities include obtaining raw content from Content Creators and other sources, performing content migration from legacy Applications and databases, entering new, engaging, user-focused content into an Application and ensuring that the content supports the customer's digital brand (e.g., has an appropriate, consistent, and authentic voice).
- **Content Editor**. A *Content Editor* is the Role that is played when a Person copy edits textual content prior to approval.
- **Content Approver**. A *Content Approver* is the Role that is played when a Person approves content for incorporation into an Application and release to the users. A Content Approver typically also has responsibility for evaluating content for correctness, currency, and consistency with the digital brand.

- **Content Publisher**. A *Content Publisher* is the Role that is played when a Person publishes approved content to an Application, such as to a Website.

Database Administrator

A *Database Administrator* is the Role that is played when a Person administers one or more databases in the production environment. Their specific responsibilities include reinstalling the database(s) and the associated software; reconfiguring the database(s) and continually tuning the database code to optimize database performance. To fulfill these responsibilities, a Database Administrator typically should have the following expertise, training, and experience:

- Knowledge of Data Definition Languages.
- Knowledge of Data Manipulation Languages.
- Knowledge of Query Languages (e.g., SQL, OSQL, JDBC, ODBC).
- Knowledge of relational and object database management systems.

Database Engineer

A *Database Engineer* is the Role a Person plays when designing, implementing, and installing an Application's databases. A Database Engineer typically has the role-specific responsibilities of performing logical and physical data modeling to produce the database schemas; producing the database layer of Software Components; initially tuning the database code to optimize database performance; and producing database loading and batch-processing routines. A Database Engineer may also use stored procedures.

Designer

A *Designer* (a.k.a. Modeler) is the Role played by a Person who creates, documents and maintains the design of an individual Component, Package or Class. Designers are typically members of Package Teams.

A Designer needs to be able to translate the Requirements and Architecture into an associated Design, to make all relevant tactical design decisions and to be responsible for documenting the design in the appropriate Design Document. To fulfill these responsibilities, a designer should have knowledge of OO design Techniques and patterns and of OO Modeling Languages and be able to understand the relevant Requirements and the Architecture of the Application.

The OPF repository supplies the following predefined classes of Designers:

- **Class Designer**. A *Class Designer* is a Designer who designs an individual class including how the class design implements its abstraction, responsibilities and contractual obligations.
- **Component Designer**. A *Component Designer* is a Designer who designs Components for third party reuse.

- **Database Designer**. A *Database Designer* is a Designer who designs the various parts of the database used to store, retrieve and delete persistent objects or data. Database Designers are concerned with logical and physical database schemata. When relational databases are used, Database Designers are concerned with such issues as table and row definitions, existence and functionality of stored procedures, triggers and how objects access the database.
- **Package Designer**. A *Package Designer* is a Designer who designs a package of collaborating classes. A Package Designer is concerned with the abstraction, responsibilities and public interfaces of classes and how they collaborate.
- **Graphic Designer**. A *Graphic Designer* is the Designer who works in the artistic domain and will have skills in photography, music, video and other visual arts. He or she works closely with the Website Designer and between them they bring together the worlds of print media and programming.
- **User-Interface Designer**. A *User-Interface Designer* is a Designer who designs, prototypes, and leads the evaluation of user interfaces. User Interface Designers are concerned with usability.
- **Website Designer**. A *Website Designer* is the Designer who works in the domain of HTML/XML for page content design and of scripts (e.g. Javascript, CGI, JSP, ASP). A Website Designer has a particular focus on the technical aspects of contemporary Web technologies as well as the regular skills and responsibilities of other Application Designers. He or she works closely with the graphic designer and between them they bring together the worlds of print media and programming.

Domain Expert

A *Domain Expert* (a.k.a. Subject Matter Expert) is the Role played by a Person who provides expertise in the Application domain. A Domain Expert therefore has the responsibility of thoroughly understanding some subset of the Application domain and offering support to the Requirements Engineers during the Requirements Elicitation Activity by providing authoritative answers to questions. He or she must also take the responsibility of evaluating the Requirements Specifications for correctness and completeness.

To fulfill his or her responsibilities, a Domain Expert should have deep knowledge of some subset of the Application domain as well as the ability to articulate Business Requirements and Rules.

Hardware Engineer

A *Hardware Engineer* is the Role that is played when a Person fabricates the Hardware Components of an Application. They have the overall responsibility for producing or obtaining the Hardware Components (e.g., servers, networks, and network connection devices), for installing the Hardware Components and for configuring these Hardware Components.

Integrator

An *integrator* is the Role played by a Person who integrates baselined Components into Builds. This Person has the responsibility of planning Application Integration and of setting up the integration environments (hardware and workspaces). They must also be the Person responsible for integrating Components into Builds.

To fulfill his or her responsibilities, an Integrator should have knowledge of the Implementation Languages used, of the development, integration, test, and production environments (i.e., operating systems, hardware platforms, browsers) and of the Configuration Management process.

The OPF comes with the following predefined classes of Integrators:

- **Component Integrator**. A *Component Integrator* specifically integrates together a number of Components, usually acquired from third parties.
- **Software Integrator**. A *Software Integrator* is an integrator of Software Components, Classes, Packages etc.
- **System Integrator**. A *System Integrator* is an integrator of System Components.

Methodologist (OO and/or CBD)

A *Methodologist* is a Person who is an expert in object-oriented (OO) development and/or Component-Based Development (CBD) methods.

- An OO (CBD) Methodologist therefore has the major responsibility of studying and evaluating existing, published OO development (CBD) methods. This means that the OO methodologist needs broad knowledge of a number of OO development (CBD) methods, including their strengths and weaknesses.

Metrics Analyst

A *Metrics Analyst* is the Role played by a Person responsible for Metrics on an Endeavor. Their responsibility focusses on the identification and collection of relevant Metrics as well as taking charge of the Metrics analysis and then reporting on the results.

To fulfill his or her responsibilities, a Metrics Analyst should have the following abilities: knowledge of object-oriented Size, Productivity and Quality Metrics; the ability to determine which Metrics are practical and cost-effective; and knowledge of Metrics collection, analysis and reporting Tools.

Modeler

A *Modeler* is the Role played by a Person who produces Models. This Person also needs to have the skills to verify, validate and maintain these Models. To do this, he or she needs in-depth knowledge of appropriate Modeling Techniques.

The OPF comes with the following predefined classes of Modelers:

- **OO Modeler**. An *OO Modeler* is a Modeler who produces Object Models.
- **Use Case Modeler**. A *Use Case Modeler* is a Modeler who produces Use Case Models.

Network Administrator

A *Network Administrator* is the Role that is played when a Person administers one or more networks in the production environment. A Network Administrator typically has the following Role-specific responsibilities:

- To administer one or more networks.
- To ensure proper network routing.
- To perform network load balancing.
- To ensure continuous network availability.
- To perform network capacity and scalability planning.
- To perform network disaster recovery.

Process Engineer

A *Process Engineer* is the Role played by a Person who is responsible for the process. This Person is responsible for creating the organization-specific process and maintaining it. Specifically, they need to identify the process needs of the specific Endeavor; instantiate the process from the framework to meet the needs of the specific Endeavor and then generate process Work Products (i.e., procedures, guidelines, standards, templates and inspection checklists). They are also responsible for identifying useful upperCASE Tools to support the process, for inculcating the use of the process Work Products across the Endeavor and, finally, for seeking to continually improve the process during the development effort.

To fulfill his or her responsibilities, a Process Engineer should have knowledge of the process to be used on the Endeavor, and good communication skills.

Programme Manager

A *Programme Manager* is the Role played by a Person who is responsible for the administrative management of the overall Programme or suite of Projects. Their responsibilities are similar to those of the Project Manager (q.v.) but at the scope of the Programme rather than the individual Project.

To fulfill his or her responsibilities, a Programme Manager should have the following abilities: knowledge of OO Project Management issues and techniques, good people skills, the ability to set priorities and, sometimes most importantly, the ability to delegate.

Programmer

A *Programmer* is the Role played by a Person who produces source code. In some organizations, the Roles of Programmer and Class Owner may be equated. He or she is directly responsible for producing code in accordance with the design documentation and approved programming standards, as well as being responsible for producing unit test software and for performing unit testing (running unit tests and identifying failures). As a consequence, the Programmer is also the Person responsible for debugging the source code. This includes identifying and fixing the defects and then providing some verification that these defects have been correctly modified.

To fulfill his or her responsibilities, a Programmer should have a good knowledge of the Programming Languages to be used, including their idioms and coding standards (international or organizational), as well as a good knowledge of the Modeling Languages used to document the design to be implemented. He or she must be familiar with Unit Testing Techniques and be skillful in their application. It is also highly useful if he has some knowledge of the Application domain.

A specialized kind of Programmer is the *Peer Programmer*, who shares the responsibility for the production of an individual class with another Peer Programmer (using the Technique: Pair Programming).

Project Manager

A *Project Manager* is the Role played by a Person who is responsible for the administrative management of a Project, including producing the system or software development plan; interfacing with the Customer/User Organizations (aiming to limit requirements "churn"); allocating financial and staffing resources; managing personnel issues (e.g., performance reviews, vacation schedules); and enforcing project schedules.

To fulfill his or her responsibilities, a Project Manager should have the following abilities: knowledge of OO Project Management issues and techniques, good people skills, the ability to set priorities and, sometimes most importantly, the ability to delegate.

Prototype Developer

Although the Role of *Prototype Developer* is useful for Application developments, it is included in OPEN with a Web focus. The Prototype Developer is the Role played by the Person who is responsible for creating and testing the White Site i.e. the prototype Website which does not yet have the full rich textual content necessary in the completed Website.

Quality Engineer

A *Quality Engineer* is the Role played by a Person who performs independent Quality Engineering Tasks on a Project. This means ensuring that the product meets the stated quality goals and assisting in inculcating a quality ethos in the Project Team and the larger Organization.

To fulfill his or her responsibilities, a quality engineer should have knowledge of quality assurance and of quality processes, perhaps including TQM (Total Quality Management). He or she would probably benefit from an understanding of the CMM (Capability Maturity Model) from the Software Engineering Institute (SEI). Metrics knowledge is critically important as is knowledge of processes and process improvement. An added benefit would be understanding capability assessment procedures such as ISO 15504 (a.k.a. SPICE) and, in the near future, OOSPICE.[2]

Requirements Engineer

A *Requirements Engineer* is the Role played by a Person who performs Requirements engineering on an Endeavor. He needs to collaborate with the Process Engineers to identify the appropriate Requirements Set of Work Products and develop the Requirements Engineering Procedure, and with the Toolsmith to identify the appropriate Requirements Analysis, Specification and Management Tool(s). The Requirements Engineer also performs Requirements Elicitation for operational, quality and design needs including any specific constraints as well as Requirements Analysis together with Requirements Specification (including those Requirements needed for the interface). The Requirements Engineer is also the Person most likely to produce Vision Statements and to perform Requirements Management.

To fulfill these important responsibilities, a Requirements Engineer should be familiar with Requirements Engineering Tools and have a wide knowledge of modern Requirements Engineering Techniques (including use cases). Finally, they need to have good communication skills for working with domain experts, customers and users during Requirements Elicitation.

The OPF provides the following predefined classes of Requirements Engineer:

- **Business Requirements Engineer**. A *Business Requirements Engineer* is a Requirements Engineer who deals with the overall Requirements of a business.
- **Software Requirements Engineer**. A *Software Requirements Engineer* is a Requirements Engineer who deals with the Software Requirements of an Endeavor.
- **Systems Requirements Engineer**. A *System Requirements Engineer* is a Requirements Engineer who deals with the system-level Requirements of an Endeavor.

Reuse Librarian

A *Reuse Librarian* is the Role that is played by a Person who manages the reuse library of Classes and Components. Particularly in a Component-Based Development Organization, they have major responsibilities. These include ensuring that the quality of Components added to the library is of an acceptable standard; cataloguing and classifying Components added to the library; and managing both additions and usage of Components into and out of the library.

2 http://www.oospice.com

To fulfill these responsibilities, a Reuse Librarian should be a methodical and a strategic thinker. He or she also needs to have knowledge of a large number of the Projects within the Organization, perhaps by being a part-time member of these Project Teams. Sometimes, secondary membership on a Development Team for a short period can be highly beneficial.

Scheduler

A *Scheduler* is the Role that is played by a Person who identifies work schedules and delivery dates, taking into account available personnel. He or she is thus responsible for timeboxes, delivery dates, cost and effort estimation (with the Metrics Analyst), as well as for contracting (between Developer and User/Client).

To fulfill his or her responsibilities, a scheduler should have the ability to balance and assess relative merits of various options. He needs, therefore, to be a good and equitable decision-maker. He or she needs some technical knowledge as to what is and is not technically feasible as well as management understanding as to the realities of business life in the twenty-first century.

Security Analyst

A *Security Analyst* is the Role that is played when a Person engineers an Application's Security Requirements. Typically this Person is responsible for performing threat analysis at the data center and Application levels; for developing the customer's security policy, for determining the Security Requirements for individual Applications, for performing security testing, and for training the security personnel.

Security Engineer

A *Security Engineer* is the Role that is played when a Person engineers Components, Applications and data centers to meet Security Requirements. This Person is responsible for implementing security mechanisms, installing and configuring Security Components, taking part in design and code inspections for security defects, providing input into the design and coding standards, and performing security testing.

Stakeholder

A *Stakeholder* is the Role played by any Person who is significantly affected by an Application.

The OPF has the following predefined classes of Stakeholders:

- **Administrator**. An *Administrator* is a Stakeholder who has responsibility for one or more aspect of the system construction. He will be involved in contractual obligations to third parties and will likely be responsible for their fulfillment. Their orientation may be loosely categorized as either technical (as in "systems administrator") or non-technical (as part of the Management Team).

- **Customer (a.k.a. Client) Representative**. A *Customer Representative* is a stakeholder who purchases an Application from a Development Organization. Customers provide funding for Development and Support Organizations. Because customers are responsible for officially approving Requirements and the acceptance of deliverables, customers also have final responsibility for go/no go decisions at major Milestones.
- **Operator**. An *Operator* is a Stakeholder who is responsible for the effective operation of the hardware and the environment in running the Software Application.
- **Developer**. A *Developer* is a Stakeholder who invests time and effort in creating the software.
- **Manager**. A *Manager* is a Stakeholder who has skills in managing all aspects of the creation of the software intensive system.
- **Subcontractor Representative**. A *Subcontractor Representative* is the Role played when a Person represents a subcontractor Organization in interactions with members of the Development Organization.
- **User**. A *User* (a.k.a. End-User) is a Stakeholder that uses the Application.
- **Vendor Representative**. A *Vendor Representative* is the Role played when a Person represents a Vendor Organization in interactions with members of the Development Organization.

Strategist

A *Strategist* is a Person playing a Role focussing on strategic analysis and decision-making. The OPF repository supplies the following predefined classes of Strategist:

- **Brand Strategist**. A *Brand Strategist* is the Role that is played when a Person develops the digital brand strategy for a customer's business. He or she has overall responsibility for collaborating with the User Analysts and Business Strategists to develop the Customer's Requirements for their digital branding strategy and for employing appropriate strategies for producing an appropriate digital brand (e.g., brand identity) that will help the Customer Organization to build its desired relationships with the users of its Applications, for maintaining a clear understanding of the customer's business issues and objectives, for communicating branding information with customer representatives and Project members, and for collaborating with the Process Engineer to ensure that the branding aspects of the project process are appropriate, efficient, and effective.
- **Business Strategist**. A *Business Strategist* is the Role that is played when a Person develops the business strategy for a customer's business. He or she is typically responsible for analyzing the Customer's Organization and business including products and services, for analyzing the customer's market and competitors, for analyzing the users of the customer's products, services, and Applications, for modeling the customer's business and business processes, for developing business cases for potential Applications, for recommending and envisioning new Applications and for documenting and implementing the customer's business strategy.

- **Technology Strategist**. A *Technology Strategist* is the Role that is played when a Person develops the technology strategy for a customer's business. He or she is typically responsible for determining the Customer Organization's technology capabilities and needs, analyzing available technology for relevancy to the Customer Organization, developing the technology strategy for a customer's business, providing technology vision and thought leadership and advising customers on technology decisions.

Systems Administrator

A *Systems Administrator* is the Role that is played when a Person administers a data center and its associated production environments. A Systems Administrator typically has the following Role-specific responsibilities:

- To install, configure, maintain, and upgrade hardware, operating systems, browsers, and other system software (e.g. middleware).
- To detect, diagnose, analyze, resolve, and report related problems.
- To install patches.
- To perform ongoing performance tuning.
- To manage user accounts including user identification, authentication, and authorization.
- To perform system backups.
- To perform system capacity and scalability planning.
- To perform disaster recovery and system rollback.

Technical Leader

A *Technical Leader* is the Role that is played by a Person who is responsible for decision-making in the technical areas of the Project. The Person playing this Role will be responsible for evaluating current Tools offerings and for taking decisions on the technical environment, both hardware and software, for the Project.

To fulfill his or her responsibilities, a technical leader should have the following abilities: be knowledgeable about current Tools; be knowledgeable about current directions in object technology and Component-Based Development; and enjoy the confidence of his/her Team that the choices made will be acceptable.

Technical Writer

A *Technical Writer* is the Role that is played by a Person who writes Documents. These are the end-user support material such as user guides, installation guides and release notes. As well as being responsible for the creation of these Documents, the technical writer is also likely to be able to be of assistance in developing the engineering Documents.

To fulfill his or her responsibilities, a Technical Writer should have excellent writing skills, a good understanding of the Application and a good understanding of the technology itself.

Tester

A *Tester* is the Role that is played by a Person who performs testing. Test plans have to be generated and suites of test cases designed. A set of procedures for testing need to be developed and documented. For the Application, a suite of test cases then needs to be developed and these tests executed and test reports written and evaluated for completeness and effectiveness. All these Tasks fall within the remit of the Tester.

To fulfill his or her responsibilities, a Tester should have the following abilities: Training and Testing Tasks and Techniques, a destructive attitude, and good communication and social skills to interface with developers.

The OPF model contains the following predefined classes of Testers:

- **Build Tester**. A *Build Tester* is responsible for the operational, performance and stress testing of a Build.
- **Class Tester**. A *Class Tester* is responsible for the testing of a Class.
- **Component Tester**. A *Component Tester* is responsible for testing and evaluating (a) home designed and built Components and (b) third party, imported Components.
- **Integration Tester**. An Integration Tester is responsible for performing integration testing of an Increment.
- **Model Tester**. A *Model Tester* is responsible for the testing of a Model.
- **Package Tester**. A *Package Tester* is responsible for the testing of a Package.
- **Regression Tester**. A *Regression Tester* is responsible for performing regression testing of a Component.
- **Test Participant**. A *Test Participant* is a Person, usually external to the Development Team, who participates in the testing of the Application.
- **Usability Tester**. A *Usability Tester* is responsible for performing Usability Testing of a user-interface Component or Application.
- **Website Tester**. A *Website Tester* is responsible for performing all the necessary tests on the Website.

Toolsmith

A *Toolsmith* is the Role played by any Person who is responsible for the development environment of an Endeavor. He or she must work with the Process Engineers to identify Tools to support the development process, evaluate the development Tools, and purchase these Tools where practicable. If Tools cannot be purchased, the Toolsmith is responsible for creating Tools for the Organization. Whether bought or made, the development Tools must be installed and integrated into an IDE (integrated development environment). This IDE must be maintained, usually by the Toolsmith, who is also responsible for answering users' questions regarding the IDE.

To fulfill his or her responsibilities, a Toolsmith needs to have knowledge of the relative strengths and weaknesses of the relevant development Tools.

Trainer

A *Trainer* is the Role played by any Person who is responsible for training the staff of an Endeavor. They are responsible for the identification of the training needs of all the Roles participating in the Endeavor. They then develop the training plan, and organize and oversee the training of their staff in the development process.

To fulfill his or her responsibilities, a Trainer should have the following abilities: (a) technical knowledge of the areas in which training is to be offered, (b) educational skills and experience in adult learning, (c) patience and (d) skill in explaining both simple and difficult concepts to both novices and experts.

The OPF model contains the following predefined classes of Trainers:

- **Classroom Trainer**. A *Classroom Trainer* provides formal, classroom training.
- **Mentor**. A *Mentor* provides informal, one-on-one, on-the-job training.

Usability Engineer

A *Usability Engineer* is the Role that is played by a Person who implements the human interfaces. This Person has overall responsibility for implementing the human interfaces (e.g., GUIs), optimizing the human interface to the platform (i.e., hardware, operating system, and browser) and for collaborating with the Programmers.

User Analyst

A *User Analyst* (a.k.a. user researcher) is the Role played when a Person analyzes users and User Organizations in order to determine the users' desires and needs. His or her responsibilities include classifying and analyzing different kinds of users, analyzing User Organizations, documenting user analyses, developing and performing usability tests and maintaining competency in (and staying abreast of) the latest user experience, methods, Techniques, and Tools.

Tools

A *Tool* is a software Application that is used to generate, document, or manage a Work Product. The OPF contains a number of predefined types of Tools which are divided into Documentation Tools (for example a word processor) and CASE Tools. CASE, standing for Computer-Assisted (or Aided) Software Engineering, is often used as a generic term for any software Tool used to assist in improving the productive development of a software product. These are often divided into *upperCASE*

Tools and *lowerCASE Tools*, the names referring to the early/late stage of the life cycle in which they tend to be used. UpperCASE Tools include Tools for management, configuration, and modeling as well as metrics collection and/or evaluation. LowerCASE Tools are appropriate to coding activities and thus include Tools such as compilers, debuggers, interpreters and the like.

Natural Language Tools

A *Documentation Tool*, such as a word processor, is a Tool used to generate Documents.

CASE Tools

A *Computer-Aided Software Engineering (CASE) Tool* is a Tool specifically designed to support software engineering. As noted above, these may be either upper- or lowerCASE Tools.

UpperCASE Tools

An *upperCASE Tool* is a CASE Tool that works above the code level. The OPF includes definitions for:

- Configuration Management Tools
- Documentation Management Tools
- Metrics Tools
- Modeling Tools
- Requirements Management Tools.

LowerCASE Tools

A *lowerCASE Tool* is a CASE Tool that works at the code level. The OPF includes definitions for:

- compilers
- browsers
- debuggers
- interpreters
- JavaDoc (for generating documentation in a Java programming environment).

Development Environment

As well as being individually useful, Tools are often grouped together in an integrated fashion such that they can easily transfer information between individual Tools within the same Development Environment. Two terms often used are:

- A *Development Environment*, which is a collection of Tools used to develop an Application.
- An *Integrated Development Environment* (IDE), which is a Development Environment in which the Tools are integrated to work together (e.g., the output of one Tool is the input of another).

Indirect Producers

An *Indirect Producer* is any Producer that indirectly produces Work Products. The OPF comes with the following predefined classes of Indirect Producers:

- Team
- Organization.

Teams

Teams are cohesive aggregations of Roles that collaborate to perform the Tasks necessary to generate a cohesive collection of Work Products. Teams may be either atomic (i.e., composed directly of Roles) or aggregate (i.e., composed of subTeams).

Teams should have the following characteristics. They should be cohesive, generating a well-integrated collection of products; and they should be complete, containing all of the Roles necessary to generate the products. A Team should also have high internal coupling, signifying the high degree of collaboration among the Team members, together with low external coupling to other Teams, so that Teams can work relatively indepently. Finally, a Team should have a well-defined interface, allowing other Teams to interact with it without being impacted when the implementation of the Team changes (e.g., Team membership changes, Team member Tasks are given new implementations or Techniques).

Each Team is characterized by its definition, its responsibilities and its membership. The membership of a Team is determined by the size and complexity of the Application, the available budget and the availability of appropriate staff.

Individual Team members have personality characteristics and their own individual skill set. While there are many ways to categorize people's traits, the approach suggested by Belbin[3] and used in DSDM[4] is advocated here in order to identify both strengths and weaknesses in order to avoid areas in which the weakness will be a disadvantage; sometimes to build on a second strength in order to complement another's major strength; and to construct Teams in the clear knowledge that some strengths are complementary and others incompatible. For instance,

3 Belbin, R.M. (1981) *Management Teams* and (1993) *Team Roles at Work*, Butterworth Heinemann.

4 Stapleton, J. (1997) *DSDM: Dynamic Systems Development Method. The Method in Practice*, Addison-Wesley.

clearly two individuals who are strong "movers and shakers" is probably a recipe for disaster as is a Team full of conciliators (but no leaders).

Teams should be empowered to make decisions and as far as possible be autonomous and proactive with a focus on solutions. Small Teams often work best; with larger Teams, the overheads associated with inter-Team member communication are often just too large. The Team culture is created by the Team, not imposed on it, and social Team-building exercises are to be encouraged.

An Organizational Chart is often used to document the overall structure of the Project in terms of its Teams, although we should note that only a small percentage of the relationships that exist between Teams are often documented.

The OPF comes with a list of predefined classes of Teams. The characteristics of some of these are now described briefly.

Architecture Team

An *Architecture Team* is the Project subTeam that is responsible for an Architecture. The OPF suggests the need for four types of Architecture Team: Business Architecture Team, Software Architecture Team, System Architecture Team and Web System Architecture Team.

Business Architecture Team

The *Business Architecture Team* is the Project subTeam that is responsible for the Architecture of the Business Model. Specifically, the Business Architecture Team is responsible for developing and documenting the overall Architecture of the business and for maintaining the Business Architecture Document. It is important that the focus of this Team is not software-related. The Business Model and its Architecture is *totally* within the business domain.

Software Architecture Team

The *Software Architecture Team* is the Project subTeam that is responsible for the Software Architecture. Specifically, the Software Architecture Team is responsible for developing and documenting the overall Software Architecture including both the Domain and Infrastructure Architectures; and for creating and documenting the major architectural design decisions. The software Architecture Team is also responsible for ensuring consistency of the package designs with the overall Software Architecture and of the overall Software Architecture with reusable corporate software Components. This Team also supplies members to the Change Control Board and is responsible for the development and maintenance of the Software Architecture Document. The Team also needs to inspect both the Software Requirements Specifications and the Package Design Document. Finally, they are responsible for developing and maintaining the Team Schedule.

The Software Architecture Team typically consists of a Software Architecture Team Leader, the Software Architect(s), an OO Methodologist(s) and a Reuse Librarian.

System Architecture Team

The *System Architecture Team* is the Project subTeam that is responsible for the System Architecture. Specifically, the System Architecture Team has the following responsibilities: (a) produce the overall System Architecture including both the Domain and Infrastructure Architectures, (b) make the major system-level architectural design decisions, (c) Document the System Architecture in the System Architecture Document, (d) ensure the consistency of the Software and Hardware Architectures with the overall System Architecture, (e) ensure the consistency of overall System Architecture with reusable corporate Components, (f) supply members to the Change Control Board, (g) inspect the System Requirements Specifications and (h) develop and maintain the Team Schedule.

Web System Architecture Team

The *Web System Architecture Team* is the Project subTeam responsible for the overall shape of the Website. This includes development of the Information Architecture and the way in which it couples with the Functional Architecture of the system. It does not extend to detailed consideration of actual content. In designing the Architecture, the Team will also need to take into account the impact of performance issues such as response times, throughput, and scalability.

Business Engineering Team

The *Business Engineering Team* is most useful in business modeling and business re-engineering Projects but also as the pre-technology component of a software or software-intensive system development. There are three areas that need to be addressed by Component Teams:

Branding Strategy Team

The Branding Strategy Team is the Team that produces the customer's digital brand and associated strategy. The Branding Strategy Team typically has the following responsibilities:

- Analyze factors influencing the digital brand strategy.
- Produce the customer's digital brand strategy.

Business Strategy Team

The Business Strategy Team is the Team that produces the Customer Organization's new business strategy during the activities of Business Engineering. The Business Strategy Team typically has the following responsibilities:

- Analyze factors influencing business strategy.
- Recommend new Business Models with improved business processes.
- Recommend new organizational structures.
- Develop reusable intellectual capital.

Technology Strategy Team

The Technology Strategy Team is the Team that produces the customer's technology strategy.

Change Control Board (CCB)

The *Change Control Board* (CCB) is the Team that is responsible for approving proposed changes to a baseline. The CCB evaluates the impact of proposed changes to the configuration and approves or rejects proposed changes to the configuration, including defects reported to them by the Test Team.

The Change Control Board typically has the following membership: Configuration Manager (Team Leader), Requirements Engineer, Architect, and Independent Tester.

Component Acquisition and Integration Team

The *Component Acquisition and Integration Team* is the Team responsible for both identifying and procuring Components from third-party vendors and for integrating these together as well as with in-house developed Components.

Configuration Management Team

The *Configuration Management Team* is responsible for configuration management including:

- *Configuration Identification* – the identification and designation of Components as configuration items and the identification of baselines.
- *Configuration Control* – the management of changes to baselined configuration items including requesting, evaluating the impact of, approving/rejecting and implementing changes.
- *Configuration Status Accounting* – the recording and reporting of information needed to effectively manage a configuration. This consists of identifying the configuration items and baselines, and managing the documentation of (a) the status of proposed changes, deviations, and waivers to the configuration and (b) the implementation status of approved changes.
- *Configuration Auditing* – the auditing of a baseline to verify if it is complete, correctly identified and properly versioned.

A Configuration Management Team is responsible for maintaining an effective Configuration Management Activity including configuration identification, configuration control, configuration status accounting and configuration auditing; for producing and maintaining the configuration management plan or the associated section of the system or software development plan; and for overseeing the configuration management Programmes of suppliers and subcontractors.

The Configuration Management Team typically has, as members, the Configuration Manager (Team Leader) and the Build Integrator.

Database Team

The *Database Team* is charged with all aspects of data/object storage by use of persistence. Many developers still use relational databases for persistent storage of objects although objectbases have been available for many years and, more recently, object-relational databases. This Team is responsible for choosing the appropriate database product and for managing it effectively and efficiently.

Deployment Team

The *Deployment Team* is responsible for taking the tested Application and ensuring that it operates correctly and successfully in its production environments. This involves deciding on an appropriate strategy for "phasing in" the new Application when it is to replace an existing one or when it is replacing a manual system. Consideration must be given to strategies such as a rapid switchover to a period of parallel running of the new and old systems. The Team must be customer-focussed since it is an important link between the Software Development Organization and the clients.

Documentation Team

The *Documentation Team* is the Project subTeam that is responsible for supporting the documentation of the software. The Documentation Team has the responsibility for creating and keeping up-to-date documentation (of Requirements, of the Business Model, of the System Model, of the Implementation Model and the user manual(s)).

The Documentation Team performs the following activities: (a) liaising with the Product Development Teams to ensure adequate and current knowledge of the product; (b) creating all necessary Documents and (c) using Version Control in updating all Documents. The documentation usually consists of the Documentation Team Leader and Technical Writers.

Environment Team

The *Environment Team* is the Project subTeam responsible for creating the development and production environments in which the Application will be developed. They are responsible for choice of CASE Tools, debuggers, testing Tools and so on, perhaps integrated together as a suite of Tools or an IDE (integrated development environment).

The Environment Team therefore performs the following activities: (a) identifying possible support Tools, (b) evaluating the available products from vendors, (c) identifying vendor support and likely long-term stability of the vendor company, (d) taking a decision on which Tools to recommend for purchase, and (e) deploying the appropriate Hardware and Software Components.

Hardware Development Team

A *Hardware Development Team* is responsible for fabricating new hardware components. In particular they need to understand and be able to use various hardware platforms, networks and peripheral devices such as CD, DVD, backup facilities and so on. They are responsible for analyzing these Requirements and for constructing the tender Documents and then for initiating and managing the competitive tendering process and, from that, recommending and purchasing the appropriate hardware for acquisition.

Hardware Prototyping Team

A *Hardware Prototyping Team* is responsible for testing and evaluating hardware by use of a prototyping approach.

Integration Team

An *Integration Team* is responsible for all aspects of integration. This will include planning for and executing the strategy for the involvement of third-party Components into the Organization; for integrating sections of the Application, perhaps developed as Packages, together; and for ensuring a smooth integration of new systems with existing Applications.

Management Team

The *Management Team* is responsible for performing administrative management on an Endeavor. The Management Team has the responsibility for managing Project Teams directly; for managing risk; and for ensuring that the Requirements are achieved.

The Management Team comprises the Administrative Manager, Project or Programme Manager, Technical Leaders, and the Scheduler.

On large Projects, there are likely to be one to three specialist subTeams:

- Hardware Management Team
- Software Management Team.

Hardware Management Team

A *Hardware Management Team* is responsible for the hardware management. In particular they need to have knowledge of various hardware platforms, networks and peripheral devices such as CD, DVD, backup facilities and so on.

Software Management Team

A *Software Management Team* is responsible for all aspects of software construction and delivery to the client.

Metrics Team

A *Metrics Team* is responsible for collecting, analyzing, and publishing Endeavor Metrics. A Metrics Team typically comprises the Metrics Team Leader and one or more Metrics Analysts.

Package Team

Each *Package Team* is a Project subTeam that is responsible for the development of an individual Package or a cohesive collection of related Packages. This subTeam consists of the Package Team Leader, Package Modelers and Class Owners.

Peer Programmer Team

A *Peer Programmer Team* is a Project subTeam that is responsible for a cohesive collection of Classes. It is responsible for designing, coding and unit testing the Classes. The subTeam usually comprises two Class Owners, although in some processes (e.g. XP), the notion of class "ownership" is deliberately weakened.

Process Team

The *Process Team* is the Endeavor subTeam that is responsible for the development process. Its membership usually comprises the Process Team Leader, the OO Methodologist and the Process Engineer.

Project Team

The *Project Team* is the overall Team that is responsible for creating all Project Work Products. The Project Team typically has the following composition: Configuration Management Team, Documentation Team, Hardware Development Team, Independent Test Team, Management Team, Process Team, Software Development Team, Software Requirements Team, System Development Team and System Requirements Team.

Project initiation Team

The *Project Initiation Team* is the Project subTeam that is responsible for initiating the Project including: developing the Vision Statement and the development process. This is done by tailoring and instantiating the Object-Oriented Development Process Framework and identifying and obtaining the development environment. This Team is also likely to be responsible for the provision of initial training as well as developing the initial Systems Requirements and System Architecture and the initial Project Estimates and Project Schedule.

A Project Initiation Team typically has the following composition: Project Initiation Team Leader, Management Team, Metrics Team, Process Team, Project Initiation Team, System Architecture Team and System Requirements Team.

Quality Team

The *Quality Team* is the Project subTeam that is responsible for independently evaluating and reporting the quality of the Application development process and Work Products. It is composed of the Quality Team Leader and one or more Quality Engineers.

Requirements Team

The following describes three identified kinds of Requirements Team, in the OPF: (a) Hardware Requirements Team, (b) Software Requirements Team and (c) System Requirements Team:

Hardware Requirements Team

The *Hardware Requirements Team* is the Project subTeam responsible for engineering Hardware Requirements. They need to elicit the overall Requirements for hardware within the contracted system.

Software Requirements Team

The *Software Requirements Team* is the Project subTeam responsible for the Software Requirements. The responsibilities of the Software Requirements Team include eliciting the Software Requirements; analyzing the Software Requirements; specifying the Software Requirements and maintaining the Software Requirements Specifications.

Membership of the Software Requirements Team includes the Software Requirements Team Leader, the Requirements Engineer, the Domain Expert, the Librarian, the Architect and the Application Tester.

System Requirements Team

The *System Requirements Team* is the Project Team responsible for the system-level Requirements including eliciting the System Requirements; analyzing the System Requirements; specifying the System Requirements; and maintaining the system Requirements Specifications.

Reuse Team

The *Reuse Team* is responsible both for the strategic direction and the operational parameters of enjoying the benefits of a reuse-based development environment, whether it is based on Objects or Components. They are responsible for creating and maintaining the reuse repository, for deciding buy or build options and for maintaining (and improving) quality of reusable artefacts.

The members of the Reuse Team will include the Reuse Librarian, a representative Designer and Domain Expert, the Quality Engineer and a Technical Writer. A member from the Development Team, in the Role of an *Application Conscript*, is also advocated in OPEN – a Person who is normally playing the Role of Programmer or Designer but who is assigned part time to the Reuse Team for a short fixed period.

Security Team

The *Security Team* is responsible for all aspects of security. This ranges from how users access their workstations/PCs, the security levels on the filewall, the permissions for file transfer to and from users' machines, and the decision on whether to install a firewall, through to physical security of the machine rooms or users' cubicles.

Software Development Team

The *Software Development Team* is the Project subTeam responsible for developing the Application software. This Team operates via its component Teams in taking responsibility for, *inter alia*, the engineering of the Software Requirements, the development of the Software Architecture and, subsequently, of the software and, finally, the testing of the software. This Team typically comprises (as its component Teams) the Software Requirements Team, the Software Architecture Team, the Software Architecture Team, the Package Team and the Software Test Team.

System Development Team

The *System Development Team* is the Project subTeam responsible for developing the system Application. The System Development Team performs the following Tasks:

- constructing the schedule against which external suppliers will tender;
- managing the tendering process;
- contracting with the preferred software supplier.

Test Team

There are three kinds of Test Team: those with specific expertise in (a) hardware, (b) software and (c) systems and systems integration. Ideally, the members of the Test Team should be independent of the Development Team.

- The *Hardware Test Team* is the Project subTeam responsible for testing the Hardware Components.
- The *Software Test Team* is the Project subTeam responsible for testing the integrated software. Typical membership would be the Software Test Team Leader and Application Testers.
- The Integration Test Team that is responsible for performing software and system integration testing.
- The *System Test Team* is the Project subTeam responsible for testing the integrated system including operational testing, load testing, stress testing etc.
- The *Usability Test Team* is the Project subTeam responsible for testing the usability of the Application.

Training Team

The *Training Team* is responsible for identifying skills shortages and deficiencies and contracting internal or external trainers and mentors to undertake necessary training. Membership of the Team includes the trainers themselves but also representatives of the strategic direction-setters for some training elements. It is after all a strategic decision to adopt a process like OPEN, a specific CASE Tool and one or more OO Languages, to invest in a Component-Based Software Development economy, or to adopt an XP style approach.

Usage Phase Team

The *Usage Phase* follows the delivery of the completed Application to the site and for the use of the business "end-users". This Phase is one of operation but also supports the growth of the product in the business environment. There are four areas to which individual subTeams may be allocated.

Operations Team

The *Operations Team* is the Team that keeps an onsite Application, perhaps including a data center and all of its Applications and Components, operating properly. The Operations Team typically has the following responsibilities:

- Keep the Applications functioning properly.
- Keep the databases functioning properly.
- Keep the hardware environments functioning properly.
- Keep the networks functioning properly.
- Maintain the operations manual.

Maintenance Team

The *Maintenance Team* is the Team that maintains one or more Applications focussing not only on correcting previously unidentified defects but, more importantly, managing the demand for further enhancements to the product. The Maintenance Team typically has the following responsibilities:

- Make minor fixes and enhancements to the Application and its Components.
- Update the associated Development and User Documents to keep them consistent with the Application.
- Pass on requests for major enhancements to the Development Team for the next version of the relevant Application.

Content Management Team

The *Content Management Team* is the Team that manages the content of an Application, particularly relevant to contemporary Websites and Web Applications. The responsibilities of this Team are to perform content management for an Application and to perform content management for a program of related Applications.

Support Team

The *Support Team* provides internal and external user support out of a contact center. The responsibilities of this Team include answering users' questions and registering users' complaints.

User Interface Team

The *User Interface Team* is charged with creating the GUI for the software. Members of the Team need skills which are largely not technical but focus on issues of usability. Their concerns must reflect those of the end-users (rather than the customers but in the context of the customer's stated Requirements), taking into account their skills levels and the way they *wish* to use the forthcoming product. The job is easier if the user group is small and/or identifiable. For Teams involved in producing shrink-wrapped software for the mass market, the issues of usability must rely on information gained by random sampling of the end-user population.

Web Development Team

The *Web Development Team* comprises Team members who possess skills for handling all the necessary architectural, graphics and technical aspects of Web development. The Team is responsible not only for the look and feel of the Website, but also the technical aspects such as response time and interface to backend transaction processing systems. Members of the Team include the Graphic Designer, the Web Designer, the Web Architect and preferably some members of the Application-focussed Development Team (particularly if both Website and Application are being synchronously and newly developed).

XP-style Team

When using a lightweight methodology such as XP or a Version of OPEN that mimics this style, the Team that is needed is essentially an aggregation of several Peer Programmer Teams – except that the pairing is fluid.

In an *XP-style Team* (which must be small – less than ten), everyone is paired with someone. While there are many Roles played by Team members, two important categories are the Programmer and the User, representing the technical and business aspects of software development. It is important that the user is fully involved in the process. They will most likely play the Role of Tester and must learn how to write stories – narratives from which the Programmers can implement the software. All other Roles are played by Team members. This means that a successful XP-style Team is one which is highly cohesive and mutually supportive. It is therefore easily disrupted by anyone who "doesn't fit in".

Organization

An *Organization* is a large Indirect Producer consisting of one or more Teams. The OPF comes with the following predefined classes of Organizations:

- *Customer Organization* – an Organization that funds Application development by a Development Organization. The customer provides the Requirements and the resources for the Development Organization to be able to deliver the product.
- *Development Organization* – an Organization that develops one or more Applications. Ideas for Applications may come from internal sources or may be from Customer Organizations.
- *Maintenance Organization* – the Organization responsible for maintaining existing Applications. This logical Organization may be the same physical Organization as the Development Organization but in which the Organization is playing a different Role.
- *Marketing Organization* – an Organization that markets Applications to Customer Organizations. It is also responsible for generating the Application Vision Statement and the System Marketing Requirements.
- *Reuse Organization* – the Project-independent Organization that is responsible for Enterprise reuse including documentation, deliverable software, and test software. Its membership is, typically, that of the Librarian, the Class Owner and the Toolsmith together with representation from the Support Organization and the User Organization.
- *Support Organization* – an Organization that supports Customer and User Organizations. This might include services, such as staffing helpdesks or contact centers, or sending technicians to customer sites to correct technical problems.
- *User Organization* – an Organization that uses Applications developed by a Development Organization. It may or may not be the same physical Organization as the Customer Organization. The difference is seen in the fact that members of the User Organization are those who actually use the created software on a daily basis.
- *Vendor Organization* – an Organization whose main purpose is to supply third-party hardware or software (Applications and Components) to the Development Organization.
- *Partner Organization* – an Organization which collaborates in some way with the Development or Customer Organization.
- *Subcontracter Organization* – an Organization that subcontracts a part of the development from the Development Organization.

Endeavors

Affiliated with Producers, particularly Indirect Producers, are *Endeavors*. An Endeavor is a business venture undertaken to meet a specific business mission. The OPF comes with the following predefined classes of Endeavors:

- *Project* – a Project is an Endeavor that consists of all Activities directly related to the development and maintenance of an individual Application. For software development, this is often the prime focus. Project Teams are created in order to create a specific Application; Endeavors are often resourced at this Project level.
- *Programme* – a Programme is an Endeavor consisting of a set of related Projects that are managed as a group. For example, product-line software development would fall into this category. When developing a Programme, the Organization can amortize its investments (people, hardware, software Tools) over many Projects and can benefit from a strategic approach to reuse and domain modeling.
- *Enterprise* – an Enterprise is an Endeavor consisting of all Programmes when managed as a group. Such an Endeavor may collect together all the Programmes within a particular Organization or, more recently, cross organizational boundaries. Virtual Enterprises no longer adhere to the notion of organizational boundaries. They flourish and change as companies create partnerships around the world for specific, sometimes short-duration, purposes.

E Work Units

In OPEN, Work Units describe Activities, Tasks and Techniques, as described in Chapter 5. The list of Tasks and Techniques provides a "pick-list" of recommended approaches. These are discussed below and, in more detail, in other OPEN publications (see Bibliography for details).

Activities

While Tasks are crucial for actually building and delivering Applications and other Work Products, their number (in any one process) is likely to be too large for "seeing the big picture". Thus, we recommend grouping together a number of logically related Tasks into larger, now heterogeneous, collections called Activities. In general, existing Activities tend to be fairly stable while not constraining the creation of new Activities if these are deemed appropriate. In this Appendix, we start with a number of those stabilized Activities. However, it is important to realize that the creation and stabilization of these Activities has not resulted from a single Project nor even from a single Project kind. Some have come from simple, small Projects in which Project management is highly integrated and not explicitly drawn out as an Activity; others, on the other hand, relate to significantly larger-scale Endeavors in which there are multiple Teams, a formal Project Management and reporting structure together with medium to high ceremony.

Thus it is crucial to appreciate that *some pairs of Activities are mutually exclusive* in their use – they may overlap or one may be appropriate for a large Project and the second only for a small Project. Furthermore, some of these Activities overlap with some of the Tasks. For example, Project 1 may use a Project Management Activity in which reside Tasks A-E; Project 2, in contrast, may have no explicit Project Management Activity but rather Project Management Tasks A-E will be found integrated into several other Activities. On some Projects, for example, Project Planning and Project Initiation will be treated as Activities, whereas on others they will be Tasks within a Project Management Activity. Thus, although we document Activities in a roughly sequential fashion, the non-orthogonality of each subsection should be remembered and taken into account when organizing your own Tasks using these or other Activities.

Project Management

Project Management is the application of knowledge, experience, Tools, and Techniques to manage a Project so that stakeholder's needs and expectations regarding the Project are met or exceeded. The typical objectives of the Project Management Activity (when used) are to ensure that:

- Overall Project Requirements are met.
- Project Activities reinforce rather than conflict with each other.

The Project Management Activity typically involves the Project Management Team performing Tasks associated with, for example:

- Project planning (plan development, communication and execution).
- Contract management (subcontractor and partner selection and oversight).
- Cost management (budgeting, cost containment and cost reporting).
- Customer relationship management (status reporting, in-process reviews and scope control).
- Human resource management (organizational structuring, staffing and team development, and task allocation).
- Resource management (software and hardware source selection, evaluation and procurement).
- Schedule management (time estimation, schedule development and control).
- Establish policies (e.g. for component acquisition, COTS and outsourcing).

The Project Management Activity results in the production of one or more of the following Work Products:

- Management plan (e.g., business modeling plan, system development plan)
- Project cost reports
- Project organization chart
- Project status reports
- Project schedule.

In rare cases where Project Management is *not* selected as an Activity, then two typical and useful activities are often created called *Project Initiation* and *Project Planning.*

Project Initiation

Beginning a Project follows from discussions of an existing business problem in the context of the business. It is largely a business issue and, as such, is frequently omitted from other discussions of development process. This may be a standalone Activity but is more likely to be a part of Project Management.

Project Planning

This is focussed on planning the Phases, Builds, and Milestones. Prioritizing and sequencing Components for the Build Activity is an important part of Project Planning. This may be a standalone Activity but is more likely to be a part of Project Management.

Configuration Management

Configuration Management, again not always seen explicitly in practice, is the Activity involved with the management and baselining of configurations of configuration items. The objectives of the Configuration Management Activity include:

- Ensuring that the configurations of major Work Products are identified.
- Ensuring that the iteration of configuration items is performed in a controlled manner that minimizes disruption within the Project or Programme.
- Ensuring that the current status of the configurations is captured and distributed to all relevant Stakeholders.

The Configuration Management Activity involves the Configuration Management Team performing Tasks focussed on:

- Configuration management planning.
- Configuration identification.
- Configuration control.
- Version control.
- Configuration status accounting.
- Configuration auditing.

The Configuration Management Activity results in the production of one or more of the following Work Products:

- Configuration identification report
- Change request form
- Configuration status report
- Configuration audit report.

Risk Management

Risk Management is the Activity involved with all aspects of managing project risk. Again, on some Projects, this is not seen to be important enough to be an independent Activity. The objectives of the Risk Management Activity, when used, include:

- Identifying risks to project success
- Avoiding risks where ever practical
- Mitigating the impact of risks that cannot be avoided.

The Risk Management Activity involves the Project Team performing the following Tasks:

- Identify potential risks.
- Analyze risks.
- Document risk potential.
- Establish risk avoidance strategy.
- Mitigate risk.

The Risk Management Activity results in the production of the following risk management Work Product:

- Risk management plan.

Metrics Engineering

Metrics Engineering is the Activity of involving all aspects of the Metrics that are used on a Project. The objectives of the Metrics Management Activity include:

- Ensuring that essential metrics are properly collected, analyzed, and reported.
- Ensuring that the use of metrics on the project is cost-effective.
- Minimizing the disruption that can be caused by metrics collection and reporting.
- Ensuring that project estimates of project productivity and progress are accurate.
- Ensuring that project estimates of the quality of the Work Products are accurate.

The Metrics Management Activity involves the Metrics Team performing the following Tasks:

- Assess metrics needs.
- Set up metrics collection programme.
- Collect metrics data.
- Analyze metrics data.
- Report on metrics data.

This leads to the Project manager acting on the Metrics Report. The Metrics Management Activity results in the production of one or more of the following Metrics Management Work Products:

- Metrics plan
- Productivity/performance reports
- Quality reports.

Quality Engineering

Quality Engineering is the Activity of ensuring that the Project will satisfy the Stakeholder's needs and expectations regarding quality. The objectives of the Quality Engineering Activity include:

- To ensure that deliverable Work Products have the required quality (Quality Control).
- To ensure that Project-specific process has the required quality (Quality Assurance).

The Quality Engineering Activity involves the following Producers and Tasks:

- The Quality Team performs the following Tasks:
  - Specify quality goals
  - Evaluate quality of the process, Quality Assurance (QA)
  - Evaluate the quality of the Work Products, Quality Control (QC)
  - Undertake in-process review (Quality Control)
  - Undertake post-implementation review (a retrospective)

The Quality Engineering Activity results in the production of one or more of the following quality engineering Work Products:

- Quality management plan
- Quality reports, which may include Inspection reports, an Inspection summary report and a Process inspection report.

Process Engineering

Process Engineering is the Activity involved with all aspects of instituting and using an Endeavor-appropriate process (a.k.a. method or methodology). The objectives of the Process Engineering Activity include:

- Instantiate the OPF to meet the specific needs of the Endeavor.
- Iterate the Endeavor process (i.e., Endeavor-specific instantiation of the OPF) as needed.
- Ensure the proper use of the Endeavor process.
- Capture process-specific lessons learned.

The Process Engineering Activity involves the process Team performing the following Tasks:

- Maintain process framework
- Instantiate process framework to construct the process
  - Tailor the process

- Document the process
- Communicate the process to stakeholders
- Enforce the process
- Report on status of process.

The Process Engineering Activity results in the production of one or more of the following kinds of Work Products:

- Process Description Document
- Conventions:
  - Standards
  - Templates
  - Inspection checklists
  - Procedures
  - Guidelines
- Process status report.

Environment Engineering

Environment Engineering is the Activity involved with all aspects of installing and maintaining the environments used on a Project. On small Projects this may not be seen to be worth identifying as an explicit Activity, although the associated Tasks must still be performed. The objectives of the Environment Engineering Activity include:

- Ensure the existence of the Project environments
- Ensure the quality of the Project environments.

The Environment Engineering Activity involves the Environment Team performing the following Tasks:

- Environment design
- Tool evaluation and selection
- Environment documentation
- Environment installation
- Environment maintenance.

The Environment Engineering Activity results in the production of one or more of the following kinds of environment engineering Work Products:

- Documents:
  - Project environments description
  - Tool selection matrix

- Environments:
  - Development environment
  - Integration environment
  - Functional test environment
  - Load and stress test environment
  - Staging environment
  - Production environment (client, data center, contact center).

Website Development

Website Development is the Activity which brings together all the Tasks involving the development, maintenance and management of a corporate Website which may or may not include access to back-end transaction processing systems. The objectives of the Website Development Activity include:

- Create a high quality Website
- Keep the Website up to date
- Ensure that site standards are met as the Website evolves.

The Website Management Activity involves the Website Development Team, consisting of, at least, a Web Designer, a Graphics Designer and a Website Prototype Developer, performing the following Tasks:

- Design Web system Architecture.
- Create navigation map for Website.
- Define acceptance criteria for Website.
- Design and implement content management strategy.
- Design and implement personalization strategy.
- Create content (on Website).
- Integrate content with user interface.
- Build White Site/Wireframe prototype.
- Design Website standards.
- Define Website testing strategy.
- Undertake testing of Website.

In undertaking these Tasks, Websites have some individualistic characteristics that need to be considered. These include the effects of unpredictable volumes of Website traffic, high and irregular numbers of users, ease of use and integration to back-end systems.

For B2B (business-to-business), there are further considerations, including

- Supply chain and flow analysis
- Role analysis

- Identification of business lines
- Scenario analysis
- Reference model development
- Business rule and usage definition
- Rich data model
- Work Flow design
- Drivers to determine protocol.

The Website Management Activity results in the production of one or more of the following Work Products:

- Website design guidelines
- Web pages
- Website
- Website content
- Statistics regarding response times and accessibility.
- Graphics
- Audio and video files
- Scripts
- CGI programs
- Usability test materials
- Storyboards
- Low and high fidelity prototypes
- Information architecture
- Site map and navigation diagrams.

With the current rapid evolution of the industry's understanding of developing on and for the Web, these Web management Work Units are still evolving. At present, they can either be viewed as a single package (as an Activity, as described above) or as Web extensions to existing Work Units already defined for "regular" Application development.[1] There is still much disagreement about whether Web Application development is essentially just one more type of Application development or significantly different. OPEN can support either viewpoint equally easily.

1 As someone who has been a chief architect who has worked on corporate processes at two major Web development and eCommerce package integration companies, Donald Firesmith personally feels that (a) Web development is just a different kind of application, (b) the OPF is flexible enough to cover Web development via process component selection and process construction often without adding a new Activity, and (c) adding new Roles, Tasks, Techniques, and Work Products (as has been done) is the best approach.

Requirements Engineering

Requirements Engineering is the subdiscipline of systems software engineering which addresses all aspects of Requirements including identifying the location and sources of Requirements, eliciting the Requirements, analyzing the Requirements specifying cross-checking to ensure consistency and formally documenting them. There is much active work in OO Requirements Engineering research at present.

In OPEN, Requirements Engineering is the Activity that is involved with all aspects of producing and maintaining Requirements including operational Requirements, data Requirements, quality Requirements and design constraints. The objectives of the Requirements Engineering Activity are to:

- Produce a formally documented consensus among all Project stakeholders (e.g., client, users, management, developers) concerning the Requirements for the next Version (incremental iteration) of the Application.
- Provide input (e.g., number of use cases and use case paths) to the Project cost and schedule estimation Task.
- Provide a basis (e.g., use cases and use case paths) for the scheduling of the Project Phases and Builds.
- Maximize the quality of the Requirements (e.g., correctness, completeness, consistency, testability and understandability).
- Maximize the productivity of the Requirements Teams (e.g., reuse of Requirements, reuse of conventions and existence of examples).

The Requirements Engineering Activity involves the Requirements Team performing the following Tasks:

- Identify client's vision.
- Identify source of Requirements.
- Identify reusable Requirements.
- Elicit Requirements.
- Analyze Requirements.
- Specify Requirements.
- Maintain trace between Requirements and the Architecture, design, and test suites.

The Requirements Engineering Activity results in the production of one or more of the following Requirements Work Products:

- Application Vision Statement
- Glossary
- System Requirements specification
- External interface specification
- Software Requirements specification
- Use case specification.

Architecting

Architecting (a.k.a. Architecture) is the Activity involved with all aspects of producing and maintaining the Architectures (i.e., strategic design decisions) of an Application (or business). The objectives of the Architecting Activity are to:

- Produce a formally documented consensus among the Project Stakeholders (e.g., client, management, developers) concerning the overall structure and major mechanisms of the next Version (incremental iteration) of the Application.
- Provide input (e.g., number, size and complexity of system Components) to the Project cost and schedule estimation Task.
- Provide a basis (e.g., Components) for the scheduling of the Project Phases and Builds.
- Maximize the quality of the Architecture:
  - Correctness, completeness, consistency and understandability
  - Meeting architecturally significant operational Requirements
  - Meeting architecturally significant data Requirements
  - Meeting architecturally significant quality Requirements (e.g., scalability, operational availability, security)
  - Meeting architecturally significant design constraints.
- Maximize the productivity of the Architecture Teams (e.g., reuse of reference Architectures, reuse of Architecture conventions and existence of example Documents).

The Architecting Activity involves the Architecture Team performing the following Tasks:

- Create a system Architecture (Component analysis, mechanism analysis).
- Create a software Architecture.
- Create the information Architecture.
- Create the database Architecture.
- Document the Architecture.
- Prototype the Architecture.
- Enforce the Architecture.
- Manage subsystems.

The Architecting Activity results in the production of one or more of the following Architecture Work Products:

- Enterprise Architecture Document
- Programme Architecture Document
- Business Architecture Document

- System Architecture Document (system Components, major mechanisms, technology selection)
- Software Architecture Document
- Web system Architecture Document
- Hardware Architecture Document
- Information Architecture Document
- Database Architecture Document
- Security Plan.

Design

Design (a.k.a. Designing) is the Activity involved with all aspects of producing and maintaining the tactical design of an Application. The objectives of the Design Activity include:

- Produce a formally documented detailed design of the major aspects (e.g., databases, data centers and human interfaces) of the Application.
- Maximize the quality of the design:
  - Correctness, completeness, consistency and understandability
  - Meeting the Requirements (operational and quality)
  - Meeting the design constraints
  - Conforming to the Architecture.
- Maximize the productivity of the design Teams (e.g., reuse of existing designs, reuse of design conventions and existence of example Documents).

The Design Activity involves a number of Teams:

- The Database Team performs the following Tasks:
  - Design the database Model
  - Map the logical database schema
  - Design and implement physical database.
- The Environment Team performs the following Tasks:
  - Design the data center(s).
  - Design the contact center(s).
- The Software Development Team performs the following Tasks:
  - Construct the Object Model
  - Develop Business Object Model (BOM)
  - Identify CIRTs
  - Capture the design

  - Document the design
  - Optimize the design
  - Refactor.
- The User Interface Team performs the following Tasks:
  - Prototype the human interface
  - Design the user interface
  - Undertake usability design
  - Capture the design
  - Document the design.
- The Design Inspection Team performs the following Task:
  - Evaluate the design.

The Design Activity results in the production of one or more of the following design Work Products; for example:

- CRC cards
- Database Design Document
- Framework User's Manual
- UI design Document
- Software Design Document
- White Site/Wireframe Prototype.

In some situations, there is no Design Activity *per se*, the Design Tasks being allocated to the Build Activity (q.v.).

Component Selection

The Activity of Component Selection focusses on identifying Components that already exist in a repository (in-site or at a vendor's site) and that may be useful in the current Application development. It requires identifying not only the required Component(s) but also the necessary granularity.

The Component Selection Activity involves the Software Development Team performing the following Tasks:

- Establish policy on Component acquisition.
- Screen the candidate list of Components.
- Evaluate the potential Components.
- Choose appropriate Components.
- Integrate Components.

In a CBD development this is a prime focus of the whole life cycle description but if Components are only a minor constituent in an OO development, the importance of

Component Selection is diminished. Traditionally, this is viewed as an essential Task that is part of the Architecting Activity, instead of as an Activity in its own right.

Build

This is a technical, highly iterative Activity and is used as an alternative formulation to separate Design and Implementation Activities. It is often used since it emphasizes the iterative nature of the software construction part of the life cycle.

The Build Activity[2] may have several subactivities. Typically three may be described in a Management Information Systems (MIS) domain (although there are many other possibilities for appropriate subactivities, particularly in different domains like building real-time control systems):

- *Evolutionary development.* This is the seamless Requirements analysis, design, code cycle as exemplified, for instance, in the fountain model, together with verification and validation.
- *User review.* A planned iteration (usually around three cycles overall) between the development Team and the users. In other words, the end-users are intimately involved with the software development and have several opportunities to give the development Team feedback and to trial interim releases as they are incrementally delivered through these planned iterations.
- *Consolidation* is a user+developer finalization after all the formal reviews have been satisfactorily accomplished. It might also consider integration issues although these are often dealt with separately under the Integration Activity. An alternative to a separate build Activity is to keep the standard Requirements engineering, architecting, design, implementation, integration, and testing activities and to achieve the same effect by using short iterative, incremental Builds during the construction Phase.

Implementation

Implementation is the Activity involved with the production of system Components. The objectives of the Implementation Activity are to:

- Acquire or produce the data Components.
- Acquire or Programme software Components.
- Acquire or fabricate any hardware Components.
- Deliver the functioning Components to the Integration Team for deployment on the integration environment.

2 Older methodologies, such as Object Modeling Techniques (OMT) basically restricted themselves to the scope of the Build Activity.

The Implementation Activity involves the following Producers and Tasks:

- The Software Development Team performing the following Tasks:
  - Software reuse
  - Programming
  - Software iteration:
    - Debugging
    - Extension
    - Refactoring
  - Software evaluation.
- The Hardware Development Team performing the following Tasks:
  - Hardware reuse
  - Hardware development
  - Hardware configuration
  - Hardware evaluation.

The Implementation Activity results in the production of one or more of the following implementation Work Products:

- Data Components.
- Software Components.
- Hardware Components.

Integration

Integration is the Activity involving all aspects of integrating system Components to form an executable Version of an Application. The objectives of the Integration Activity are to:

- Ensure that the Application is properly integrated prior to system testing.
- Regularly and frequently integrate the software and data Components from various Teams into an executable code build.
- Deliver the integrated code build to the configuration management.
- Deploy the integrated code build to the various test environments.
- Integrate the Hardware Components and produce the networks.
- Build the data and contact centers.
- Report the success or failure of the integration process.
- The integration Team performs the following kinds of integration:
  - Software integration
  - System integration.

The Integration Activity involves the following Producers and Tasks:

- The Integration Team performs the following integration Tasks:
  - Plan integration
  - Execute integration plans
  - Report on status of integration.
- The Environment Team performs the following Tasks:
  - Integrate Hardware Components
  - Build data center
  - Build contact center.

The Integration Activity results in the production of one or more of the following implementation Work Products:

- Code build
- Integration Build Plan
- Integration Report
- Increment.

Evaluation

This is the opportunity for a formal review by Team members, users and management. Inspection Techniques are often used and comprehensive "testing" (both technical and managerial/business) is undertaken. The objectives of the Evaluation Activity are to:

- decide whether authorization should be given for the Project to continue
- decide whether delivery of the Increment should be made or not
- identify potentially reusable Components
- review security issues and provide data for audit
- evaluate the current set of Metrics data
- review actual progress against planned progress
- review and approve any exception plans
- review the plan for the next Increment
- identify and review risks and their mitigation.

Alternatively, the Evaluation Activity is typically seen as part of the Quality Control Task and thus a part of the Quality Engineering Activity.

Testing

Testing is obviously an important component of software development and delivery. Although often inadequately funded or exercised, Testing is critical to the quality of the delivered software product. In some approaches, such as a lightweight process, Testing is so highly integrated that it becomes the prime focal point of the process. Then, Testing Tasks (and Techniques) are fully integrated and the execution of individual Testing Tasks may be viewed as post-conditions on other (actually all other) development Activities. In classic information systems developments, Testing is often equated with quality assurance in an old-fashioned sense of being something that occurs after everything else. In an OO and Component-Based Development this is usually regarded as inappropriate. Spreading this sort of testing out across the life cycle and allocating the responsibility for its execution to members of one or more "Testing Teams" leads to the notion that it may be useful to have a Testing Activity. If this is the selected approach, then we typically select a Testing Activity as follows.

Testing is the Activity involved with all aspects of executing a Work Product (e.g., Model, Software Component and Application) in order to cause failures so that the underlying defects may be identified and eliminated. The objectives of the Testing Activity thus include:

- Increase quality by helping identify defects in executable Work Products so that the underlying:
  - Defects in the Work Products can be identified and eliminated.
  - Human errors can be avoided in the future (e.g., via training or iterating the process).
- Maximize the productivity of the Test Teams (e.g., reuse of test harnesses and test cases, reuse of test plans and existence of example documents).

The Testing Activity involves the following Producers performing the following kinds of Testing:

- The Requirements Team, which performs:
  - Model Testing on Requirements (e.g., Use Case) Models
- The Architecture Team, which performs:
  - Model Testing on Architecture Models
- The Software Development Team, which performs:
  - Model Testing
  - Unit Testing
- The Integration Test Team, which performs:
  - Integration Testing
- The System Test Team, which performs:
  - Functional Testing
  - Fail Over and Recovery Testing

  - Performance Testing
  - Load Testing for scalability
  - Stress Testing
  - Portability Testing
- The Security Team, which performs:
  - Security Testing
- The User Experience Team, which performs:
  - Usability Testing
- The Website Development Team, which performs:
  - Website Testing.

The Testing Activity involves Producers performing the following Testing Tasks for each kind of the above kinds of testing:

- Test planning
- Test reuse
- Test design
- Test implementation
- Test capture
- Test execution
- Test reporting.

The Testing Activity results in the production of one or more of the following Test Work Products:

- Documents:
  - Project test plan
  - Test procedure
  - Test report
  - Test harness design document.
- Software:
  - Test harness
  - Test suite
  - Test case
  - Test data.

Deployment

Deployment is the Activity involved with all aspects of placing an Application into production. It includes the planning aspects as well as the "delivery" aspects.

The on-site implementation or deployment of the software needs to be carefully planned. Switchover schemes need to be in place (following the traditional options) as well as user training and user evaluation and feedback. In an incremental delivery environment there is also likely to be potential feedback to the developers.

The objectives of the Deployment Activity include:

- Transfer of control of the Application from the Development Organization to the Client Organization.
- Placing the Application into usage by the User Organizations.

The Deployment Activity involves the following Producers performing the following Tasks:

- The Management Team, which performs the following Task:
  - Deliver product to customer.
- The Deployment Team, which performs the following subTasks:
  - Determine installation process
  - Document installation process
  - Install Application
  - Train users.
- The Project Team should also hold a user-focussed post-deployment review (a "retrospective") aimed at capturing lessons learned.

The Deployment Activity results in the production of one or more of the following Deployment Work Products:

- Deployed Application (e.g. Website)
- Documents:
  - Installation guide
  - Users' manual
  - Release notes
  - Deployment plan
  - Disaster recovery plan
  - Support plan
  - Support reference materials
  - Job aids.

Note that distributed systems are deployed differently from more traditional, non-distributed Applications. In addition, Web-based Applications are not deployed in the true sense at all. They are just made available and users informed.

All the above Activities relate to the Application development i.e. typically at the Project level. The following Activities are more relevant to the Enterprise and Programme levels i.e. closer to the business domain and to strategic issues that cross Project boundaries.

Business Engineering

Business (Re)engineering is the Activity involving all aspects of (re)engineering an Organization's business, especially regarding the Applications it develops and maintains. The objectives of the Business Engineering Activity are to produce and implement an appropriate Organizational Business Model that includes the Organization's:

- business strategy
- branding strategy
- technology strategy.

One component of Business Engineering is typically Business Domain modeling. In domain modeling we expand our horizons beyond the current Application to the more generic domain of knowledge related to the current and future Applications. For instance, if the current Application is creating software support for auctions, our Domain Modeling considers (software equivalents of) all pricing mechanisms. Thus specifics (in an Application) can be made more generic – and thus more reusable – when other similar Applications are envisaged. The benefit gained is of course offset to some degree by the cost of undertaking an analysis of a problem which is currently beyond the scope of a single Project. Yet, the payoff in terms of higher flexibility and adaptability in the future can be immense. Clearly, Domain Modeling is most valuable for product line developments and is of little value if each following Application is likely to be in a different knowledge/problem domain.

Overall, the Business Modeling Activity involves the following Producers and Tasks:

- The Business Strategy Team performs the following Tasks:
  - Customer analysis
  - Market analysis
  - User analysis
  - Domain modeling
  - Modeling and re-engineering business processes.
- The Branding Team performs the following Tasks:
  - Brand development
  - Brand communication.
- The Technology Strategy Team performs the following Tasks:
  - Research technology trends
  - Evaluate and select appropriate technologies
  - Select partners and vendors.

The Business Engineering Activity results in the production of one or more of the following Work Products:

- Business Strategy Work Products:
  - Stakeholder profiles
  - Customer analysis report
  - Market analysis report
  - User profiles
  - User analysis report
  - Proposed applications list
  - Application business cases
  - Programme and Project recommendations.
- Branding Strategy Work Products:
  - Brand strategy document
  - Brand communication plan
  - Brand style guide.
- Technology strategy work product:
  - Technology strategy document.

Reuse Engineering

Reuse Engineering is the Activity involving all organizational-level support for reuse. The objectives of the Reuse Engineering Activity are to:

- Set the organizational reuse policy
- Collect and maintain the Organization's reusable Work Products and supporting documentation
- Maximize the reuse of these Work Products by Projects.

The Reuse Engineering Activity involves the following Producers and Tasks:

- The Reuse Team focusses on appropriate reusable Work Products with respect to their:
  - Identification (including individual consideration for Requirements)
  - Acquisition
  - Development
  - Documentation
  - Evaluation and Certification
  - Maintenance/Management.

They are also responsible for disseminating information regarding reuse potential to all Project personnel.

The Reuse Engineering Activity results in the production of one or more of the following Work Products:

- Reusable Components
- Reusable Component descriptions
- Reuse guidelines
- Reuse status reports
- Project harvest reports.

Programme Management

A Programme is a collection of several related Projects. It is closely akin to the notion of "product line" development. When such a suite of Applications is envisaged, the notion of a Programme allows capital expenses and investments to be larger since they can be amortized across the several Projects in the Programme.

Programme Management is the Activity involving all aspects of managing a Programme of related Projects. The objectives of the Programme Management Activity are to ensure that the:

- Overall Programme Requirements are met.
- Projects comprising the Programme remain consistent and do not unnecessarily constrain each other.

The Programme Management Activity involves the following Producers and Tasks:

- The Programme Management Team performs the following Tasks:
  - Decompose Programme into Projects
  - Identify and allocate Programme funding
  - Plan Programme
  - Report Programme costs
  - Report on Programme status.

The Programme Management Activity results in the production of one or more of the following Work Products:

- Programme plan
- Programme status reports
- Programme debrief reports.

Resource Planning

Resource Planning is a multi-Project consideration and permits resources to be gathered, evaluated and used most wisely when several Projects or a "product line" style of development is being considered. Resource Planning needs to take into account temporal ordering and any associated constraints; Work Units to be constructed; Team structures; choice of hardware and software; training; the role of reuse and the optimum introduction of a metrics programme. Typically this will not be a standalone Activity but part of Programme Management (see above).

Training

Training is the Activity involved with all aspects of providing Stakeholders (developers, maintainers, and users) with the necessary knowledge and expertise to perform their assigned Tasks. The objectives of the Training Activity include ensuring that:

- developers have the necessary knowledge, skills, and expertise to efficiently develop Applications;
- maintainers have the necessary knowledge, skills, and expertise to efficiently maintain Applications;
- users have the necessary knowledge, skills, and expertise to effectively use the Application.

The Training Activity involves the following kinds of training:

- Classroom (lectures)
- Classroom/laboratory (exercises)
- Small Projects (say about an hour) in groups
- Large Teamwork Projects
- On-the-job training/mentoring
- Off-site special training events, usually with a single focus and some interspersed social events.

The Training Activity involves the following Producers and Tasks:

- The training Team considers the aspects of training along the dimensions of:
  - planning
  - analysis of requirements
  - development of training materials
  - execution
  - cost reporting
  - status reporting.

The Training Activity results in the production of one or more of the following training Work Products:

- Training plan
- Training materials
- Training cost reports
- Training status reports.

In the specialized Application of Organizational Transition to OT, there are three activities documented in OPEN: Organization Assessment, Pre-development Acceptance and Technology Insertion.

Organization Assessment

A first Activity when using OPEN to assist in Organizational Transition is to undertake an assessment of the Organization with regard to its skills and other resources that might help (or hinder) it in moving from a traditional development environment to one based on Objects and Components. Such an assessment not only provides a picture "as is" but should also consider providing an answer to the question "Where do we want to get to?"

Tasks typical of this Activity include:

- Assess current state of Organization
- Set transition goals
- Assess transition path
- Assess Organization's resources for transition
- Assess staff skills/knowledge.

Pre-development Acceptance

In Pre-development Acceptance, we need to consider the impacts of rapid culture change and ensure that, once adopted, the new technology is successful. This requires consideration of the potential impact of changes in the Organization's culture, including people, policies, politics and business rules. Cultural change will apply to everyone within the Organization and have a strong impact on his or her roles and responsibilities. Culture change is typically slow but can be accelerated if the decision-makers within the Organization are committed to it and do everything in their capacity to facilitate its occurrence. In addition, management needs to enhance Team productivity, perhaps by adding opportunities for upskilling. The main aim of the Activity is therefore to obtain full acceptance and support from every member of the Development Team who will champion the change.

The main Tasks here are:

- Identify pilot project
- Enhance teamwork
- Create SWAT team
- Effect rapid culture change.

Technology Insertion

Technology Insertion deals with the process of transitioning. In enforcing a new technology, we seek commitment. Once over the inevitable resistance (from at least some), there should be no turning back. The ability of OT/CBD to offer benefits and fulfill promises must be fully and objectively explored and evaluated. There may still be culture change occurring in this Activity but the major Task is really the introduction and enforcement of the newly introduced technology. The two main Tasks in this Activity are therefore:

- Effect rapid culture change
- Introduce and enforce new technology.

Tasks

Tasks are linked to Activities in a fuzzy way using the matrices as described in Chapter 8. The goals of the Task are accomplished by one or more Techniques – again linked in a fuzzy matrix. Although, at least in principle, each Task may contribute to any Activity (in fact one or more Activities), in most Projects there will be a much tighter linkage. In this sense and context, we can loosely group the Tasks under the most logical and typical headings – noting that the reader should not be misled into thinking that these groups are either irrevocable or unique.

Project Management Tasks

Undertake feasibility study is the Task of comparing several possible solutions, taking into account hardware and software, likely technology changes, etc., and making a recommendation about the most feasible, both technically and budgetwise.

Undertake project planning is the Task of planning how to execute the Project. This includes the following subTasks:

- **Develop the overall project plan** is the Task of determining the intended approach to performing the major Project Management Activities and Tasks and creating, iteratively, project plans using, for example, PERT, CPM or Gantt charts or by using the dependencies in the BOM.
- **Develop iteration plan** – while iterations give flexibility, planning for major iterations and increments is vital. This contributes to the development of the project schedule.
- **Develop contingency plan** – creating plans for when things go wrong, from software failure to attacks on the hardware.
- **Develop security policy** – particularly if there is a user need for high levels of traditional security.
- **Consolidate and agree project plans** – to be effective, plans must be agreed by all stakeholders.
- **Maintain plan documentation** is the Task that includes producing, documenting and maintaining a project plan.
- **Communicate plan** is the Task of communicating the plan to all Stakeholders.
- **Execute plan** is the Task of executing the Activities and Tasks documented in the project plan.

Establish change management strategy – how to transition to OO/CBD.

Establish policy on component acquisition – there is a need to have an agreed approach to how and when to acquire outside Components including checks on quality of such third-party products.

Establish policy on COTS – there is a need to have an agreed approach as to what extent third-party COTS (Commercial Off The Shelf) products might be appropriate to be incorporated into the Organization's system development plans.

Establish policy on outsourcing – there is a need to have an agreed approach to how and when to outsource development including checks on quality of such third-party vendors and a clear policy on how the arrangement is to be managed.

Manage contract(s) is the Task of managing all contracts. This includes the following subTasks:

- **Negotiate contract(s)** is the Task of negotiating and signing the contract or statement of work for a Project. This includes contracts between the Development Organization and the Client Organization, any subcontractors and any partners.
- **Select subcontractors and partners** is the Task of selecting appropriate subcontractors or partners to work with the Development Organization on the Project.
- **Oversee subcontractors and partners** is the Task of overseeing the subcontractors and partners to ensure that they are correctly performing their assigned Tasks.
- **Sign off deliverables** is the process of obtaining formal client signoff on each deliverable of the Project.

Manage costs is the Task of ensuring that the cost of the Project is within the budgeted cost. This includes the following subTasks:

- **Create a project budget** is the Task of developing a budget for the Project.
- **Apply cost containment** is the Task of limiting the costs of the Project.
- **Report on project costs** is the Task of regularly reporting financial information on the Project.

Manage the customer relationship is the Task of managing the relationship between the Project and its clients. This includes the following subTasks:

- **Set client expectations** is the Task of ensuring that client expectations regarding the Project and Application are reasonable and accurate.
- **Keep client informed** is the Task of keeping the client informed of the Project status. This includes the following Tasks:
  - **Status reporting** is the Task of regularly reporting the status of the Project.
  - **Hold in-process reviews** is the Task of regularly holding formal reviews of the Project with the client.
- **Address client concerns** is the Task of ensuring that the client's concerns are addressed in a timely manner.
- **Scope control** is the Task of ensuring that the scope of the Project does not inadvertently grow at the expense of the schedule and budget (i.e., scope creep).

Manage human resources is the Task of making effective use of the people involved in the Project. This includes the following subTasks:

- **Create an appropriate organizational structure** is the Task of identifying the Organizational structure of the Project in terms of Teams and major Roles.
- **Project staffing** is the Task of procuring qualified staff for the Project. This includes the following subTasks:
  - Interviewing prospective staff members.
  - Hiring prospective staff members.
  - Assigning staff members to Roles and Teams.
  - Evaluating staff member performance.
  - Specifying individual goals (personal development) – a focus on the individual and helping him/her to extend their skills set.

Identify project roles and responsibilities is the need to identify what Role and responsibilities are required *before* considering which people should play those Roles.

Choose project team is the allocation of Roles to Teams and the allocation of personnel to play these Roles plus an agreement on their responsibilities. Complementary skills sets are important. The nine Team Roles of Belbin[3] can be very usefully employed here.

Allocate tasks is the Task of allocating Tasks to the Project Roles and Teams.

Manage resources is the Task of procuring goods (e.g., hardware, software) and services from outside of the Project. This includes the following subTasks:

- **Select suppliers** is the Task of selecting the sources of the resources.
- **Evaluate possible resources** is the Task of evaluating vendors and their products and services.
- **Procure needed resources** is the Task of purchasing resources from their sources.

Ensure schedule management is the Task of ensuring the timely completion of the Project and its Stages and Work Units. This includes the following subTasks:

- **Estimate time** is the Task of estimating the duration of Project Stages and Tasks.
- **Develop schedule** is the Task of producing and maintaining the Project Schedule to the appropriate level of detail (e.g., documenting Phases and major Milestones). Timeboxing might be a useful approach here whereby timeboxing permits delivery of product on a stated date with 100% certainty. Customer education is also required here!
- **Communicate schedule** is the Task of communicating and reporting the Project Schedule to all of its Stakeholders.
- **Control schedule** is the Task of ensuring that the Project staff follows (or iterates) the Project Schedule to avoid schedule slippage.

Obtain business approval A key Task in a successful Project is getting "buy-in" and ultimately official approval from the business decision-makers.

3 Belbin, R.M. (1993) *Team Roles at Work*, Butterworth Heinemann.

Configuration Management Tasks

Identify an appropriate configuration is the Task of identifying baselines and identifying and baselining Components (i.e., designating Components as configuration items in these baselines).

Control the configuration is the Task of managing baselined configuration items. This includes the following subTasks:

- Request change.
- Evaluate the impact of the requested change.
- Approve/reject the requested change.
- Implement change.

Monitor configuration status is the Task of recording and reporting of information needed to effectively manage a configuration including the:

- status of requested changes, deviations, and waivers to the configuration; and
- implementation status of approved changes.

Audit configuration is the Task of auditing a baseline to verify if it is complete, correctly identified and properly versioned.

Risk Management Tasks

Identify potential risks is the Task of identifying potential risks to the success of a Project.

Analyze (formal) risk is the Task of analyzing identified risks in terms of their probability of occurrence, its potential impacts, steps to take to avoid their occurrence and steps to take to mitigate their impact once they occur.

Document risk potential is the Task of documenting the results of risk analysis (e.g., in the risk management plan).

Establish risk avoidance strategies is the Task of taking steps to avoiding the occurrence of a risk.

Mitigate risks is the Task of taking steps to mitigate the impact of a risk once it occurs.

Metrics Management Tasks

Metrics Management Tasks include those for both management (e.g., productivity and progress) and quality:

Set up metrics collection Programme – the Task of planning the use of Metrics on the Project including the need to address corporate culture in introducing the ideas of software engineering Metrics.

Collect metrics data is the Task of collecting appropriate Metrics on the Project.

Analyze metrics data is the Task of analyzing the Metrics that have been collected.

Report on metrics data is the Task of reporting the results of Metrics analysis to the appropriate Roles on the Project.

Act on metrics report reflects the important need for management to *use* the data derived from Metrics studies in a timely and effective manner.

Quality Engineering Tasks

Assess quality needs is the Task of evaluating exactly what is meant by quality in the context of the Organization, the particular Project and the end-user. Quality is in the eye of the client or end-user.

Specify quality goals is the Task of determining the goals to be achieved by the quality assurance and quality control Tasks.

Assure quality is the Task of independently assessing and reporting the quality of the Project process, sometimes known as Quality Assurance.

Quality control is an important Task in the OPF since it addresses the critical area of ensuring that the quality of the delivered Work Products is going to be acceptable to the client. This Task has six subTasks:

- Analyze quality metrics data.
- Ensure components integrate properly with other components.
- Ensure portability to other platforms.
- Ensure no coding standards are violated.
- Evaluate usability.
- Evaluate documentation.

Useful Techniques include inspections, reviews and audits.

Undertake in-process review Reviewing is a Task that can occur frequently. It often helps Projects keep on track with little overhead in terms of spending resources (usually reviewers' time).

Undertake post-implementation review Often called a "retrospective"[4] or a "project debrief", a post-mortem following the end of the Project permits not only individuals but also the Organization to learn from the success (or failure) of the Project.

Write manual(s) and prepare other documentation Documentation to provide an organizational history and memory is important for a learning organization. User manuals (although often now online) still need to be written. Often, the worst Person to do the documentation is the developer, who will not use the software as a new user would. A technical writer or writing team is usually the optimum solution and our recommendation.

4 See, for example, Kerth, N.L. (2001) *Project Retrospectives: A Handbook for Team Reviews*, Dorset House, New York.

Process Engineering Tasks

Maintain process framework is the Task of extending or modifying the OPF based on Project experience and current research.

Instantiate process framework is the Task of instantiating the OPF to produce a project-specific process by selecting the relevant, cost-effective reusable process components of the OPF process component library:

- **Select Work Products** is the Task of selecting the internal and deliverable Work Products to be produced.
- **Select Producers** is the Task of selecting the Organizations, Teams and Roles to be used to produce the Work Products. This also includes evaluating and selecting the Tools (e.g., word-processing, upperCASE Tools and lowerCASE Tools) to support the process.
- **Select Work Units** is the Task of selecting the Activities, Work Flows, Tasks and Techniques to be performed by the Producers.
- **Select Stages** is the Task of selecting the development/life cycle, its component Phases, their component Builds and the associated Milestones that provide overall structure to the Work Units.

Tailor the process is the Task of modifying the selected process components to meet the specific needs of the Project.

Document the process is the Task of documenting the results of process framework instantiation and process tailoring so that the Project Stakeholders understand the Project process.

Communicate process to stakeholders is the Task of consulting with Project Stakeholders to ensure that they understand the Project process and how to effectively use it.

Enforce the process is the Task of ensuring that the Project Stakeholders follow the official process (or else either obtain a waiver or tailor the process).

Report on status of process is the Task of reporting the status of Project process usage including any problems requiring either consulting, enforcement, or tailoring.

Environment Engineering Tasks

The Environment Engineering Activity involves the performance of the following Tasks:

Design optimum environment is the design of a development or production environment that fulfills its associated needs.

Choose toolset is the Task of identifying, evaluating, and selecting software Tools for inclusion in an environment.

Document environments is the Task of documenting the design, Tool selection, installation plans, and maintenance approach of the Project environments.

Choose and install components is the Task of selecting, installing and configuring the Hardware and Software Components of an environment. The Hardware Components should be checked to ensure that they have no obvious defects and are properly configured.

Hardware fabrication is the Task of developing custom special purpose Hardware Components.

Maintain environment is the Task of maintaining the Hardware and Software Components of an environment in operating condition.

Website Management Tasks

Choose architectural pattern (subTask of Create A System Architecture) is the Task whose purpose is to minimize both design time and risk by selecting and adapting an architectural pattern that has already been developed and tested.

Design and implement content management strategy is the Task of managing the semantic (business) content of the Website.

Design and implement personalization strategy is the Task focussing on how a Website can be used to personalize a service to each of its clients.

Create content (on Website) is the Task of actually creating content, as opposed to structure, on the Website.

Integrate content with user interface is the Task which takes the semantic content of the Website and ensures it is smoothly integrated within the existing (or developing) user interface.

Manage content is the Task charged with facilitating the rapidly changing visual and textual information content of a Website.

Develop data standards is the Task aimed at creating extensible and scalable standards for data in Web developments.

Build white site/wireframe prototype is the Task of creating a content-poor prototype of the Website in order to evaluate understanding between client and Web Development Team.

Produce Website standards is the Task focussing on creating a set of standards for an Organization's Website so that the look and feel (and more importantly the navigability and usage) of the Website is homogeneous.

Design Web system Architecture is the Task in which the overall Architecture of the Website is decided.

Create navigation map for Website is the Task in which the navigational structure of the Website is determined.

Define acceptance criteria for Website is the important Task of pre-selecting the criteria by which the Website's success will be evaluated.

Define Website testing strategy is the Task of creating a strategy for effective evaluation of the Website.

Undertake market analysis is a Task whose main purpose is to determine market share and sector characteristics.

Test Website is the Task of executing the test suite and testing goals of the preselected testing strategy.

User Interface Tasks

Integrate content with user interface is a Task that brings together the creative world of graphical designers and editors with the technical world of members of the software engineering Team.

Design user interface, a long established OPEN Task, has three new subTasks for Web development:

- Create the UCD[5] Role Model – focussing on modeling who will use the system
- Create the UCD Task Model – focussing on the nature of the work for which the system is being created
- Create the UCD content Model – focussing on efficient user performance in their interaction with the system.

Analyze market is a Task whose main purpose is to determine market share and sector characteristics.

Prototype the human interface is a Task concerned with ensuring usability of the human interface by trialing a prototype, typically with the users themselves.

Requirements Engineering Tasks

Identify client's vision is the Task of eliciting and documenting the client's vision of the Application. This includes the following subTasks:

- **Describe application** is the Task of obtaining consensus on a concise description of the Application.
- **Elicit vision** is the Task of eliciting the client's vision of the Application in terms of its.
  - Stakeholders
  - Business goals
  - Operational goals in terms of major Application functions
  - Quality goals
  - Business, legal and technological constraints.
- **Document vision** is the Task of documenting the client's vision in the Application Vision Statement.

Identify source(s) of requirements is the Task to identify not only the Requirements but where they are to be found. This obviously precedes the actual Requirements elicitation.

Identify reusable requirements is the Task of identifying and reusing (possibly with modification) reusable Requirements on a specific Project.

Elicit requirements. The purpose of this Task is to develop and refine a formal and stable Requirements specification by eliciting the Requirements from clients, domain experts, marketing personnel, and users. This Task has several subtasks:

5 UCD stands for Usage-Centered Design (Constantine and Lockwood, 1999).

- Define problem and establish mission and objectives.
- Evaluate existing systems (if they exist) – is the Task of evaluating relevant existing competing system for potential Requirements.
- Establish Requirements for users.
- Establish user Requirements for distributed systems.
- Establish user database Requirements.

Analyze requirements – aimed at gaining an understanding, possibly through modeling, of the Requirements in order to ensure that they have the necessary quality (e.g., are complete, are consistent with other Requirements and other Work Products, are understandable etc.). This may include the following subTasks:

- **Context modeling** is the Task of identifying the context of the Application in terms of its externals and its relationships with them.
- **Use case modeling** is the Task of modeling the operational Requirements in terms of use cases and the paths through them.
- **Domain object modeling** is the Task of modeling the essential domain concepts of the Requirements in terms of object types, their responsibilities and the relationships between them.

Specify requirements. The purpose of this Task is to document the analysis of the Requirements. In this Task we formally specify Requirements in a set of Requirements Specifications. This Task may be manually performed or automated by means of a Requirements Management Tool.

Maintain trace between requirements and design. Since one of the benefits of OO is the possibility of auditability and a "common language" across all the stages of the life cycle, maintaining a trace between concepts in the Requirements and their realization in code is more feasible. It also lays the groundwork for automatic re-engineering and round-trip development.

A group of Tasks that are important in the business domain, e.g., when using OPEN in a business modeling mode, focus on understanding the market, your competitors and opportunities (useful Technique: SWOT analysis). These four Tasks are as follows:

- **Analyze customer organization(s)**. Since knowing your customer(s) is a critical success factor in business, this Task aims to understand the Customer Organization by producing an accurate and complete analysis of the customer's current business and by determining the customer's relevant business needs.
- **Analyze market**. Here we analyze the marketplace(s) in which the customer Organization competes. To do this successfully, we must produce an accurate and current analysis of each market segment and determine what the customer must do to compete effectively in each marketplace.
- **Analyze technology**. The purpose of this Task is to keep abreast of new technologies in order to evaluate which (if any) will be useful on future Projects.

- **Analyze users**. In order to create high-quality products that the user will appreciate and use successfully in their own Endeavors, we must analyze our users in order to understand them. We specifically need to understand the different kinds of users and User Organization(s) in order to provide ourselves with a foundation on which to produce creative ways to organize user Tasks and Work Flows and which will assist us in determining optimal screen layouts (especially important for Web pages) as well as good quality and usable user interface navigation.

Architecture Tasks

Create a system architecture is the Task of developing an overall Architecture of the system. This includes the following subTasks:

- **Choose architectural patterns** is the Task whose purpose is to minimize both design time and risk by selecting and adapting appropriate architectural pattern that have already been developed and tested.
- **Apply architectural patterns** is the Task of applying architectural patterns to the Architecture of the Application.
- **Reuse architecture** is the Task of identifying an overall system Architecture to reuse.
- **Determine major components** is the Task of identifying and determining the major components of the system, their responsibilities and their relationships.
- **Determine reusable system components** is the Task of identifying and evaluating opportunities to reuse both in-house and commercial off-the-shelf (COTS) System Components in the system Architecture. This includes the evaluation and selection of major COTS Hardware and Software Components.
- **Determine major mechanisms** is the Task of identifying the major mechanisms to be implemented by the Components. This includes the following subTasks:
  - **Determine process architecture** is the Task of determining the mechanisms to be used to handle concurrency.
  - **Determine persistence architecture** is the Task of determining the mechanisms (e.g., databases vs. files, object vs. relational databases, data definition language and data manipulation language) to be used to ensure persistence of data and objects.
  - **Determine exception architecture** is the Task of determining the mechanisms to handle exceptions.
  - **Determine security mechanisms** is the Task of determining the mechanisms (e.g., encryption and digital signatures) to be used to ensure that the security Requirements are met.
  - **Determine control architecture** is the Task of determining the startup, failover and shut-down mechanisms.
  - **Establish distributed systems strategy** is the Task of evaluating and incorporating the effects and constraints of distribution.

- **Select technologies** is the Task of selecting major technologies (e.g. Languages, Component Models, Databases).
- **Trace system architecture** is the Task of ensuring that each architecturally significant Requirement is implemented by one or more system Components.

Create a software architecture (mechanism analysis) is the Task of developing the Architecture of the software. This includes the following subTasks:

- **Apply architectural patterns** is the Task of applying architectural patterns to the software Architecture of the system.
- **Develop layer design** – for instance in terms of a standard *n*-tier client–server Architecture.
- **Trace software architecture** is the Task of ensuring that the relevant architecturally significant Requirements are implemented by one or more software Components.

For Websites, the following Tasks are also relevant:

- **Design and implement content management strategy** is the Task of creating a strategy by which the contents of a Website will be kept up-to-date.
- **Design and implement personalization strategy** is the Task of incorporating a strategy by which individual users interact with the Website in a fashion exactly suited to their needs.

Document the architecture is the Task of documenting the system and software Architectures, often by entering and maintaining the Architecture in an upperCASE Tool (or database).

Prototype the architecture is the Task of producing an executable software prototype which exercises the major architectural decisions of the system.

Enforce the architecture is the Task of ensuring the architectural integrity of the system by enforcing conformance of the design and implementation to the Architecture.

Develop capacity plan – the standard need to ensure software and hardware can cope with the volume of information needed today plus some future expansion.

Establish data migration strategy – determine how to incorporate existing data into the Application.

Create navigation map for Website is the Task in which the navigational structure of the Website is determined.

Manage subsystems – subsystems and packages need to be managed carefully, as do Components, in order to ensure that they actually fit together as planned.

Modeling Tasks

Develop Business Object Model (BOM) The Business Object Model is an object Model of the business focus i.e. NOT the software used by the business.

Construct the object model In this fairly Large-scale Task, the knowledge gained during Requirements and "analysis" are turned progressively into a Model of the system to be developed.

Identify CIRTs Identification of Classes, Instances, Roles and Types (CIRTs) is an integral part of object modeling. This Task has four subTasks:

- Determine initial class list
- Identify persistent classes
- Identify roles
- Refine class list.

Map roles on to classes Roles are not supported directly by OO Programming Languages but are highly useful in analysis and design. This Task shows how to map those modeling constructs to the chosen Implementation Language.

Database-related Tasks

Design the database model is the Task of designing the databases. This includes the following subTasks:

- **Design the logical data model** (e.g., using class diagrams, entity relationship diagrams).
- **Map the logical database schema.** This Task focusses on the mapping of the Object Model we have created to a database schema, typically relational (including any relevant normalization considerations).
- **Design any associated stored procedures.**

Design and implement physical database. It is important to include consideration of the database design and implementation as an OPF Task. This Task has three subTasks:

- **Distribution/replication design** – fragmentation and storage considerations.
- **Operational and performance design** – including recovery, concurrency control, security control and Versioning.
- **Performance evaluation** – assessment of whether user expectations are met.

Design the data center is the Task of designing a data center. This includes the following Tasks:

- **Design the hardware components** is the Task of selecting the hardware Components including:
  - Routers
  - Firewalls
  - Web, Application and Database Servers
  - Disk and Tape Libraries.
- **Design the networks** is the Task of designing the local area networks that connect the Hardware Components.
- **Design the layouts** is the Task of designing the floor layouts, cable layouts and rack locations.

- **Design the supporting infrastructures** is the Task of designing the infrastructure systems including:
  - Cooling system(s)
  - Power supply system(s)
  - Fire suppression system(s)
  - Physical security.

Design Tasks

Prototype the human interface is the Task of prototyping the human interfaces, especially the graphical user interfaces.

Design user interface is the Task of designing all human interfaces and associated media such as the graphical user interfaces (and Websites), audio portals, wireless devices, e-mail, fax and reports. There are three important subTasks adopted from usage-centered design. These are:

- create the Role Model
- create the Task Model
- create the Content Model.

Note that these names are those used in usage-centered design and conflict to some extent with the use of the words "Role" and "Task" in other parts of OPEN. The word "content" is also used specifically with respect to Website content in the Web Management Activity of OPEN.

Capture the design is the Task of entering and maintaining the design in an upperCASE Tool (or database).

Document the design is the Task of documenting the design in the Design Documents.

Optimize the design Design optimization is only important for certain domains, such as critical safety and/or real-time domains.

Refactor Improve the design detail without changing the external behavior of the code. Applied to working code, i.e., when both design and code already exist and are functional.

Undertake usability design Designing for usability is critical for today's software developers. In this Task, we concentrate on what aspects of usability and good human–computer interface (HCI) design need to be considered and implemented.

Component Engineering Tasks

Screen the candidate list of component frameworks is the Task of filtering out likely candidate Component Frameworks from a longer list.

Evaluate the potential component frameworks. Having screened the candidate list, a list of potential Component Frameworks remains. These are now seriously evaluated.

Choose the appropriate component framework is the Task of selecting the Component Framework from those screened and evaluated.

Establish policy on component acquisition is the Task of deciding on how/when/where Components should be acquired from third parties.

Screen the candidate list of components The goal here is to identify vendors and the Components on offer. Appropriate subTasks are:

- gather information on candidate Components
- select candidate Components
- gather preliminary cost information on selected candidates
- product first (rough) assessment.

Evaluate the potential components The goal of this Task is to undertake a full evaluation of the candidates which emerged from the screening. Appropriate subTasks are:

- generate a compliance matrix
- execute vendor-supplied examples in test mode
- obtain independent benchmark data [optional]
- develop and test context-specific examples
- document results of component evaluation
- document interactions with vendor
- rank the candidate components.

Choose appropriate components For this decision-making Task, the most appropriate Component(s) need to be chosen from those already evaluated. This Task is only activated if there is no "clear winner" already. Producers involved are technical and product managers as well as system architects. Appropriate subTasks are:

- compile a list of critical components
- discuss trade-off factors and risks
- compile list of individuals' assessments of candidate components
- arrive at overall score and ranked list (probably using a normalization/weighted aggregate approach).

Create and/or identify reusable components ("for reuse") To capitalize on reuse opportunities, the reusable Component Library must be built up. This Task focusses on how the development Team can optimize their effort in the context of create Components that will have reuse value in the future.

This Task has two subTasks:

- Construct frameworks – at a high level of abstraction, frameworks, either whitebox or blackbox, should be created.
- Optimize for reuse – sometimes designs which have esthetic quality may need further optimizing, perhaps destroying elements of good object-orientedness, in order to get a highly efficient working system.

Integrate Components

Since Components already exist, they do not need to be coded i.e. the OPEN Task: "Code" is no longer needed. Instead, Components need to be integrated together or "composed". This is, in essence, coding at a coarser granularity. The interfaces of the Components would ideally be immediately pluggable but, in many cases, "glue" will need to be written, perhaps using a scripting language or creating some other form of inter-Component "adapter".[6]

Implementation Tasks

Code is the Task of implementing a new software Class or Component in a chosen Programming Language (here an OO Programming Language).

Iteratively improve software components is the Task of iterating Software Components. This includes the following subTasks:

- **Debugging** is the Task of removing defects from new or modified Software Components.
- **Extension** is the Task of extending Software Components with new or modified capabilities or interfaces.
- **Refactoring** is the Task of iterating the Software Component to improve its quality without modifying its functionality.

Integration Tasks

Plan integration is the Task of developing plans for performing integration including identifying the versions of the configuration items to integrate and developing integration procedures and scripts to document or automate the integration process.

Execute integration plans is the Task of actually integrating Components into either larger Components or the system. This includes the following subTasks:

- **Integrate software** is the Task of integrating Software Components into larger collections of Software Components. Since Components already exist, they do not need to be coded i.e. the OPEN Task: "Code" is no longer needed. Instead, Components need to be integrated together or "composed". This is, in essence, coding at a coarser granularity. The interfaces of the Components would ideally be immediately pluggable but, in many cases, "glue" will need to be written, perhaps using a scripting language or creating some other form of inter-Component adapter.

6 D'Souza, D.F. and Wills, A.C. (1999) *Objects, Components, and Frameworks with UML. The Catalysis Approach*, Addison-Wesley, p. 388.

- **Integrate system** is the Task of integrating System Components into the system.
- **Integrate external systems** is the Task of integrating the system with external (e.g., legacy) systems.

Report on status of integration is the Task of reporting the success or failure of integration execution.

Integrate with existing, non OO/CBD systems – so-called legacy or heritage systems.

Integrate content with user interface is the Task which takes the semantic content of the Website and ensures it is smoothly integrated within the existing (or developing) user interface.

Testing Tasks

Testing is crucial for delivering high-quality software. Testing Tasks include:

Plan testing strategy is the Task of planning the Testing Activity in terms of testing Teams, Roles, Tools, Tasks, and Techniques.

Design test suite is the Task of designing test suites of test cases.

Code test suite is the Task of implementing test suites of test cases based on the associated design, perhaps reusing fragments of previous test suites.

Document test suite is the Task of entering and maintaining the test suites of test cases using a test Tool (or database).

Execute tests is the Task of executing the test suites of test cases.

Report on test results is the Task of reporting failures detected by the execution of test suites of test cases.

These Tasks are each applied over a range of granularities (Class, Component, Package etc.). This gives rise to a set of orthogonal, yet equally valid, views on testing:

- **Perform acceptance testing** – user focus
- **Perform class testing** – low-level code focus
- **Perform cluster testing** – still code focus but at the Component or Package level
- **Perform regression testing** – ensuring modified code still works as well as it did pre-modification.

Deployment Tasks

Deliver product to customer is the Task of formally transferring the final versions of the deliverable Project Work Products to the client. This includes the following subTasks:

- **Determine installation process** is the Task of determining how to install the Application. This includes installing and configuring Hardware Components, install Software Components, integrating with legacy systems and populating databases.

- **Document installation process** is the Task of documenting in an installation guide how to install the Application.
- **Install application** is the Task of installing the Application in the production environment at the client data center.

Train users is the Task of training users in the proper usage of the Application.

Other Tasks useful here are (a) **Write manual(s) and prepare other documentation** to explain to users how to use the Application (e.g. in a user manual or help feature); and (b) **Undertake post-implementation review** in which users are involved in order to ascertain the Project successes and failures as well as what should be done differently in future Projects.

The following are at the level of the Enterprise rather than the individual Project.

Business Modeling Tasks

Identify context. This Task aims to identify the needs of the business user(s). The business context is vital if software is to be successfully used in the Organization.

A number of Business Modeling Tasks refer to appropriate and consistent business strategies which may be used to guide the selection and management of multiple Applications:

Analyze customer is the Task of analyzing and documenting the client. This includes the following subTasks:

- **Determine organizational structure** is the Task of determining the client's current organizational structure.
- **Identify stakeholders** is the Task of identifying, categorizing, understanding and documenting the client's essential stakeholders.
- **Determine offerings** is the Task of identifying and understanding the client's current service and product offerings.
- **Model client's current business processes** is the Task of producing a Business Process Model that analyzes the current state of the business in terms of business Activities, Tasks, Work Products and their Producers.

Analyze market is the Task of analyzing and documenting the relevant state of the market. This includes the following subTasks:

- **Identify market trends** is the Task of identifying relevant market trends that should affect the client's business Model.
- **Analyze competitors** is the Task of identifying and evaluating the client's primary competitors and their offerings, together with their strengths and weaknesses.

Analyze users is the Task of analyzing and documenting the various user communities.

Model domain is the Task of modeling the business domain in terms of potential elements in the wider business arena which "surround" the current Application's focus but are not currently considered as being within scope. This includes the following subTasks:

- **Develop domain object model** is the Task of producing an Object Model analyzing the business domain in terms of essential types of objects, their responsibilities and their relationships.
- **Develop domain use case model** is the Task of producing an essential Use Case Model of the business domain in terms of actors, use cases and paths through these use cases.

Model and re-engineer business processes. This Task aims to evaluate and possibly restructure business processes, generally in order to use modern technologies more efficiently and more effectively. It has several subTasks:

- **Build context (i.e. business process) Model** – model the business at a high level.
- **Build Task Object Model (TOM)** – which models the business in terms of Tasks.
- **Convert TOM to BOM** i.e. convert a Task focus to an object focus.
- **Do user training** – users must understand the nature of new or revised business processes.
- **Prepare invitation to tender** – to give opportunities to various third-party vendors to submit proposals for consideration.
- **Produce new business process model** is the Task of producing an improved business process model based on the business analysis and technology strategy.
- **Improve organizational structure** is the Task of determining and recommending improvements in the client's organizational structure to support the new business process model.
- **Improve offerings** is the Task of determining and recommending improvements (e.g., additions) to the client's current service and product offerings.
- **Identify applications** is the Task of identifying potentially useful [new Versions of] Applications, which may deserve funding based on their business cases.
- **Perform feasibility study** is the Task of determining if Applications are feasible within technical, financial, staffing and scheduling constraints. This is a fairly traditional Task of comparing the various high level strategies as alternatives.
- **Develop the application business cases** is the Task of developing and documenting the business case for each feasible Application.
- **Undertake programme and project selection** is the Task of selecting the Programmes and Projects to fund, based on the business cases of the associated Applications.

Technology strategy Tasks are those Tasks involved with producing the client's strategy for applying appropriate and consistent technology across multiple Projects:

Research technology trends is the Task of researching, analyzing, and reporting relevant technology trends that may affect multiple Projects.

Evaluate and select appropriate technologies is the Task of evaluating and selecting relevant technologies for widespread use across Projects.

Select partners and vendors is the Task of evaluating and selecting partners, commercial off-the-shelf products, and vendors for widespread use across Projects.

Brand strategy Tasks are those Tasks associated with establishing the client's strategy regarding a consistent and appropriate brand identity for its Applications. This includes the following Tasks:

Develop brand identity is the Task of producing a new digital brand for the customer. This includes the following subTasks:

- analyze customer's current brand
- identify and analyze competitors' brands
- formulate new digital brand
- document new brand
- perform market evaluation of new brand.

Communicate the brand identity is the Task of communicating the new brand to the client, user communities, and other stakeholders in the marketplace. This includes the following subTasks:

- plan communication.
- implement communication plan.

Reuse Engineering Tasks

Identify appropriate reusable Work Products ("for reuse") is the Task of identifying potentially reusable Work Products for addition to the Organizational reuse repository. It is a slightly more generic form of Create and/or identify reusable Components described earlier in the context of CBD.

Identify reusable requirements is a special case of the above Task, focussed solely on the Requirements domain

Optimize reuse ("with reuse"). In a reuse environment, one Task is to locate, identify and evaluate existing Components in order to see if there will be a business and technical advantage in (re)using them. This is a slightly more generic form of Choose appropriate Components described earlier in the context of CBD.

Acquire reusable Work Products is the Task of acquiring potentially reusable Work Products for addition to the Organizational reuse repository.

Develop reusable Work Products is the Task of developing reusable Work Products (e.g., Documents, Classes, Frameworks, Software Components and Test Cases) for addition to the Organizational reuse repository.

Manage library of reusable components. As well as creating and using reusable Components, an important Task is that of maintaining and managing the library or Organizational repository in which they reside. This typically involves updating the

Work Product (e.g., by refactoring, debugging or providing adequate test software). Two subTasks are:

- **Evaluate reusable Work Products** is the Task of evaluating potentially reusable Work Products for addition to the Organizational reuse repository.
- **Document reusable Work Products** is the Task of documenting reusable Work Products for addition to the Organizational reuse repository.

Disseminate information regarding reuse opportunities is the Task of advising Project personnel regarding the existence and appropriateness of reusable Work Products in the Organizational reuse repository.

Programme Management Tasks

Decompose Programmes into Projects – Programmes are suites of Applications, whereas Projects usually focus on a single Application.

Obtain Programme funding is the Task of producing approval and funding for the Programme.

Plan Programme is the Task of producing, documenting and maintaining a Programme plan.

Report Programme cost is the Task of regularly reporting the overall financials of the Programme including summarizing the financials of its component Projects.

Report Programme status is the Task of regularly reporting the overall status of the Programme including summarizing the status of its component Projects.

Establish policy on Component acquisition is the Task of identifying an important Organizational policy on the extent to which third-party Components will be considered preferentially for use.

Training Tasks

The Training Activity involves the performance of the following Tasks for each type of training (e.g., client training and user training):

Develop education and training plan is the Task of planning the Training Activity in terms of its associated Roles, Responsibilities, Requirements and approach to meet those needs (e.g., classroom training, on-the-job training and individual mentoring), courses including intended audience and prerequisites, and the general schedule.

Analyze training needs is the analysis of the training Requirements of the Organization, its Project and its individual staff members.

Develop training materials is the Task of developing the necessary materials for a training course.

Identify training vendor is the Task of deciding upon which third-party training company will be hired to supply your Organization's training needs.

Perform training is the Task of providing training at the Organizational, Project, or individual level. This could be time to attend in-house training or to send people to third-party training vendor courses.

Report on training costs is the Task of reporting the costs of training.

Report on status of training is the Task of reporting the status of training in terms of training provided and the degree to which training Requirements have been met.

Transition Tasks

Tasks associated with the transition of an Organization or Organizational group from a regular to an OO or CBD environment and mindset are associated with three Activities – those of Organization Assessment, Pre-development Acceptance and Technology Insertion. The Tasks themselves are:

Assess current state of Organization – it is critical that an audit of the resources of the Organization (or perhaps only Project Team) that is intended to transition to OT/CBD be carefully reviewed. Some of the elements of this Task are:

- Measure the Organization's maturity using, say, the Capability Maturity Model (CMM). This allows the maturity of the existing software processes to be assessed and key practices identified that are required to increase the maturity level.
- Define the current problem(s) and the compelling reason for transition.
- Define alternative and/or possible solutions e.g. Adopt new technology, Outsourcing.

Set transition goals acknowledges that the whole Team/Organization will not transition in a single "big bang", so careful planning is needed for a Phased or incremental transition. One way of setting the goal would be in terms of forecasting the final CMM level that might be achieved following a successful transition exercise.

Assess transition paths supports the evaluation of the several options that might be available for assisting the transition. The Team members and management must define a path appropriate to their specific organizational group which will assist them to go from the current situation to the desired one.

Assess organization's resources for transition considers the need to:

- Identify the available processes/methodologies, supportive (CASE) Tools, availability of books and other reference material for the transition process.
- Identify the approved fund or budget.
- Identify the available human resources to carry out the transition.
- Identify the available processes/methodologies, supportive (CASE) Tools, availability of books and other reference material for the software development process itself (technology insertion).
- Define measure(s) of success. An existing OPEN Technique: Critical Success Factors will be useful here.

Assess staff skills/knowledge

- Measuring the current level of skills and knowledge of people involved in the Project.

- Recommending the appropriate Techniques and/or methods to bring their skills and knowledge up to the level required for successful transition (this links with Training issues).

Identify pilot Project, which is recommended to be

- smaller rather than larger but large enough to keep attention of senior management;
- in a well-known domain.

Enhance Teamwork. This can be done in many ways, both technically and socially. For some, the provision and employment of new Tools may be a significant way of improving Teamwork, as might the provision of easy access to resources such as Internet/Intranet, Emails, Lotus Notes etc.

Create a SWAT Team, which is a core Team of highly responsible and high-profile leaders who set an example and act as a conduit for good practice, new ideas, etc. Essentially, the members of this elite Team become the "in-house gurus".

Effect rapid culture change focusses on dealing with the human reaction to change: resistance, denial, blaming others and, finally, acceptance. People resist change and rapid culture change should work on building willingness for change by tackling appropriate actions to educate and persuade people to move to the desired culture. Rapid culture change can be achieved by using some Techniques such as interviewing of individuals and organizing special meetings for the development Team. During interviews and meetings, we identify and explain to people the current situation stating the problem, suggesting and exploring possible solutions and giving people the chance to comment and give their feedback. The main goal of those interviews and meetings is to make people feel that they are an important part of the organization and that they are responsible for contributing significantly to solving the current problem. The more people become involved, the better the change behavior will be achieved.

In summary, the key issues here are:

- Defeat resistance to change.
- Remove or eliminate any conflicting goals which have been developed as a result of many levels of bureaucracy involved.
- Identify barriers to success and ways to overcome them.
- Identify risk factors and how to minimize them.
- Explore the potential aspects of the adoption of OT.
- Obtain a full commitment and readiness for commencing the transition.

Introduce and enforce new technology, a Task that seeks commitment. Once over the inevitable resistance (from at least some), there should be no turning back. The ability of OT/CBD to offer benefits and fulfill promises must be fully and objectively explored and evaluated.

Techniques

In this section, we merely list the current Techniques in OPEN. For further details, see references in the Bibliography and the OPEN Website.

User Requirements

- Action research
- Active listening
- Activity grid construction
- Analysis of judgements
- Brainstorming
- Concept maps
- Context modeling
- CRC (Class Responsibility Collaborator) card modeling
- Domain analysis
- Expected value analysis
- Interviewing
- JAD (Joint Application Development)
- Kelly grids
- Meetings
- Power analysis
- Questionnaires
- RAD (Rapid Application Development)
- Record and playback
- Rich pictures
- Roleplay
- Scenario development
- Simulation
- Social systems analysis
- Soft systems analysis
- Special events
- Storyboarding
- Throwaway prototyping
- Videotaping
- Workshops

Project Management and Business Issues

- Approval gaining
- BPR (Business Process Re-engineering)
- Business process modeling
- Configuration management
- Cost–benefit analysis
- Cost estimation
- CPM charts
- Critical success factors
- Customer (on-site) training
- Envisioning
- Gantt charts
- Hierarchical Task analysis
- Impact analysis
- Impact estimation table
- Library management
- Package construction
- Package co-ordination
- PERT charts
- Pistols at dawn
- PLanguage
- Priority setting
- Project planning
- Prototyping
- PSP (Personal Software Process)
- Risk analysis
- Role assignment
- Scenario development
- Simulation
- SMART goals
- Social systems analysis
- SWOT analysis (Strengths, Weaknesses, Opportunities, Threats)
- Systems acceptance
- Systems audit
- Team-building
- Throwaway prototyping

- Timeboxing
- TQM (Total Quality Management)
- Use of dependencies in the Business Object Model (BOM) to generate first-cut Project plan
- Versioning (DBMS)
- Walkthroughs
- Workflow analysis

Quality

Testing

- Acceptance testing
- Beta testing
- Dependency-based testing
- Integration testing
- Package and subsystem testing
- Regression testing
- System acceptance
- Unit testing
- Usability testing

Inspections

- Defect detection
- Inspections
- Reviews
- Walkthroughs

Metrics

- Cohesion measurement
- Complexity measurement
- Cost estimation
- Coupling measurement
- Function points
- Law of Demeter
- Metrics collection

- Reuse measurement
- Statistical analysis of data
- Task points
- Thresholds
- Web Metrics

Other Quality Techniques

- CIRT (class, instance, Role or type) indexing
- Class naming
- CMM (Capability Maturity Model)
- Contract specification
- Exception handling
- Formal methods
- GQM (Goal Question Metric)
- Hierarchical Task analysis
- Literate programming
- Quality templates
- Refactoring
- Rule modeling
- Standards compliance
- Timeline

Modeling

Concepts/philosophy

- Abstraction
- Classification
- Encapsulation and information hiding
- Generalization (see also Classification)
- Responsibilities and Responsibility-Driven Design

Technical/low-level "analysis and design"

- Abstract class identification
- Class internal design
- Class naming

- Collaborations analysis
- Contract specification
- Creation charts
- Delegation analysis
- Design templates
- Event modeling
- Generalization and inheritance identification
- Genericity specification
- Granularity
- Hierarchical Task analysis
- Interaction modeling
- Layering
- Mixins
- Petri nets
- Qua-types
- Refactoring
- Relationship modeling
- Responsibility identification
- Robustness analysis
- Rule modeling
- Scenario development
- Service identification
- State modeling
- Stereotyping
- Time-threads
- Visibility analysis

Other Modeling Techniques

- Abstraction utilization
- Application scavenging
- Blackboarding
- Business process modeling
- Completion of abstractions
- Connascence
- CRC card modeling
- Dataflow modeling

- ER modeling
- Event charts
- Exception handling
- Formal methods
- Function points
- Fuzzy logic and fuzzy modeling
- Gap analysis
- Hierarchical Task analysis
- Hotspot identification
- Hypergenericity
- Information engineering
- Intelligent agent identification
- Object life cycle histories
- Ownership modeling
- Pattern recognition
- Protocol analysis
- PS-PPS
- Refinement
- Reverse engineering
- Revision of inheritance hierarchies
- Role modeling
- Roleplay
- Screen scraping
- Simulation
- Textual analysis
- Transformations of the object Model
- Viewpoints
- Visualization Techniques
- Zachman frameworks

Database

- Access analysis
- Audit Requirements
- Clustering (in databases)
- Collapsing of classes
- Database authorization

- Database fragmentation
- DBMS product selection
- DBMS type selection
- Indexing
- Interfacing to relational DBMS and legacy code
- Mapping to relational databases
- Normalization
- Object replication
- Object retention Requirements
- Path navigation
- Query optimization
- Reliability Requirements
- Storage of derived properties
- Tuning of database
- Versioning (DBMS)
- Volume analysis

Distributed computing

- DCS classification
- DCS optimization
- Distributed system partitioning and allocation
- Implementation of distributed aspects of system
- Scenario development

User Interface

- Dialog design in UI
- Screen painting
- Usability testing

Reuse

- Access analysis
- Application scavenging
- CIRT indexing

- Collaborations analysis
- Completion of abstractions
- Framework creation
- Gap analysis
- Genericity specification
- Granularity
- Layering
- Library class incorporation
- Library management
- Pattern recognition
- Reuse measurement
- Revision of inheritance hierarchies
- Scenario development
- Variant analysis

Coding

- Class internal design
- Creation charts
- Generalization and inheritance identification
- Inspections
- Implementation of distributed aspects of system
- Implementation of rules
- Implementation of services
- Implementation of structure
- Law of Demeter
- Mixins
- Pair programming
- Screen scraping
- Storage of derived properties
- Wrappers

Training and education

- Computer-based training
- Games

- Group problem-solving
- Internet and Web technology
- Lectures
- Roleplay
- Simulation
- Train the trainer
- Videotaping
- Workshops

Components

- Checklists
- Compliance matrix templates
- QESTA

Web support

- Development spikes
- Digital branding
- Reuse of graphical components
- System metaphors
- Web metrics
- Web template

Organizational transition

- Meetings
- Special events

F Example Work Flow

External Interface Specification Work Flow

In this appendix we describe a lone, illustrative example – that for the External Interface Specification or EIS (Figure F.1). The *objective* of this Work Flow is to produce an external interface specification that documents the Application programmer interfaces of an Application.

The following *Producers* perform the Tasks comprising the External Interface Specification Work Flow:

- Teams:
  - Configuration Management Team
    - Configuration Manager
  - Inspection Team:
    - Inspector, played by
      - Customer
      - System Architect
      - System Tester
      - User
  - Management Team:
    - Project Manager
    - Scheduler
  - System Requirements Team:
    - Requirements Engineer
    - Domain Expert
- Tools:
  - Configuration Management Tool
  - Requirements Management Tool
  - UpperCASE Tool that supports object modeling
  - Word processor to document the External Interface Specification

The following are *pre-conditions* for this Work Flow:

- The Process Team specifies creation of the External Interface Specification by the System Requirements Team.

The following example collaboration lists the *Tasks*, performed in an iterative, incremental and parallel manner, that could comprise this Work Flow:

- The Management Team requests specification of the External Interface Specification by the System Requirements Team.
- The Scheduler obtains a schedule for the External Interface Specification from the System Requirements Team.
- The System Requirements Team produces the initial version of the External Interface Specification:
  - A Requirements Engineer uses the associated Template to produce an initial empty version of the External Interface Specification.
  - The Requirements Team members read the Vision Statement.
  - The Requirements Team members read any relevant customer/user Documentation.
  - The Requirements Engineers interview the Domain Experts.
  - The Requirements Team members specify the Application Programmer Interfaces.
  - The Requirements Team members ensure consistency with the:
    - Vision Statement.
    - System Requirements Specification.
- The System Requirements Team hosts an External Interface Specification inspection:[1]
  - The Requirements Team schedules the inspection.
  - The Requirements Team identifies the inspectors.
  - The Requirements Team distributes copies of the External Interface Specification to the inspectors.
  - The inspectors review the External Interface Specification.
- The System Requirements Team updates the External Interface Specification based on the results of the Inspection.
- The System Requirements Team delivers the updated version of the External Interface Specification to the Configuration Management Team.
- The Configuration Manager baselines the parts of the External Interface Specification that passed the Inspection.

The following are *post-conditions* for this Work Flow:

- The parts of the External Interface Specification that passed the Inspection are baselined.

The following are *usage guidelines* for this Work Flow:

- The External Interface Requirements can be specified using a Requirements Management Tool so that the External Interface Specification can be automatically generated and printed from the associated database.

1 This can be done incrementally on different parts of the document, as they become available.

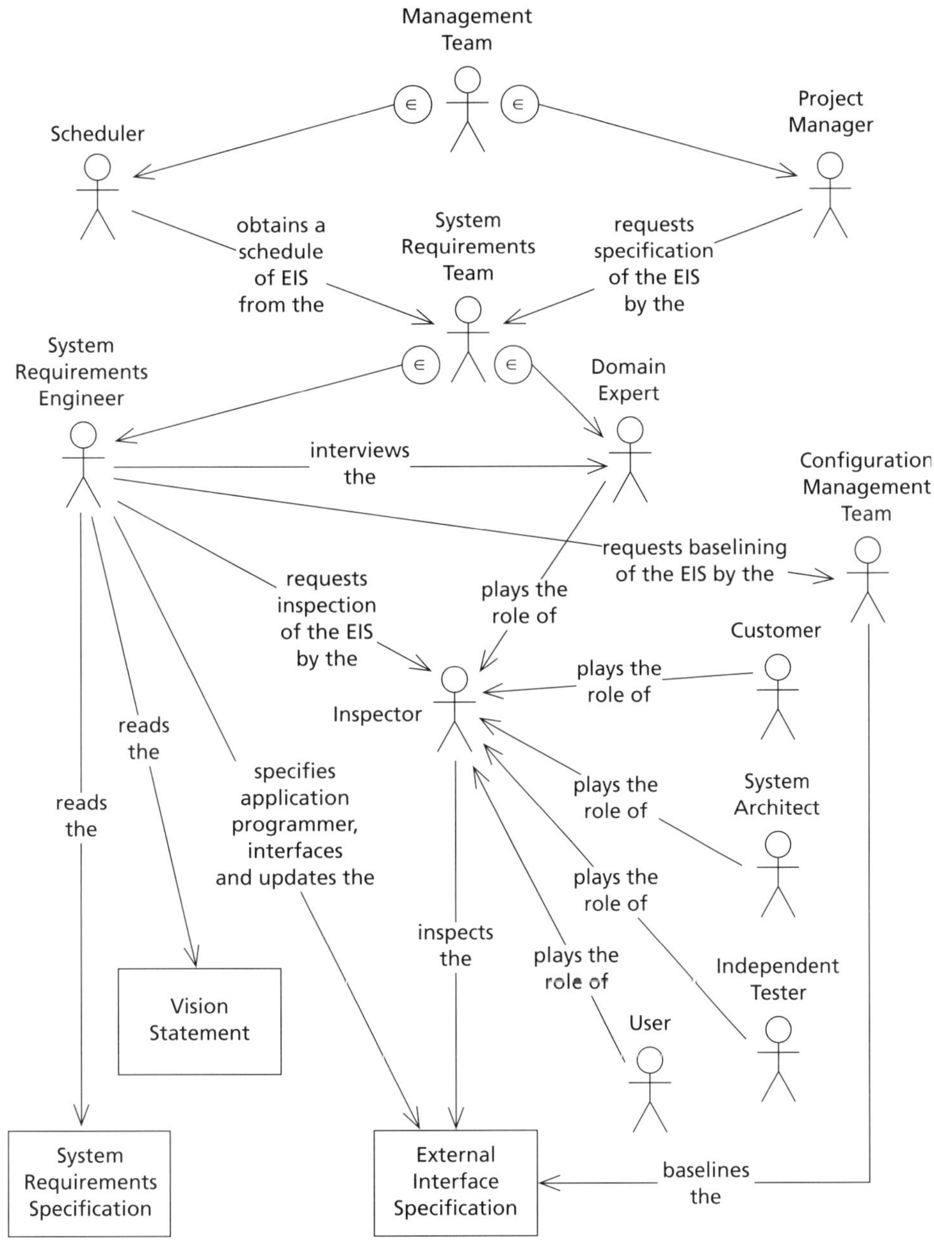

Figure F.1 Example of External Interface Specification Work Flow. To illustrate the modeling language independence of OPEN, we here choose, as an illustration only, to use the OML notation of Firesmith *et al*. (1997)

G Metamodel Diagrams

The OPF metamodel is a model of the entities in any process and the rules governing how they can interact. It is said to be at the M2 level (Figure G.1). For example, some of the entities in the OPF metamodel are Producers, Work Units and Work Products (Figure G.2). The metamodel also states which pairs of the entities can interact. The metamodel thus delineates the rules of the process. To construct an actual process or process instance, we must first instantiate the entities in the metamodel. This creates several examples (instances) of each class in the metamodel. The "process components" are then stored in the OPF repository or class library (Figure G.3). These M1 level components are then put together to create a personalized development process, again at the M1 level. This is the level at which most organizations will "adopt a process".

Since we are instantiating a process from a metamodel, there is, of course, no unique instantiation. In this sense, the OPF can be said to be a "family of processes", each generated from the same process metamodel. (Figure G.1 also shows that when you take the organizational standard process (labeled M1 in this diagram) and apply it to a specific project then you are in fact instantiating the organization's process as a *project-specific process* in which individual, named people played named roles with calendar deadlines and actual product delivery. This is known as the M0 level. Some organizations even have several, different, M0 instances in

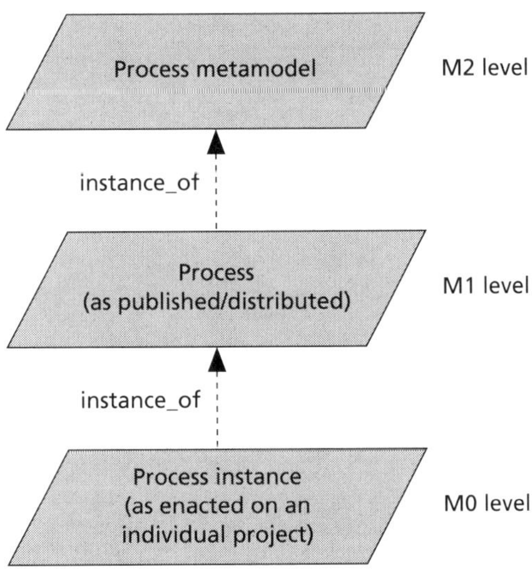

Figure G.1 Three of the levels in the metalevel architecture

action concurrently across several projects because of the contrasting process Requirements of these different projects.)

Figure G.2 summarizes the relationships between the following main process metatypes:

- **Work Products**. While specific Work Product types are discussed below, we note here that a Work Product Set is an aggregate of one or more related Work Products, each of which is composed of one or more Work Product Versions. The most important Work Products Sets are Applications that are developed for customer Organizations for use by User Organizations and Business Models – for example, those that are used to support Business Process Re-engineering.
- **Producers**. Producers may be People or Software or Hardware.
- **Work Units**. Work Units represent things that need to be done i.e. units of work or achievement. To perform them, effort needs to be expended – by Producers. The result of this expenditure of effort will be the creation and completion of one or more Work Products. Work Units are often sequenced by the use of Assertions.
- **Stages**. Stages provide a macro-organization to the triad of essential process Components.
- **Languages**. Languages are used to document the various Work Products.

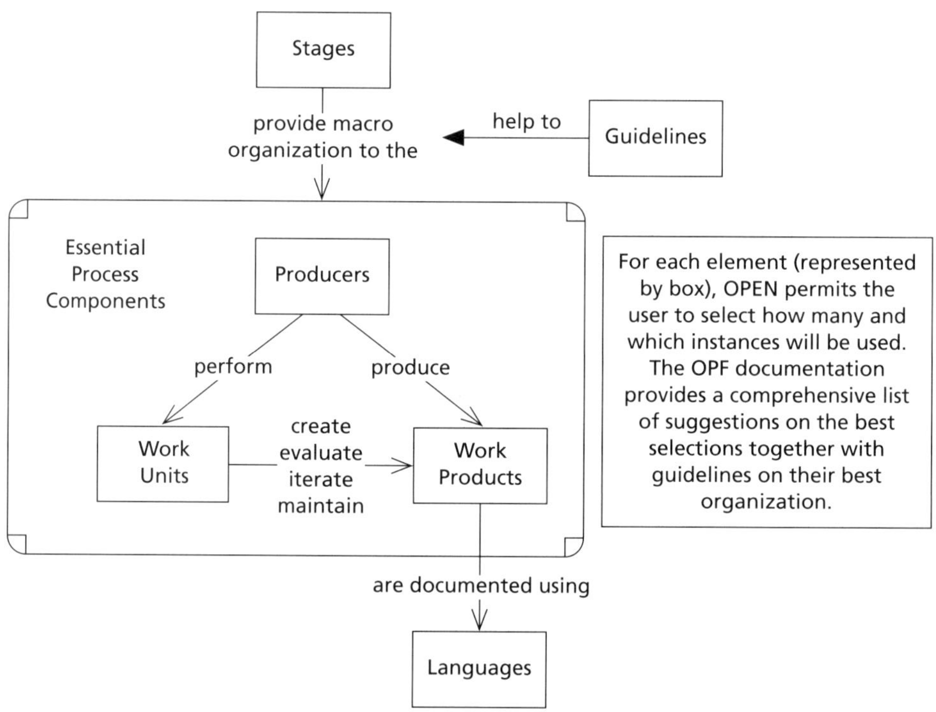

Figure G.2 The basic metatypes of OPEN Process Framework

Within the triad of core or essential process components, Producers perform Work Units (usually in the form of Tasks grouped together as Activities: Figure G.4) in order to incrementally produce and deliver Work Products.

Guidelines are available to assist in configuring the process by selecting Components from the Class Library of Predefined Process Components (Figure G.3) and possibly tailoring of these Components. This creates (see Chapter 8) a specialized OO development process for a particular Organization or, more frequently, for a particular Project or suite of Projects.

There are a large number of Work Products specified in the OPF's metamodel definition. These are shown in Figure G.5 along with the concept of an Increment which is a kind of Work Product Version. Work Products include:

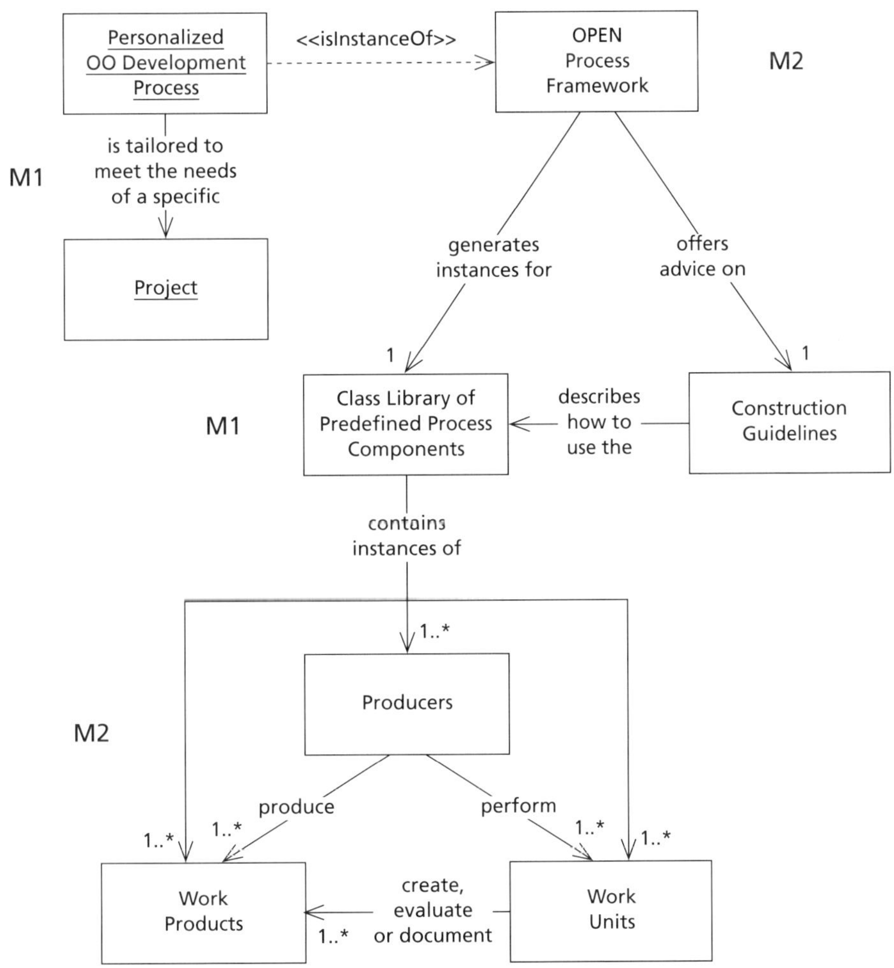

Figure G.3 The structure of a Development Process Framework

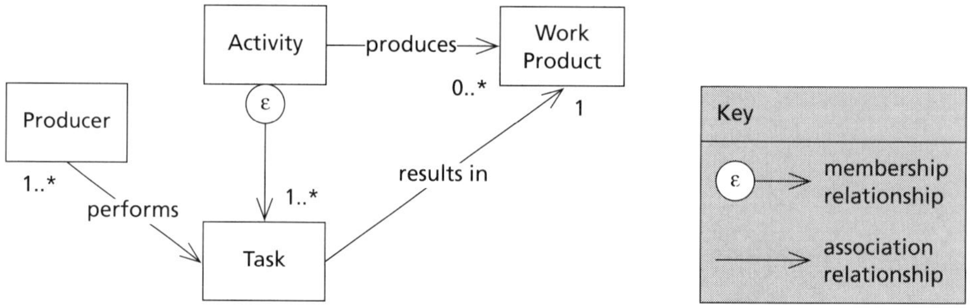

Figure G.4 Relationship between Producers, Tasks (using Activities) and Work Products

- **Architecture** – descriptions of the large-scale Architecture. Example instances (M1 level) include
  - Software Architecture
  - System Architecture
  - Web System Architecture
  - Business Model
- **Component** – various style of reusable Components focussed in the areas (Figure G.6) of:
  - Data
  - Hardware (with four subtypes of Device, Computer, Network and Storage)
  - Software
  - Wetware (personnel)
  - Paperware
  - Components can be made up of other Components.

However, Wetware is really another viewpoint on Roles as played by individual People, and Paperware can be equated with Document Work Products.

- **Application** – the product being constructed. This may be either a:
  - Software Application which consists of one or more Software Components (e.g. Website which consists of all the Web pages, the navigational structure, Web system Architecture and links to backend transaction processing software);
  - System Application which consists of Software, Hardware, Wetware (a kind of Role) and Paperware (a kind of Document) Components (Figure G.6).
- **Document** – used for describing Models and Applications. There are many kinds of Document. The six kinds shown in the metamodel are:
  - Conventions (with subtypes of Procedures, Guidelines, Standards, Templates and Inspection Checklists)

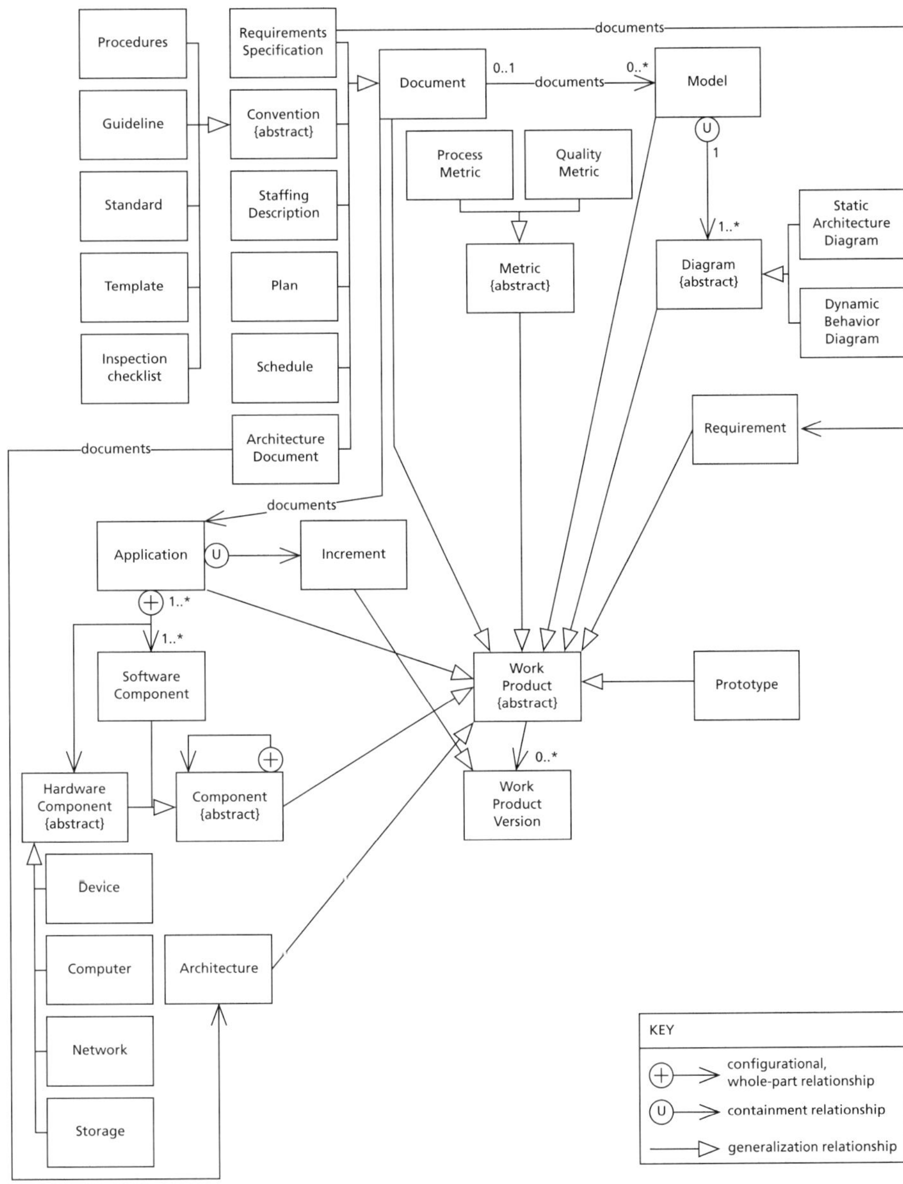

Figure G.5 Predefined classes of Work Products

  - Plans
  - Architecture Documents
  - Requirements Documents
  - Staffing Descriptions
  - Schedules
- **Metric** – a measure of some aspect of the system. Generally divided into
  - Process Metrics
  - Quality Metrics (often Design or Code Metrics of the static structure of the software)
- **Model** – a conceptual underpinning. In OO terms, usually described at the M1 level by either an OO Model or a Use Case Model described by some kind of Document.
- **Diagram** – readily divided into two subtypes: those for the Static Architecture and those depicting the dynamic behavior of the system or some portion of it.

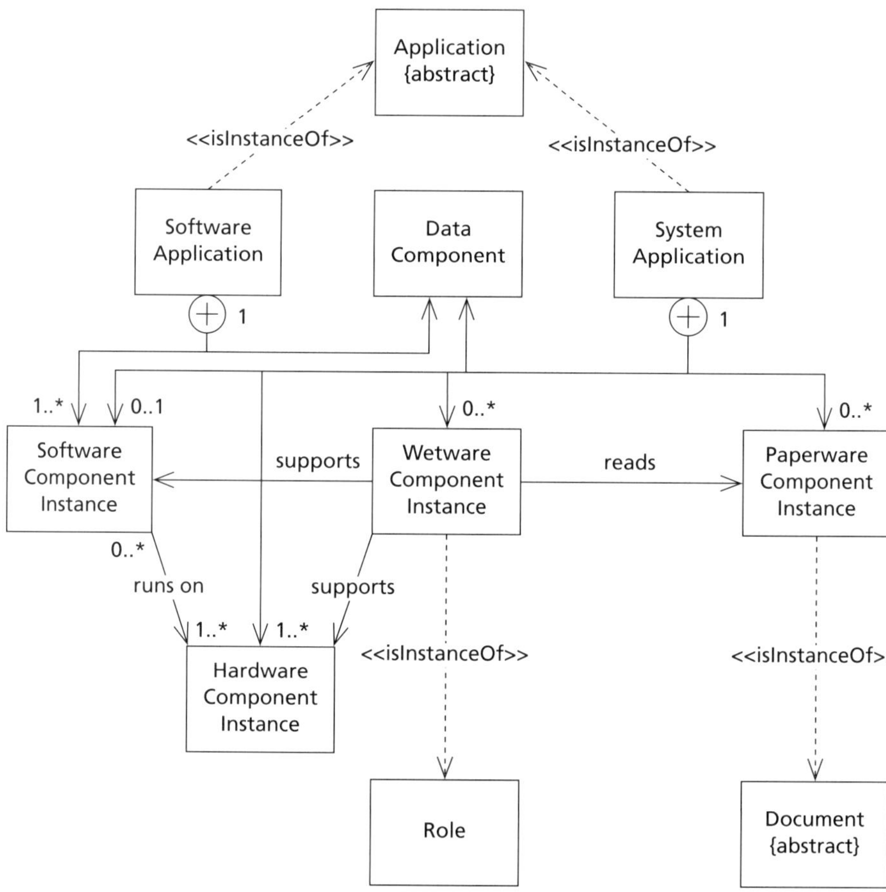

Figure G.6 M1 level kinds of Applications and their Components

- **Requirement** – description of the desired characteristics of the system and/or the software. Requirements may be instantiated (at the M1 level) as
  - Operational Requirement
  - Quality Requirement
  - Information Requirement
  - API Requirement
  - Design Constraint
- **Prototype** – various "first attempts" for either the Application or the Website.

Figure G.7 depicts the various kinds of Languages in the OPF metamodel. A Language is a medium used to document a Work Product. The most important Languages, as shown here, are:

- **Natural Languages** such as English that are used to capture narrative information in Documents.
- **Modeling Languages** that are used to document Use Case and Object Models. A Modeling Language consists of a notation plus a metamodel.
- **Specification Languages** that are used to specify Requirements.
- **Constraint Languages** that are used to constrain Models and specify business rules.
- **Implementation Languages** that are used to implement software. They can be classified, for examples, as Coding Languages, Database Languages, Constraint Languages and Interface Languages.

Producers of Work Product Versions are shown in Figure G.8. These are concurrent objects that may be either:

- **Direct Producers**, which may be Persons, Roles played by those Persons or the Tools used by those Persons.

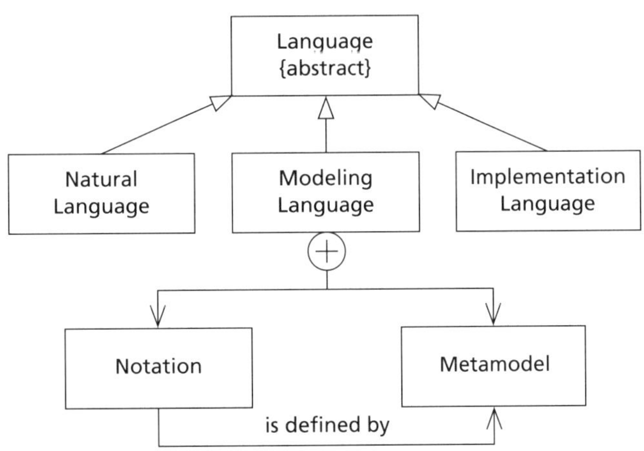

Figure G.7 Predefined classes of Language

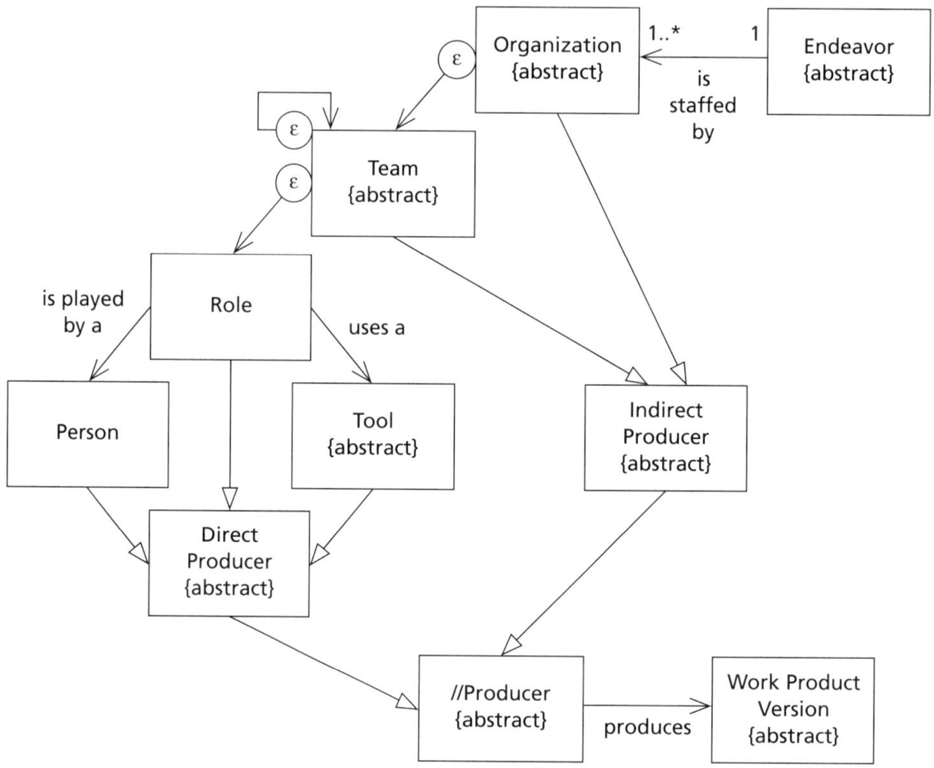

Figure G.8 Predefined classes of Producers

- **Indirect Producers**, which may be *Teams*, the members of which are Roles; or *Organizations*, the members of which are Teams.

Endeavors are staffed by one or more Organizations. Endeavors (Figure G.9) may be *Projects*, which produce either an Application or a Business Model; *Programmes*, which are aggregations of two or more related Projects; or *Enterprises*, which are aggregations of one or more related Programmes. Projects are resourced for their duration.

There are many kinds of Roles needed for OO/CBD. Figure G.10, lists the most useful instances. These are all described in detail in the OPF repository, along with other Role instances:

- Architect:
  - Business Architect
  - Software Architect
  - System Architect
- Class Owner.
- Configuration Manager.
- Designer:

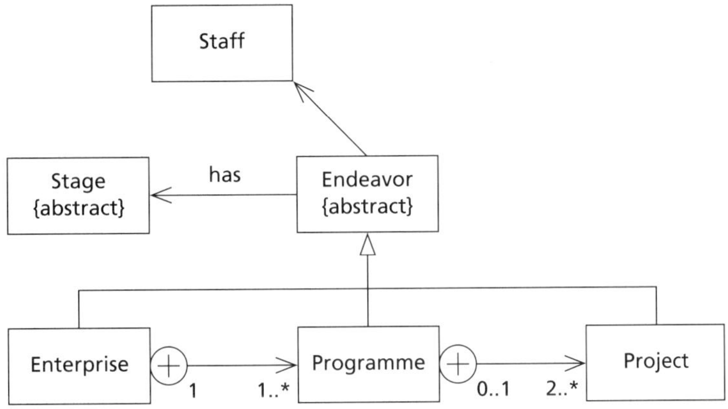

Figure G.9 Various kinds of Endeavors

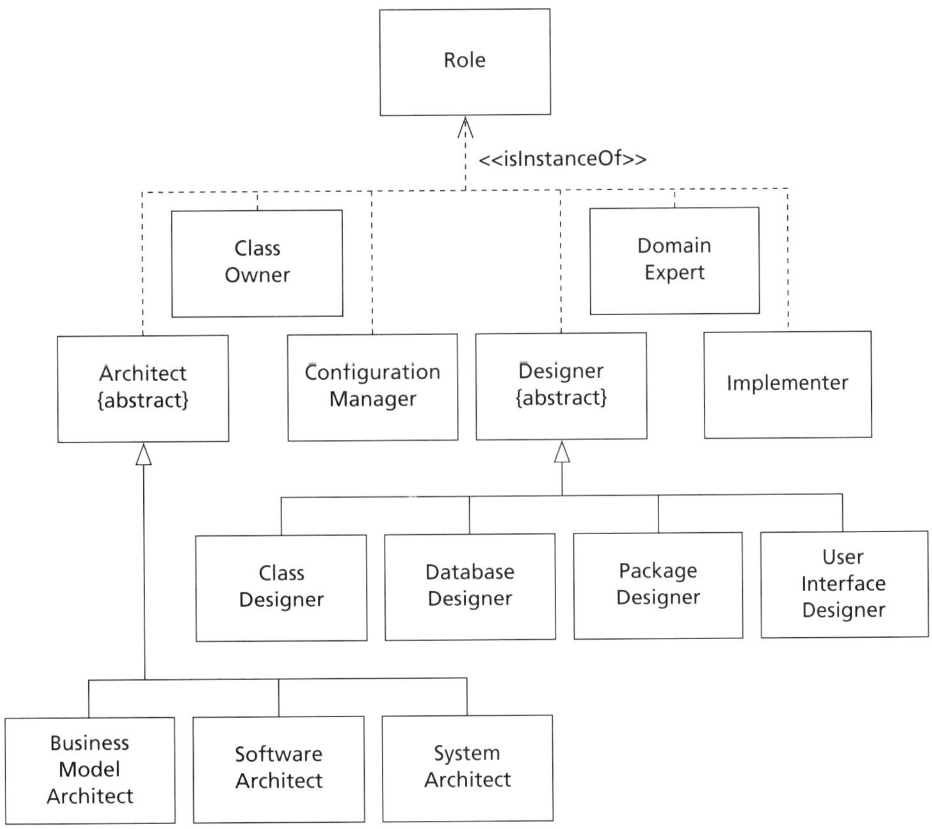

Figure G.10 A selection of the predefined classes of Roles (see text for full list)

  - Class Designer
  - Database Designer
  - Package Designer
  - User Interface Designer
- Domain Expert.
- Engineer:
  - Hardware Engineer
  - Quality Engineer
  - Requirements Engineer
  - Security Engineer
- Implementer.

In constructing software and software-intensive systems, many Tools are used (Figure G.11). These are collected together in a Development Environment. A particular kind of Development Environment, the Integrated Development Environment or IDE, is one in which the Tools are highly integrated and configured within it.

Tools may be Documentation Tools, Process Engineering Tools, Database Management Tools or CASE Tools. CASE Tools, in turn, may be classed as either Lower- or UpperCASE Tools. Particular examples (M1 level) of the former (Figure G.12) are:

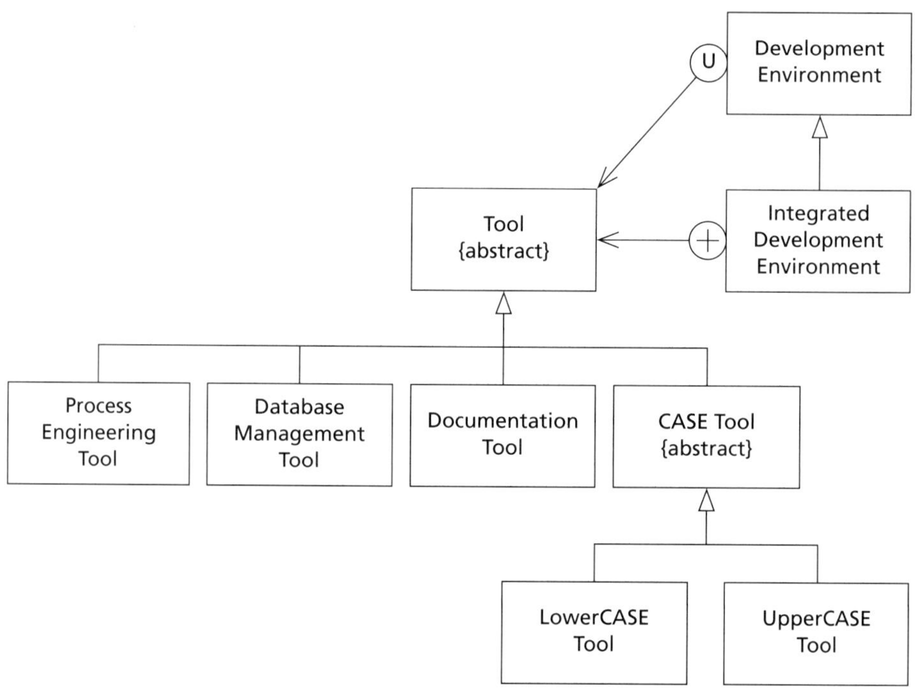

Figure G.11 Predefined classes of Tools

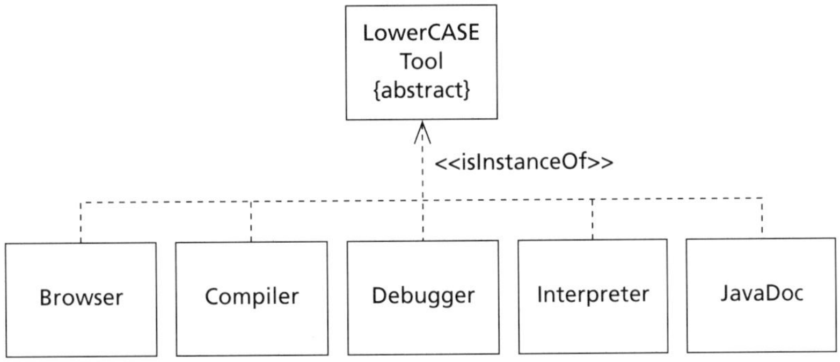

Figure G.12 Examples of LowerCASE tools

- Browser
- Compiler
- Debugger
- Interpreter
- JavaDoc.

while UpperCASE Tools (Figure G.13) include:

- Metrics Tools
- Configuration Management Tools
- Documentation Management Tools
- Modeling Tools
- Requirements Management Tools
- Project Management Tools.

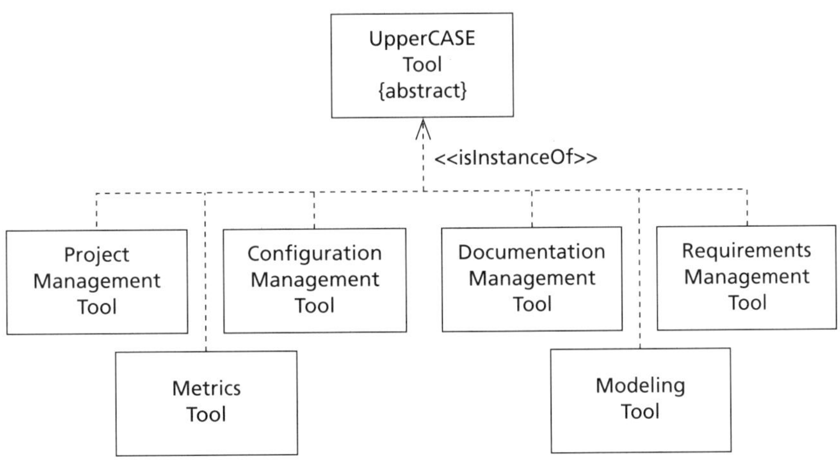

Figure G.13 Examples of UpperCASE tools

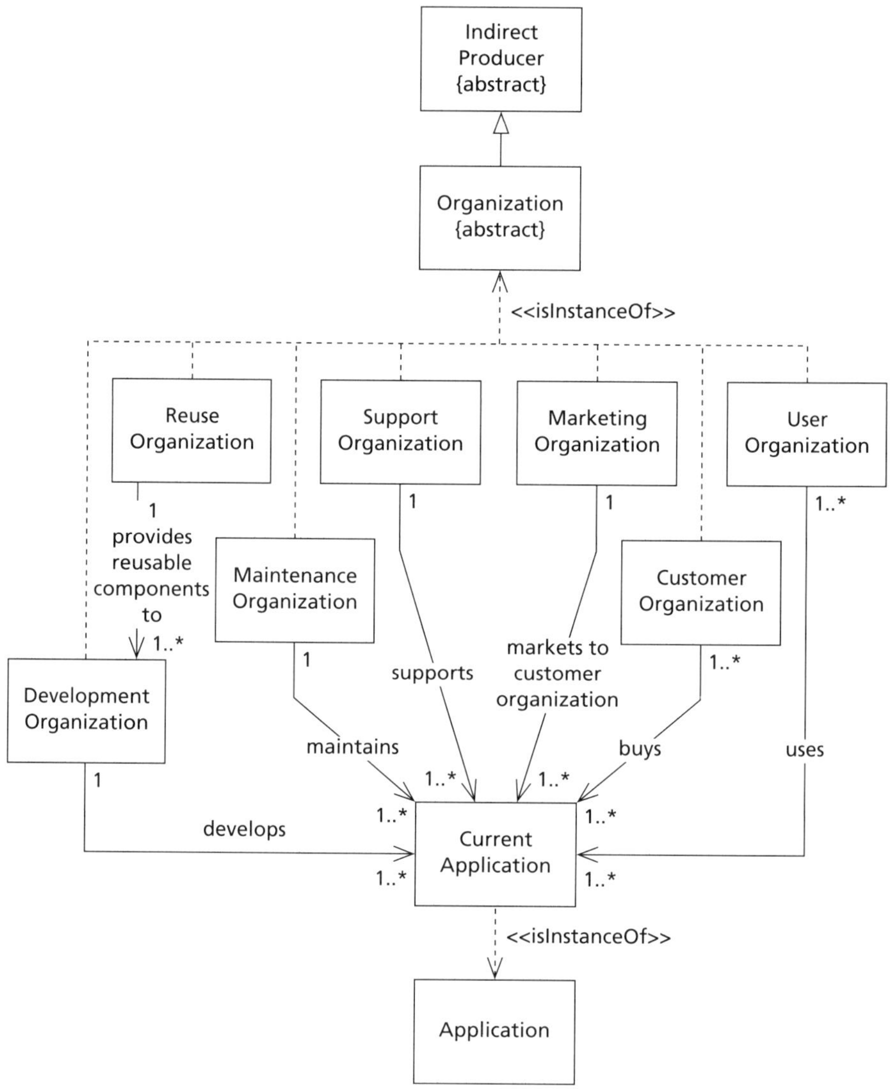

Figure G.14 A selection of the predefined kinds of Organizations in the OPF

The important roles of Organizations are shown in Figure G.14. Here we see seven example Organizations that can each play a part in creating and/or maintaining ongoing support for a current Application (the product and therefore the focus of the development effort). In the OPF repository, there are several others. For example, we have identified of interest the following Organizational categories:

- Customer Organization
- Development Organization
- Maintenance Organization
- Marketing Organization

- Operations Organization
- Partner Organization
- Reuse Organization
- Support Organization
- User Organization
- Subcontractor Organization
- Vendor Organization.

Figure G.15 gives a single example of the detailed structure of one selected Team – the Software Development Team. This Team (along with most others) has a hierarchical structure in that it has subteams which in Teams may have subteams (here the Package Team, for example).

Work Units (Figure G.16) are those items that focus on the ways of producing Work Products. They are classified as either Activities, Tasks or Techniques.

- **Tasks** are operations performed by Direct Producers.
- **Activities** are large-scale operations performed by Indirect Producers and modeled as cohesive collections of one or more related Work Flows (a kind of Stage q.v.). They can also be broken down into a set of Tasks and may even, on some occasions, consist of two or more subactivities.

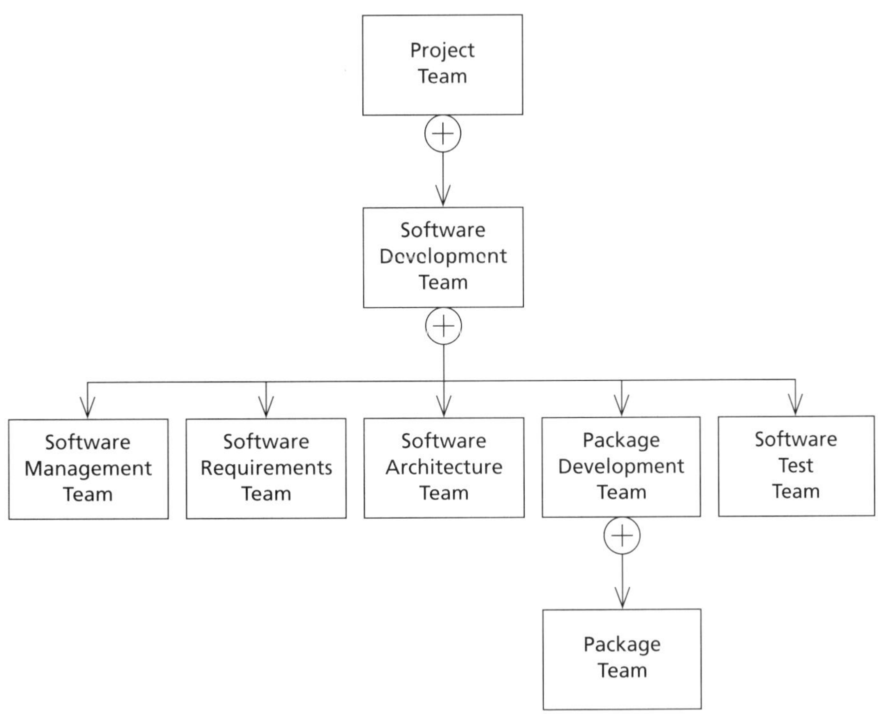

Figure G.15 Example Software Development Team Aggregation Structure

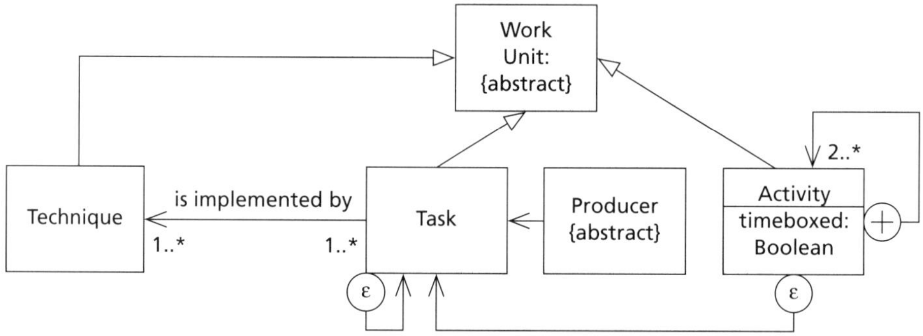

Figure G.16 Predefined classes of Work Units

- **Techniques** are realizations of the Tasks in that they tell the developer *how to* achieve the aims set by the Tasks and, to a lesser extent, by the Activities.

A *Work Performance* represents the interaction of the Producer with a Work Unit and is a major concept in bringing together work with the Producers of that work (Figure G.17). There are two kinds of Work Performance: *Task Performance* (an aggregation of Task and Performance) and *Work Flow* (a collection of Task Performances).

Work Flows (Figure G.18) result in the production of a Work Product Version. Work Product Versions provide a collection which together comprise the Work Product itself. The final aim of the Work Flow is to produce a Work Product via its various incarnations in the Work Product Versions.

As noted earlier, Work Products may be grouped under various headings. In Figure G.19 we show, as an example, the various kinds of process Work Product (an informal grouping of instances of Document) and, specifically, how they interact with the instances of Work Flow and Work Product.

Stages provide a macro-Organization to Work Units and are scheduled by Milestones (Figure G.20). Stages may be classified in one of two ways: Instantaneous Stage or as Stage With Duration.

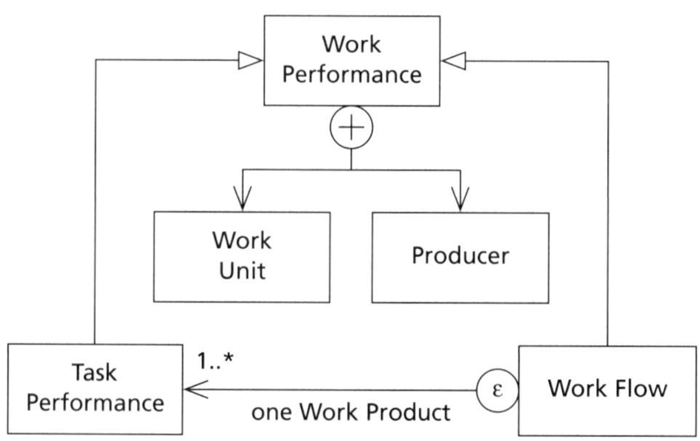

Figure G.17 Work Performance, Task Performance and Work Flow

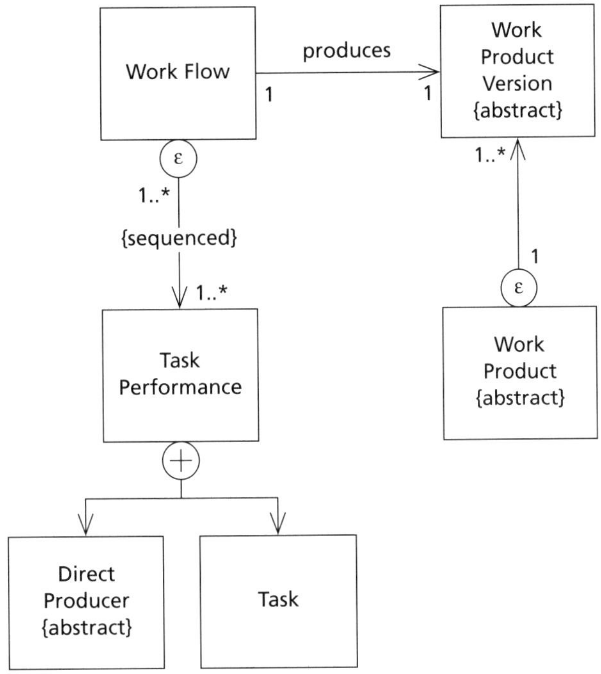

Figure G.18 Work Flows as Sequences of Task Performances

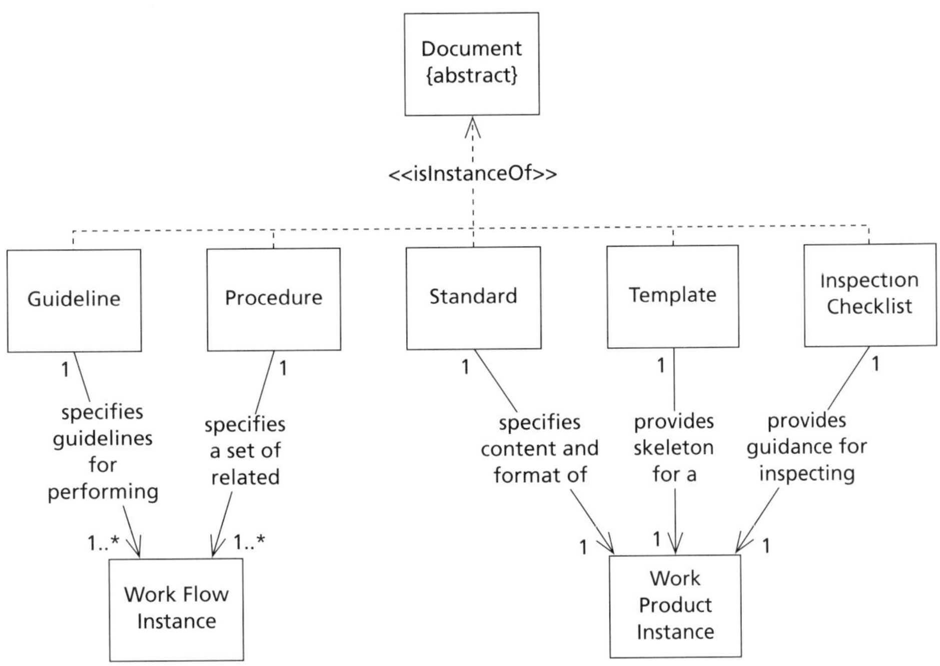

Figure G.19 Process Work Products

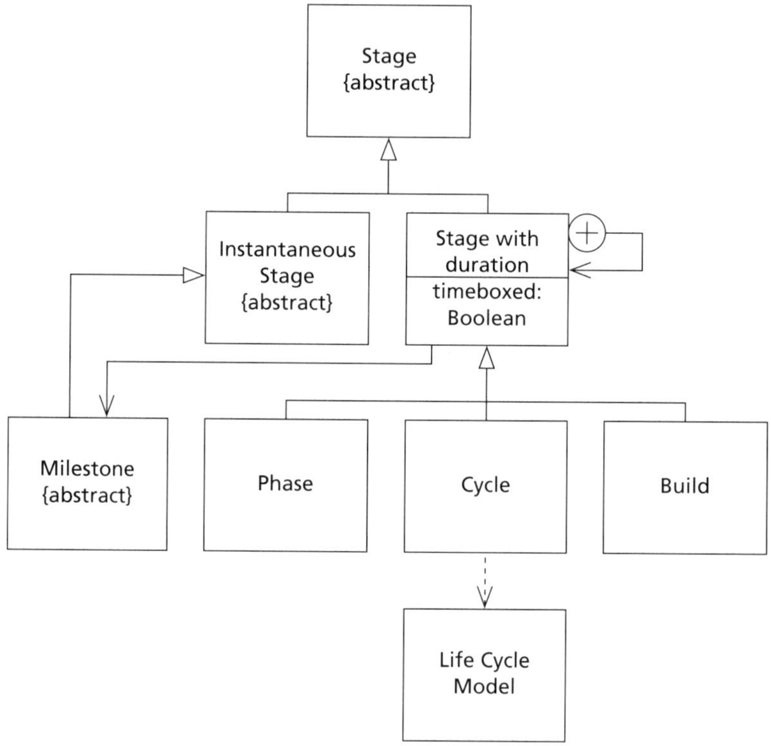

Figure G.20 Predefined subtypes of Stage

- **Instantaneous Stage**
  - Milestone
- **Stage With Duration**. There are three subtypes, each with various instances in the repository:
  - **Phases**, which are large-scale structures in which Builds and Releases occur.
  - **Cycles**, which are large-scale Stages. Three typical instances are:
    - **Development Cycles**, which are aggregations of one or more Phases of a Project.
    - **Life Cycles**, which describe the Cycle of the underlying philosophy, such as waterfall, contract-driven, spiral (described by a Life Cycle Model).
  - **Cycles** are made up of Phases (the "aggregation" relationship inherited from Stage With Duration).
  - **Builds**, which are major Increments of development. Some of these may be stereotyped as «release». Releases are Builds delivered to an external client.

Stages With Duration may be timeboxed.

When constructing your process, the largest granularity is generally the Cycle. Cycles can comprise a number of Phases (Figure G.21), the aggregation relationship being inherited from Stage With Duration. Each Phase may then, via the same mechanism, consist of other instances of Stage such as Builds, Releases and Milestones.

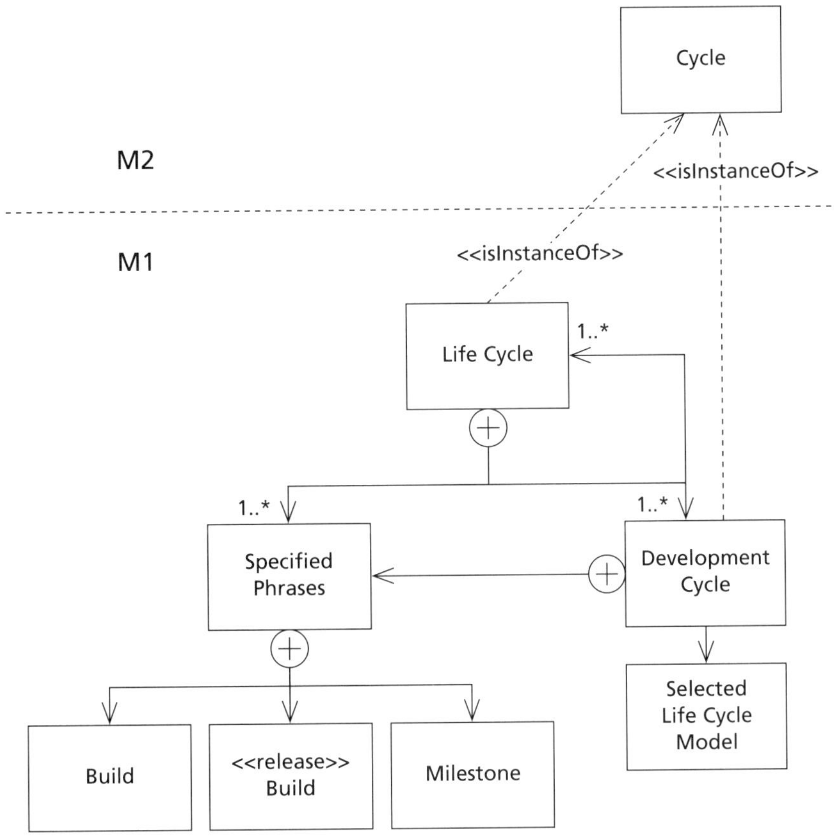

Figure G.21 Cycles consist of Phases which, in turn, consist of Builds, Releases and Milestones (M1-level model)

One such very specific instantiation is shown in Figure G.22 in which we see that eight Phases have been instantiated together with four Cycles. In each case, it can be seen that the Cycles consist of Phases.

In Figure G.22 two things should be noted. First, the OPF supports Application development via Programmes and Projects; but it also supports the improvement of Enterprises via its Enterprise Life Cycle and associated two business-focussed Phases (although Application of the Programme Life Cycle Phases is also possible). Secondly, while a Project Life Cycle produces an Application (multiplicity of 1 in Figure G.22), a Programme extends over two or more Applications (cardinality of 2..*).

The main two kinds of Milestone are the Technical Milestone and the Management Milestone. While there are only two recommended instances of Technical Milestone (Document Drop and Code Drop) in the OPF repository, there are four kinds of Management Milestone (Figure G.23). These occur when:

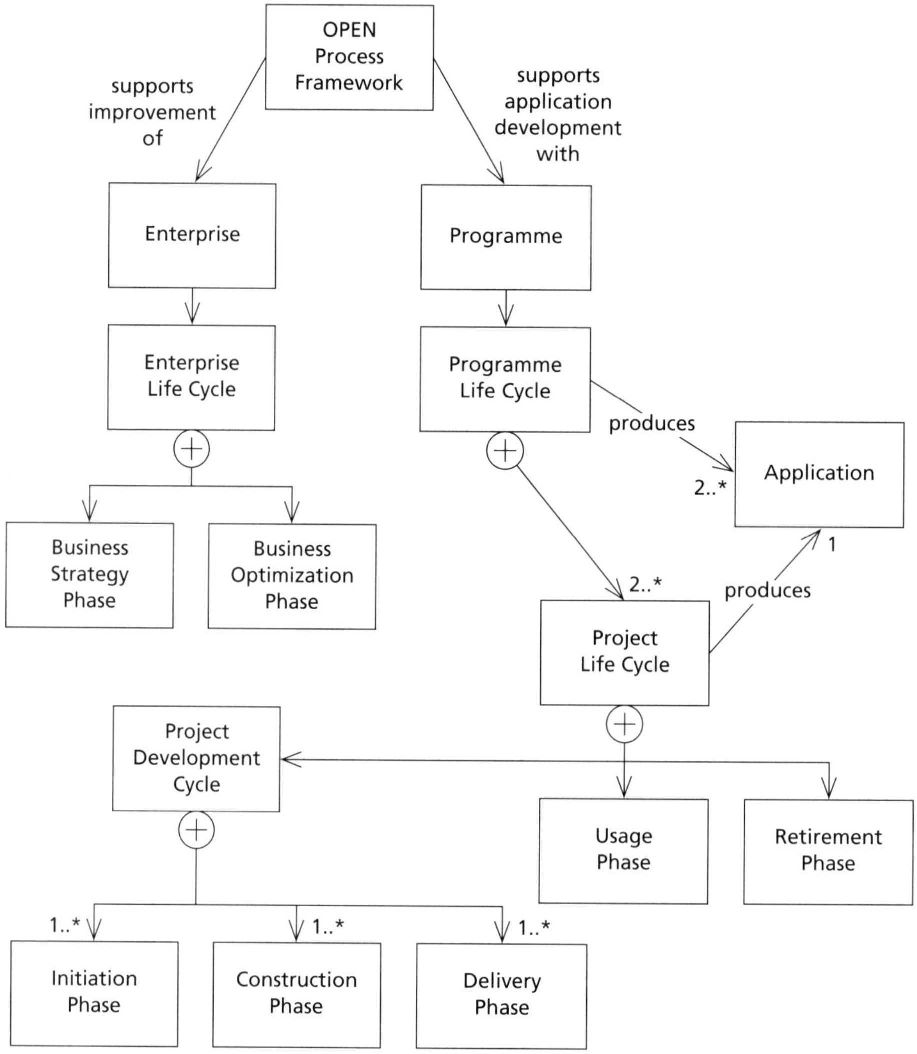

Figure G.22 A schematic of Enterprise and Programme life cycles and their constituent parts (an example described at the M1 level)

- the Vision Statement is baselined
- the Requirements are relatively stable and complete
- the Architecture is relatively stable and complete
- the Application is released to the customer.

Figure G.24 gives a final, summary-style diagram of the OPF. While many classes have been omitted for clarity, it shows the connections between the various fragments of the OPF metamodel shown in Figures G.1–24. In particular, we would draw your attention to the following:

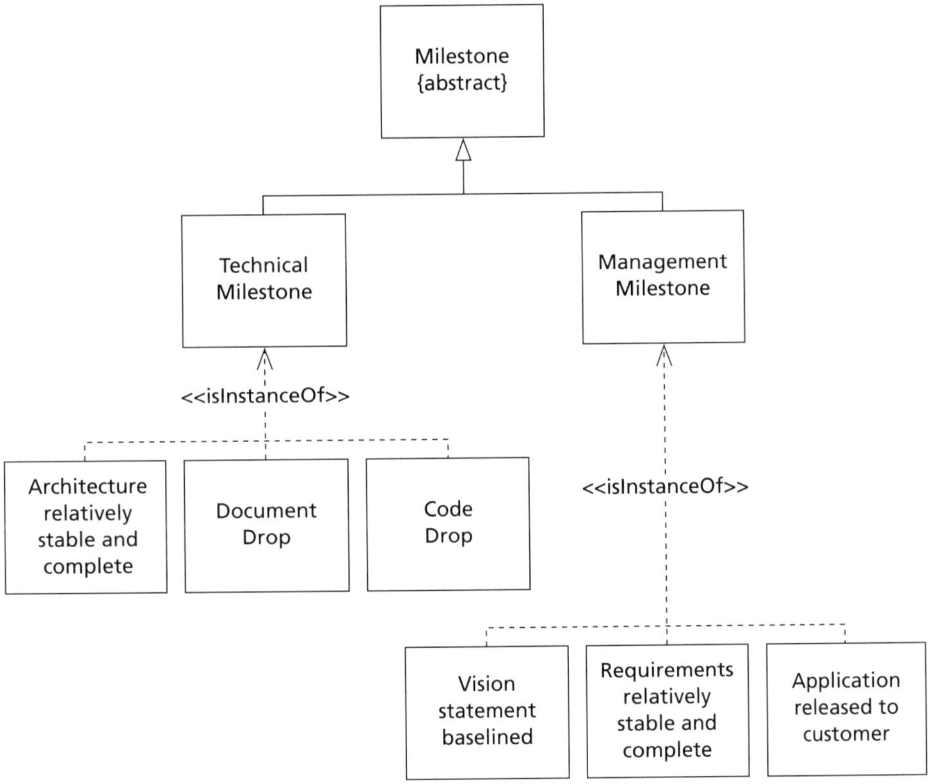

Figure G.23 Predefined classes of Milestones

- The way in which the Stages interact with Work Units.
- The sequencing of Work Units by Assertions.
- The relationship between Activity, Task, Technique, Work Flow and Task Performance noting that their supertypes are different: Work Unit for Activity, Task and Technique and Stage for Work Flow.
- The relationship between (subtypes of) Project and Work Products.
- The complex interactions between kinds of Producers, Roles, Tools, Teams and Organizations and Endeavors.

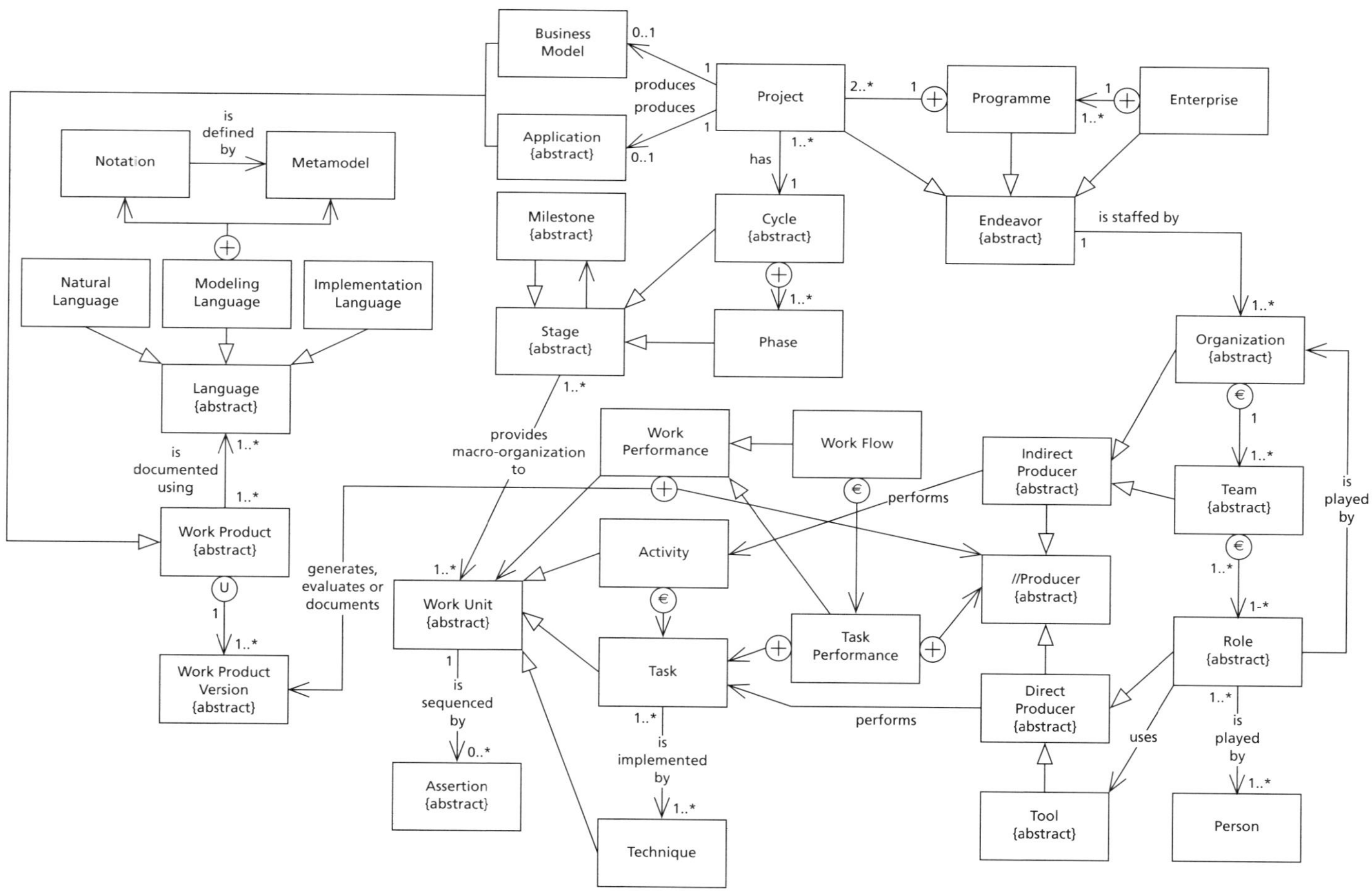

Figure G.24 Overview of the Object-Oriented Development Process Framework depicted as an M2-level metamodel

Bibliography and References

Ambler, S.W. (1998) *Process Patterns*, Cambridge University Press.

Beck, K. (1999) Embracing change with extreme programming, *IEEE Computer*, October 1999, 70–77.

Beck, K. (2000) *Extreme Programming Explained*, Addison-Wesley.

Belbin, R.M. (1981) *Management Teams: Why They Succeed or Fail*, Butterworth Heinemann, Oxford.

Belbin, R.M. (1993) *Team Roles at Work*, Butterworth Heinemann, Oxford.

Cheesman, J. and Daniels, J. (2001) *UML Components: A Simple Process for Specifying Component-Based Software*, Addison-Wesley.

Constantine, L.L. and Lockwood, L.A.D. (1999) *Software for Use*, Addison-Wesley/ACM Press.

Cook, S. and Daniels, J. (1994) *Designing Object Systems*, Prentice-Hall.

D'Souza, D.F. and Wills, A.C. (1999) *Objects, Components, and Frameworks with UML. The Catalysis Approach*, Addison-Wesley.

Firesmith, D.G. (1993) *Object-Oriented Requirements Analysis and Logical Design. A Software Engineering Approach*, John Wiley and Sons, New York.

Firesmith, D.G. (1999) Use case modeling guidelines, in *Procs. TOOLS 30* (eds D. Firesmith, R. Riehle, G. Pour and B. Meyer), IEEE Computer Society Press, 184–193.

Firesmith, D.G., Hendley, G., Krutsch, S.A. and Stowe, M. (1998) *Documenting a Complete Java Application*. Addison-Wesley.

Firesmith, D.G., Henderson-Sellers, B. and Graham, I. (1997) *OPEN Modeling Language (OML) Reference Manual*, SIGS Books/Cambridge University Press.

Fowler, M. (1999) *Refactoring. Improving the Design of Existing Code*, Addison-Wesley, Reading, MA.

Ginsberg, M.P. and Quinn, L.H. (1995) *Process Tailoring and the Software Capability Maturity Model*, Technical Report CMU/SEI-94-TR-024.

Goldberg, A. and Rubin, K.S. (1995) *Succeeding with Objects. Decision Frameworks for Project Management*, Addison-Wesley, Reading, MA.

Graham, I.M. (1995) *Migrating to Object Technology*, Addison-Wesley.

Graham, I. *et al.* (1997) Associations considered a bad thing, *Journal of Object-Oriented Programming*, **9**(9), 41–48.

Graham, I., Henderson-Sellers, B. and Younessi, H. (1997) *The OPEN Process Specification*, Addison-Wesley.

Haire, B., Henderson-Sellers, B. and Lowe, D. (2001) Supporting Web development in the OPEN process: additional Tasks, *Procs. COMPSAC 2001*.

Henderson-Sellers, B. (1997) *A BOOK of Object-Oriented Knowledge*, Prentice Hall, New York.

Henderson-Sellers, B. (2001) An OPEN process for Component-based development. Chapter 18 in *Component-Based Software Engineering: Putting the Pieces Together* (eds G.T. Heineman and W. Councill), Addison-Wesley, Reading, MA.

Henderson-Sellers, B. (2001) Adding CBD to OPEN, *JOOP/ROAD*, **13**(12), 24–28.

Henderson-Sellers, B. and Barbier, F. (1999) Black and white diamonds, in *«UML»'99. The Unified Modeling Language – Beyond the Standard*, (eds R. France and B. Rumpe), Springer LNCS 1723, 550–565.

Henderson-Sellers, B. and Bulthuis, A. (1998) *Object-Oriented Metamethods*, Springer-Verlag.

Henderson-Sellers, B. and Edwards, J.M. (1994) *BOOKTWO of Object-Oriented Knowledge. The Working Object*, Prentice-Hall, Sydney.

Henderson-Sellers, B. and Serour, M.K. (2000) Creating a process for transitioning to object technology, *Proceedings Seventh Asia-Pacific Software Engineering Conference. APSEC 2000*, IEEE Computer Society Press, Los Alamitos, CA, USA, 436–440.

Henderson-Sellers, B. and Unhelkar, B. (2000), *OPEN Modeling with UML*, Addison-Wesley.

Henderson-Sellers, B., Simons, A.J.H. and Younessi, H. (1998) *The OPEN Toolbox of Techniques*, Addison-Wesley.

Henderson-Sellers, B., Atkinson, C. and Firesmith, D.G. (1999) Viewing the OML as a variant of the UML, in *«UML»'99. The Unified Modeling Language – Beyond the Standard*, (eds R. France and B. Rumpe), Springer LNCS 1723, 49–66.

Henderson-Sellers, B., Haire, B. and Lowe, D. (2001) Adding Web support to OPEN, *JOOP/ROAD*, **14**(2).

Kerth, N.L. (2001) *Project Retrospectives: A Handbook for Team Reviews*, Dorset House, New York.

Lilly, L. (1999) Use case pitfalls: Top 10 problems from real Projects using use cases, in *Procs. TOOLS 30* (eds D. Firesmith, R. Riehle, G. Pour and B. Meyer), IEEE Computer Society Press, 174–183.

OMG (1999) OMG Unified Modeling Language Specification, Version 1.3, June 1999, OMG Document 99–06–09.

Stapleton, J. (1997) *Dynamic Systems Development Method*, Addison-Wesley.

Warmer, J.B. and Kleppe, A.G. (1999) *The Object Constraint Language. Precise Modeling with UML*, Addison-Wesley.

Some useful Websites are:

www.open.org.au

www.donald-firesmith.com

Index